NIMBY Wars

NIMBY Wars

The Politics of Land Use

■ ■ ■

P. Michael Saint

Robert J. Flavell

Patrick F. Fox

Saint University Press
Hingham, Massachusetts

Library of Congress Control Number: 2009906549

Text design, typesetting, and project management: Books By Design, Inc.

Manufactured in the United States of America.

ISBN: 978-0-615-30652-0

CONTENTS

Foreword   vii

1   All Politics Is Local, All Land Use Is Political   1

2   A Primer on Land Use Regulation in Western Democracies   18

3   What Is Land Use Politics?   28

4   Common Approaches to Influencing Land Use Decisions
(and Why They Don't Work)   45

5   Land Use Politics Is a Different Discipline   62

6   Why Use a Land Use Politics Approach?   81

7   The Differences Between Offense and Defense Land Use
Politics Campaigns   110

8   Legal Foundations for Defensive Actions   137

9   Reports from the Field: Offense and Defense Case Studies   148

10   The Future of Land Use Politics   185

11   The Saint Index   202

Bibliography   215

FOREWORD

■　　■　　■

IN THE SUMMER OF 1984, a college classmate called me to say that he planned to build 250,000 square feet of class A office space on an 11-acre site in Massachusetts. For 40 years the site had been used as an auto parts junkyard where 2,000 junked cars dripped transmission fluid into the ground.

I knew the area; I lived less than half a mile up the street. I also knew the local political climate because I had been employed in both journalism and politics in the area, and I told him he would have opposition from neighbors.

"Get out of here," my classmate responded. "We're going to create two beautiful office buildings with atrium-style open architecture and Italian granite facades and state-of-the art fiber optics, and the people who work there will come at 8 a.m. and leave at 6 p.m. Who would object to this replacing a junkyard?"

I told him the neighbors would not care about the features and benefits of the buildings. They would only worry about the possible negative impacts on them, and they would fight against the city's giving him permission to build.

His advisers counseled him to "sneak it in" to city hall in mid-August, when many people were on vacation. He tried. But 40 neighbors and a city councilor showed up and told the zoning board, "Over our dead bodies!" The only ones speaking for the developer were his out-of-town lawyers. The zoning board listened to the neighbors and turned down the request. The next day, my classmate called me and said, "Okay, wise guy. Since you know so much, fix it."

Four months later, we won unanimous approval, after having built political support for the project from real neighbors. And the new science of land use politics was born.

More than 25 years have passed, and we have worked successfully on more than 1,400 controversial real estate development projects, both in support and in opposition, in 44 U.S. states, in Canada, and in the United Kingdom. We have developed strong views on how the approval process works and what you must do to make sure your side prevails.

Former U.S. House Speaker Tip O'Neill used to say, "All politics is local." Lesson number one is that all land use approvals are political. You need to understand the local politics and figure out what to do to get a majority of the board members to vote for your side. Getting locally elected officials to approve something new in the face of overwhelming neighborhood opposition is nearly impossible, especially if the developer or project manager decides "to let the facts speak for themselves" or takes the attitude that the new scheme can be sold based on its features and benefits, like a tube of toothpaste.

When we first worked on behalf of that Massachusetts office park in 1984, only a few localities would say no to new real estate development. All the others were of the opinion that growth meant jobs, taxes, and progress in the community. Smoke a cigar with the building inspector, pick up your permit, and invite the mayor to the groundbreaking photo was the rule, not the exception.

Then came smart growth, the anti-sprawl and antienvironmental movements, historic preservationists, NIMBYs (those who said "not in my backyard"), and competitors who realized that using land use regulations to keep competitors out could protect profits far better than cutting prices after the new guy opened his location. Today, based on national polling results in our Saint Index poll, 78 percent of Americans say they want nothing new built in their communities. Nothing.

Americans may say, in theory, that they like affordable housing, windmill farms, new single-family homes, or new hospitals (never power plants, casinos, quarries, or landfills). But when the proposals are made, they swarm city hall and say, "It's a great proposal, but the wrong location." They then point out how the plan, if allowed, will worsen traffic, block views, reduce green space, increase crime, degrade the environment, lower property values, or destroy the character of their community. Those who fear adverse consequences from development are reacting emotionally, and they quickly become passionate in their opposition and convert that passion into political action. When elected local officials look out into an auditorium and see 300 button-wearing and banner-waving constituents chanting "no" and three out-of-town lawyers and engineers saying "yes," it is not surprising that they vote no.

Since land use approvals are subject to local politics, we believe in hiring experienced political campaign managers, training them on the rules and regulations of land use and environmental law, and sending them out to organize local voters into grassroots campaigns to demonstrate support for (or opposition to) what is proposed.

Our side needs to have as many or more citizens as the other side in order to convince the politicians to vote our way. This means we will generate 300 phone calls to a councilor at home in favor of a supermarket, or get 150 people to attend a public hearing for a quarry, or solicit 18,000 signatures on a petition in favor of a hospital.

It is easier to get real voters in a community to oppose a project than to support one. Opponents are afraid and demonstrate that with political action. Those who support a project are usually intellectually, not emotionally, involved. Getting them to participate in the process requires experienced and persevering operatives who can motivate them to communicate with their public officials on behalf of it.

This book looks at the land use process and describes, in detail, how to win. Bob Flavell, who wrote the book, is a lawyer, former journalist, and political campaign manager who has been a colleague at Saint Consulting since 1988. He is one of the nation's leading experts on land use politics.

I hope you read his book, enjoy it, and learn from it. We believe that the process of getting things built will become more controversial and difficult in the years to come. A proponent who does not understand that the process is inherently political, and act accordingly, will spend thousands — or even millions — of dollars and still lose.

P. Michael Saint
CEO, The Saint Consulting Group

ACKNOWLEDGMENTS

■   ■   ■

THIS BOOK would not have been possible without the assistance of many people. First and foremost, the entire staff of The Saint Consulting Group has been instrumental in building our expertise in the field of land use politics. This book is a result of the diligence, hard work, and constant innovation of everyone on our team, and we are humbled and proud to stand with them. The process of publishing this book was made far easier by the generous assistance of Suzanne Lowe. Thanks also to Marie Gendron and to Nancy Benjamin and the team at Books By Design. Greg O'Brien's advice and guidance were invaluable. Steve Shepherd, Seth Cargiuolo, Carol Murphy, Jeff Gould, Nick Keable, and Paul Mindus all contributed their ideas, thoughtful criticism, and expertise. Lastly, thank you to our families who put up with our crazy hours, ridiculous travel schedules, and obsessive dedication to handheld electronic devices. Their love, support, and encouragement make everything else possible.

NIMBY Wars

CHAPTER 1

■　■　■

All Politics Is Local,
All Land Use Is Political

ALTHOUGH THE NEWS MEDIA harp on national and international issues, it is the political soap opera of everyday life that concerns most people. They care less about the doings of the Pakistani government than they do about local officials' inability to get the potholes fixed. They focus less on the latest tsunami in Asia than they do on their neighbor's loud music or refusal to clean up the yard.

It does no good to define *politics* narrowly. Politics is not about elections; they are merely a formal manifestation of it. Politics is about how people define themselves, their society, and their environment, including their quality of life. That's why people feel strongly about political issues — war and taxes, just to mention two. And it's why they organize and unite for a cause or against a common enemy, whether a person, an issue, or a shopping center that will spoil their view.

Political can mean any controversial issue in a Western-style democracy where the rights to free speech and assembly combine with the right to petition the government for redress of grievances. Add in the sense of entitlement that exists today among many adults and their children, and you have a highly political society whose members insist on their rights. These American-style rights, enshrined in a written Constitution, may not be expressed in the exact

1

same fashion in other Western representative democracies, but they are there, just the same. The rights of Englishmen and the Canadian Charter of Rights and Freedoms are held just as dear in England and Canada as the American Bill of Rights is held in the United States.

National or global issues may affect people's lives, but there's little or nothing most people can do about them. They can write letters to their representatives or to the local newspaper editor, and even join national organizations to carry the message. But a check written to the Sierra Club does not stop global warming, and a letter to the editor does not bring peace to the Middle East. Local issues that affect people most directly, however, are subject to local action and direct democracy. Citizens can talk face to face with the public officials who have authority over local controversies. They can organize and attend meetings and hearings and make their position on the issues plain. They can support candidates who share their views, oppose those who don't, or seek office themselves.

Among the most riveting controversies at this level is land use, which is mostly controlled by local ordinances and local boards. In the United States, zoning is created, amended, enforced, and excepted at the local level. This makes zoning and rezoning a local, political issue and affords citizens considerable influence over matters that will directly affect their lives and those of their families, neighborhoods, and communities.

Controversial development projects become controversial because citizens oppose them. This might seem obvious, but it's also true that projects are not intentionally designed to be controversial and usually they don't start out that way, unless the developer has failed to do his research and preparation. If the only opposition to a project proposal is from competitors or outside interest groups, local officials aren't generally going to pay much heed. But fill the hall with angry constituents with their built-in credibility and right to vote, and local public officials will sit up, listen, and usually act accordingly.

Local citizens oppose a project because they perceive that it will adversely affect them. It will bring traffic or noise. Or it will attract undesirables. Or it will change the character of the community. Whatever the stated reasons for opposition, the real reason is usually that it represents change, the unknown. Nothing galvanizes a neighborhood like the prospect of change. Change makes people uncomfortable, particularly if they perceive that the change is likely to affect their property values adversely. The single most important investment for most Americans (and Brits and Canadians) is their home. Millions of them are counting on the value of that home to ease their retirement. Anything perceived as reducing or endangering the value of that investment is likely to stir a strong response.

Land use decisions are inherently political: each side wants a political solution that favors its position. Land use both reflects and determines where economic activity takes place and how communities develop. It also makes or breaks property owners and ultimately affects the quality of life of all who inhabit the environs.

Perception Is Reality

Land use proposals affect people's perceptions — and in politics, perception is reality. A person who lives on a river will oppose construction of a chemical plant upstream, regardless of how much he is assured that there will be no pollution. His perception of the potential danger is real, and it is irrelevant whether the perception reflects objective truth. What counts is that the person believes it and acts accordingly. A person who farms in a semirural environment will oppose development of a gambling casino resort, no matter that it will be built five miles away in a clearing in the woods, and no matter what mitigation the proponents offer. A suburbanite will oppose development of a big-box store in her community, even if she and her family habitually shop at the same store elsewhere, and even if the developer promises millions of dollars in buffers, traffic improvements, and other mitigation. Whether the perception that the big-box store is undesirable is based on rumor, news reports, experience, or gut instinct, it cannot be denied or ignored. The Saint Index® (which is discussed in detail in Chapter 11) has consistently found that people want shopping centers, but not nearby; they want electricity, but not the power plant; they want cell phones, but not the towers; they want schools, but not next door; they want trash disposal, but not in their backyards.

Because these projects are objectionable, citizens will oppose them, organize against them, and bring political pressure to influence public officials who have the authority to approve them. Those who use political pressure most effectively win the vote. Whether opponents are dismissed as short-sighted reactionary practitioners of NIMBY (not in my backyard), CAVE (citizens against virtually everything), or BANANA (build absolutely nothing anywhere near anything), the fact is that citizens today are better organized and far more effective at delaying and blocking development projects than ever before.

Nearly everyone will object to a hazardous waste plant, garbage-processing facility, or sewage treatment plant in the neighborhood. Because of their unpopularity, such undesirable LULUs (locally unwanted land uses) have historically been sited in poor and minority communities lacking political influence and therefore unable to effectively object. In 1984 the California Waste Management Board paid a consulting firm $500,000 to define communities that wouldn't resist siting LULUs, particularly trash incinerators. The resulting report is now used (and posted on the Internet) as an aid in siting LULUs. The communities least likely to resist, according to the study, included those described as southern or Midwestern, rural, conservative, Republican, low-income, less educated, and blue collar. Among those most likely to resist were communities described as Northeastern or western, urban, liberal, Democrat, middle- and upper-income, college educated, and white-collar professional.[1] The social justice movement now fights the imposition of LULUs on the defenseless, but the point is that LULU-receptive neighborhoods would not be victimized in the first place if they had political clout.

Land use experts often distinguish between "real" and "perceived" controversies in land use planning in the belief that once opponents are disabused of their confusion, they will applaud a project that they formerly opposed. This is not the case. The neighbors'

---

[1]Center for Health, Environment and Justice, "Targeting 'Cerrell' Communities," http://www.ejnet.org/ej/cerrell.pdf.

opposition is not based on logic, and a controversy is no less real because it is perceived. In land use, as in all political debate, perception is reality; people act on their perceptions, whether or not those notions are objectively true. What people think and believe informs how they act, speak, and vote, even (or especially) if they are, objectively speaking, wrong. Besides, in land use, there's plenty of room for subjectivity. Is a traffic study ever "accurate" in an objective sense? Do the buffer zones really shield the neighbors? It's all subjective, and it doesn't matter anyway because political fights are based on emotion, not logic. If neighbors believe their neighborhood is being treated unfairly, the developer's insistence that it is not carries no weight whatsoever.

Populism and Cynicism

In the populist view, public officials do what is best for the community and keep the best interests of the community in mind when they weigh the pros and cons of a project proposal. In the cynical view, politicians do what best ensures their reelection or reappointment to office. These viewpoints might seem inconsistent, but they are not; the best interests of the community coincide politically with the best interests of the people who live (and vote) there.

A "visionary" planner or social engineer might contend that public officials should look beyond the short-term wishes of their community's residents and think about the long-term needs of future generations. But future generations don't vote in the next election. Those who do vote are the residents currently living and paying taxes in that community. Thus, they have the right to determine what is in the public interest; they are the public, and their interest is the public interest. The public official knows what those citizens want (and have a right to want); that same official cannot know what future generations will want.

Perception as reality goes both ways: a public official who doesn't respect the neighbors' perceived fears of a development should not expect them to perceive him as responsive to their needs. Based on their conclusion that he is nonresponsive, they'll vote for someone else in the next election and urge others to do likewise. The fact that the public official may feel he is doing what's best for the community is irrelevant, and even objectionable, because he elevates his own presumed wisdom above and against that of the voters.

Public officials usually have a good instinct for survival. They are acutely aware that a public official who annoys enough people will be voted out of office, and one who really infuriates a smaller number will have made devoted enemies. This latter point is especially true at the local land use level because an infuriated constituent has a long memory. Public officials voted to allow the sewage treatment plant, and now it stands upwind from the constituent's front porch. She can't sit outside in the warm weather, can't leave her windows open in the summer, has to tolerate the plant, and her property value is destroyed. She and her family are permanent enemies of the officials responsible.

Politicians who survive know this instinctively, which is why they are sensitive and deferential to neighborhood concerns. An out-of-town developer has no political clout in a confrontation with voters, even if he has given money to the politicians. Contributions don't win elections; votes do, and neighbors vote. Besides, a developer, even if he is local, is unlikely to mount a revenge campaign against an official who votes against his project; it's a risk of doing business, and there's always another project. But a group of residents adversely affected by a project will remember who approved it. They will hold a grudge, tormented by the sight of the monstrosity—and the traffic and noise it generates—each time they open the front door.

Some commentators rely on the model of the median voter to determine how politicians will act. (The median voter is the person in the exact middle of a ranking of voters along some issue dimension, such as from the most left wing to the most right wing.) The theory is that government officials will act as if there were a referendum on every question presented and will vote according to the presumptive winner of the referendum, the median voter. There are many flaws in this theory, not the least of which is that it assumes that the referendum result can always be predicted, that minds cannot be changed, and that each issue is sufficiently important to cause people to vote against the politician. But experience shows that politicians defer to those who pose the greatest threat to their reelection, not necessarily the majority of voters.

The median voter feels strongly about only a few issues, most of which never arise at the local level. Most people simply vote for the incumbent, regardless of the incumbent's voting record, unless given good reasons not to do so. Those reasons come from the politician's enemies, who have an agenda they seek to realize and who seek to turn the median voter against the politician at reelection time. The enemies pose a greater threat to the public official than does the disconnected median voter, which is why most politicians will not stand up to a group of intransigent constituents at a hearing. The group does not represent the majority of voters; indeed, its members likely are neighbors of the project promoting their own interests. But they do represent the core of an opposition group that might coalesce against the incumbent if she fails to vote the way they demand. Discretion being the better part of valor, the politician defers to their wishes. This explains why it takes so few neighbors at a hearing to kill a project.

The Age of Entitlement

This deference to citizen entitlement represents a sea change in local government attitude toward developers and citizens. Today, local boards will bend and stretch the rules to reach the desired outcome: what the neighbors want. They will make sure that evidence that needs to get on the record gets there, and they will vet their written decision through the city legal department to make sure the decision is well-grounded, neither arbitrary nor capricious, and that the developer's appeal will fail. Before this new era of citizen entitlement, local boards would do the bending and stretching in the other direction, to achieve what the developer wanted, because growth equaled progress.

Today, however, citizens consider themselves treated fairly only if their public officials vote the way they want them to vote. A developer will think otherwise, but he does not have the entitlement that the citizens do. In fact, developers are often their own worst enemies, demanding relief when they have no right to it.

Citizens have no duty to be fair toward the developer, but the local board does have a quasi-judicial duty to be even-handed, or at least to appear to be so. This is why local boards that succumb to political pressure from neighbors must not say that they are doing so, and why public hearings often resemble an elaborate dance, with posturing and playing to the crowd.

Holding [onto] Public Office

Why does a local public official want to keep his office? For the same reason he ran for it in the first place: power, prestige, recognition, ego boost, desire to serve, public spirit. It takes a particular type of personality to seek a public office whose duties will subject the holder to midnight phone calls demanding to know why the burned-out streetlight hasn't been repaired. Whether the local official enjoys the public recognition, relishes being in charge, or has less noble reasons for wanting public office, he wants to keep the office once he wins it.

Politicians seldom leave office voluntarily. Short of running up against a term-limits law or facing a personal scandal or crisis, politicians seldom resign from office. A local official who resigns to give someone else a chance to serve is a rare bird indeed.

Good Projects Do Not Necessarily Get Approved

Some projects are sure to tickle the NIMBY bone in abutters and nearby neighbors, and some projects are simply objectionable LULUs. But what about developers who work hard to make their projects "green," set just the right density, produce marketing materials and public relations programs touting the projects' benefits to the community, provide all sorts of mitigation and linkage, contribute to local charities, and even install floodlights at the local soft-ball diamond? Do their projects get approved? Not necessarily.

What makes a project good is subjective. Sometimes *good* means politically correct or environmentally sensitive. Sometimes it reflects a belief that the community needs the proposed project, such as housing, mixed-use rehabilitation of an old factory, or a distribution center that will provide 200 jobs. Sometimes it means architecture that residents consider attractive or a design that somehow enhances its surroundings. But what the developer and his team think is a fabulous design often generates real hostility among potential neighbors, and it makes no difference that the mayor and city council have promised to support the project. Confronted with angry constituents, public officials will back off their support. Unless the developer is sophisticated enough to have built support for the project in the community and gives public officials the political cover they need, the project will fail.

Good projects do not automatically get approved. Being good is necessary but not sufficient, just as water is necessary but not sufficient to sustain human life; we also need food, air, sunlight, and moderate temperatures. Projects need to be perceived as good by the people who count: abutters, neighbors, and, most important, citizens in general. Adding 200 jobs to the local economy is a benefit, unless neighbors view it as adding 200 cars (or 400 vehicle trips) per day to their residential streets.

Some experts argue that community opinion leaders are necessary in this process. They believe in organizing support at the "grass-tops" level—former elected officials, members of the clergy, prominent businesspeople, a local celebrity or two—to help influence public officials and bring ordinary citizens along. Others think a project needs a "champion," an elected or appointed public official who leads the charge in favor of the project. Either approach might produce results in rare circumstances, but the good old days of political influence peddling are waning. Today, citizens organize, set up Web sites, call on national organizations for advice and help, produce flyers on their home computers, and turn out an angry crowd at a hearing.

In the old building-is-progress days, nobody came to hearings or raised a fuss, so projects got approved. Public officials were seen as powerful and unapproachable, part of an impenetrable political machine run by party bosses and big shots, and the little guy could not fight city hall.

The champion approach is particularly outmoded and unrealistic. This tactic was used in the late 1970s and early 1980s, when people thought they needed a politician to get anything done. Today, citizens are far more activist and assertive. They realize that the politician needs them more than they need her, and that a public official who double-crosses her constituency might well find herself voted out of office. It is highly unlikely that an elected official would stick out her neck to support a controversial project that her constituents oppose. It's also likely that an appointed official who decided to publicly promote that same project would be told to sit down and be quiet, since his role as champion will reflect on the elected official who appointed him.

Whether the approach be grass tops or champion, Americans are far less prone today than they were in decades past to follow the leader in land use fights, be the leader a prominent local clergyman or a former mayor, especially if he is seen as promoting the project. In any case, neighbors who oppose a project because they think it will ruin their neighborhood are not going to sit on their hands just because some local politician or celebrity says so.

What Constitutes Good?

What might be good for the community (let's say, affordable housing) may not be good for the neighbors if they perceive it as lowering their property values, attracting an undesirable element, or diminishing the character and quality of life in the neighborhood. Again, it's not the reality (if that could be measured) that counts; it's the perception. People associate publicly assisted housing (often derisively called "the projects") with poverty, drugs, and crime. All publicly assisted housing does not have these problems, but middle-class neighbors don't see any reason to take the risk that the project proposed for their neighborhood will meet the stereotype.

From the neighbors' point of view, "good" means a project that is minimally invasive of their peace and quiet, their lifestyle, and the qualities of their neighborhood that they value. Noisy, dusty, smelly traffic magnets are not going to be greeted as good.

For activists, "good" may mean minimal impacts on wetlands, wildlife habitat, and natural processes, little or no air or water pollution, a small carbon footprint, "green" development, and an unobtrusive profile.

"Good" for a local politician means generally that a vote in favor of the project will generate chits toward reelection — that the project will be popular among constituents, so that she can point to it with pride and take some credit for bringing it to the community. Of course, it might also mean that the developer feels grateful enough to make a contribution to the politician's campaign fund and rounds up a few of his friends to do likewise.

"Good" for interest groups answers the question "What's in it for me?" In other words, will the group or its members benefit? The trade unions, for example, will want to know how many well-paying jobs the project will generate, and for how long. The electrical, plumbing, roofing, and other supply houses will want to know that they'll have an opportunity to bid on the project. The local merchants will want to know whether the project will be good for business, whether it will bring new customers to their stores and shops. The municipal assessor, school superintendent, and mayor will wonder how much tax revenue the project will generate, and the mayor will especially want to know how many permanent jobs will be offered.

Everyone Has an Agenda

The legal basis for zoning has always arisen from more lofty sentiments — protection of public health, welfare, and morals, for example. The reality is that everyone involved in zoning and land use — the applicant, the neighbors, the town officials, the supporters, the opponents, the applicant's competitors—has a political agenda. Public health is a consideration, but let's be honest: gone are the days of slaughterhouses built next to orphanages. Gone, too, are the days when a developer could fill in a marsh or clear-cut a forest without anyone saying a word.

In local land use politics, as in almost everything else, everyone has an agenda. Even the pure of heart who don't realize they have agendas actually do, because it's human nature to think about how a given proposal will affect you, your friends, and your community. Some agendas are easily spotted and straightforward. But others may not be, and it falls to the project proponent to figure out what a given person or group's real agenda may be, and to act accordingly. Often, the neighbors' agenda is simply to see how they can benefit in exchange for dropping their opposition to a project. What will the developer offer for their silence or support? Can they make the developer buy their homes for twice their value? If not, can they exact some sort of damage payment from the developer? Can they at least force the developer to donate land for a playground?

Opponents who are intractably against a project may focus on adverse environmental impacts, claiming to be friends of nature. But often their real agenda is to make sure nothing gets built. Generally, such opponents use a kitchen-sink approach, throwing every conceivable objection and obstacle at the proposal to see what sticks. Sophisticated opponents will use a serial objection approach, pressing one issue at a time until it is resolved, and then raising another, ad infinitum.

The developer's team will assert that the project is for the greater good. Such an argument is not persuasive to people who believe that the development's noise, crowds, traffic, and odors will adversely affect their quality of life and, worse, their property values. Who could argue that any structure, including a church or an old folks' home, will not be more problematic than a vacant lot? No matter how well designed, attractive, or environmentally sensitive a project may be, it still represents change to the neighbors and brings a danger that bad things will result from it.

There are exceptions for projects that reclaim eyesores, such as vacant shopping malls, brownfield sites where environmental contamination demands remedy, and the rehab and conversion of old factories to mixed uses. But even when the project is seen as a plus for the community, neighbors will demand the least possible intrusion on their lives, and they will often demand a mitigation pound of flesh beyond the pocket park included in the design. This is their neighborhood: they have a sense of ownership, possession, and entitlement, and they want some acknowledgment of their importance in allowing the project to proceed. Besides, this may be their one and only chance to force a developer to make neighborhood improvements that the city won't make and the neighbors can't afford.

Building As-of-Right: An Old-Fashioned Misnomer

Old-timers in the development business will remember when as-of-right development was the rule, not the exception. How times have changed.

As-of-right means that the development proposal meets the requirements of the zoning ordinance or bylaw, so no type of approval, hearing, or discretionary zoning relief is needed and therefore no forum is available for opponents to hound their elected public officials. The developer simply files the plans and application for a building permit, which the building department rubber-stamps and issues.

Modern citizens and New Age planners, who consider themselves stakeholders in other people's property, don't like as-of-right development because it robs them of what they consider their right to dictate the design of someone else's project. So modern ordinances, by and large, severely limit the property owner's ability to get a building permit as a matter of right, and some regimes—the form-based zoning variety—eliminate it entirely. Instead, ordinances require discretionary relief: a special permit, a conditional use permit, a special use permit, and, of course, site plan review. Although an even-handed board would treat hearings on such permits as formalities, the reality is that once a forum is required, opponents have an opportunity to object, suggest changes, cause delays, pressure the board members, and call for the plans to be withdrawn and resubmitted with a much less ambitious design.

In some states, developers (and some local boards) confuse as-of-right with discretionary permitting. The fact that the developer appears before the local board and makes a presentation that addresses each required element does not automatically give him a right to discretionary zoning relief. While he might truly believe that he has satisfied each element of the required showings, that belief does not constitute objective truth. Board members are not supposed to decide the case based on legally irrelevant factors outside the scope of the statute or ordinance, but their perceptions and the developer's may differ—and theirs is the perception that counts. If the question is whether the proposed project sufficiently protects the environment, does enough to screen the neighbors, or effectively blocks pollution—all subjective judgments—the decision the board reaches on whether the developer has satisfied the requirements will be binding.

The developer can appeal, but courts broadly defer to the judgment of the local board that, after all, heard the testimony and viewed the evidence. If the board says no, the courts will ordinarily uphold that decision, unless the developer can prove that the board acted either corruptly or in an arbitrary and capricious manner. This is very difficult to do and illustrates why so few developers win appeals of discretionary decisions.

Once again, all land use decisions are political. It might be argued that board members voted against the project for legally improper reasons—because the neighbors oppose it, for example—rather than because the proposal failed to meet the ordinance criteria. But saying it and proving it are two different things.

As-of-right is also an old-fashioned misnomer in the modern world because of the litany of compliance regulations and reviews that offer opponents further opportunities to complain. In addition to the traditional bulk and dimensional issues, environmental, ecological, historic, and archaeological reviews are now common. New federal, state, regional, and local compliance elements are added every year as bureaucracies grow and justify themselves.

In some states, like California and Connecticut, the development's economic impact must be examined, while in others, compliance with the urban growth limit and agricultural zone limits must be met. Imaginative New Age planners are now including "viewscape" and "odorscape" requirements in their squishy and highly discretionary review requirements, making development permitting uncertain and undermining the developer's ability to secure and maintain financing. This latter issue is one that sophisticated modern-day opponents have come to cherish: delay a project long enough, and the developer's financing will dry up, or the carrying charges will overwhelm her, and she'll simply go away.

Even if the developer is able to secure a building permit, there will be numerous other permits, certificates, and sign-offs that provide a range of opportunities for opponents to throw up obstacles. Will the project require a state-issued curb cut to discharge traffic onto the public way? Opponents will write letters and corral their state legislators. Does the project need sewer and water hookups to municipal services? Opponents will demand a study measuring the impact of the development on the sewer and water systems' capacity, and the resulting effect on both water pressure and the flow rate through sewer discharge pipes. They'll ask for the fire chief's ruminations on whether the project will make it difficult to fight a serious inferno elsewhere in town, and inquire of the water department whether the development will result in watering restrictions on homeowners' lawns. Does the project require a gravel or soil removal permit? A tree-cutting permit? Fire department access? A trash disposal permit? A dust remediation permit? Runoff booms and erosion barriers? Excavation in the public way to install pipes and wires? In each case, opponents have an opportunity to object, raise issues, and cause delays.

Where the developer is the tenant, as when major retailers build stand-alone stores so they can control the site, or where the anchor tenant's identity is known, obvious, or assumed, operational issues enter the fray, making the problem more complicated. Why should the greenhouse on a big-box development be allowed to use 50,000 gallons of water per day when abutting residential neighbors are pro-hibited from watering their lawns all summer? So the owner can make a profit? Shouldn't the store's roof and parking lot runoff be collected in a tight tank? If not, how will the owner remove pollu-tants that will otherwise get into the groundwater? What types of chemicals are the store's photo developing and garden departments going to pour down the drains? Why should the big-box be open 24 hours a day when working people nearby are trying to sleep? Should the store be allowed to leave its parking lot unpatrolled when teenagers are likely to use it to execute "donuts" with their screech-ing tires, yell obscenities, take drugs, and smash beer bottles? Why should the taxpayers pay the police to quell these disturbances when the owner can hire a guard service?

These questions demonstrate why big-box tenants typically seek to remain anonymous and place their out-front developers in the laughable position of claiming that they don't know who the tenant will be. In other words, they want people to believe that they're going to clear a 10-acre site and build a 250,000-square-foot box on speculation.

A further point about as-of-right building is that, even though the project may appear to meet all the legal and zoning criteria, the community can hastily amend the zoning ordinance, or declare a building moratorium, or find technical fault with the design or docu-ments, thereby staying the hand of the building commissioner or overruling his decision. Will this lead to litigation? Maybe, but as noted earlier, courts will try hard to defer to the local government. Even if the court finds against the community, it will simply refer the matter back to the local board for a rehearing. A developer who thinks a local board, once sued and defeated in court, will then approve a project it deplores is living in a fantasyland. Meanwhile, the community is rewriting the bylaw, rezoning the land, and expanding the list of developments that are required to obtain discre-tionary permitting before they are allowed.

The point is that the local land use permitting process is totally political and is thus controlled by those who control the ballot box. Even where regional or state bureaucrats are responsible for issuing various permits and certificates, they and their supervisors are likely to comply with the request of a legislator, mayor, or other elected official representing the community. It seldom needs to get down to whether their agency budget will be cut, or whether heads should roll at the permit-issuing desk, or even whether the requesting party belongs to the same political party as the governor. The politics of favor trading are more subtle than that, and more effective.

Modern project opponents are both resourceful and determined, and the political pressure they can bring to bear easily short-circuits the supposed right to build. Challenging the building permit as improvidently granted, attacking the ancillary permits, demanding a full environmental impact report (EIR), finding listed endangered species on site, and uncovering an archaeological or historic site are all within their knowledge and ability to do at the local level. They are not above appealing to higher authority—the Army Corps of Engineers, the Federal Aviation Authority (FAA), the Federal Communications Commission (FCC), the Environmental Protection Agency (EPA), the Interior Department, the National Park Service, or whatever bureaucracy might have some jurisdiction. And they are not shy about going through their congressional delegation to make sure their concerns are heard.

Finally, project opponents know that state and national organizations of all stripes—environmental, ecological, antidevelopment, anti–population growth, anti–big-box, pro-planning, preservationist, historical, archaeological, maritime, utopian—are readily available through Web sites and e-mail to offer advice and ideas that are, on analysis, nothing more or less than political strategies and tactics.

CHAPTER 2

■ ■ ■

A Primer on Land Use Regulation in Western Democracies

CITIZENS DID NOT ALWAYS wield such power in the development process. Under the long-settled English common-law principle of *sic utere tuo ut alienum non laedas* (use your own [land] so as not harm others' [land]), a landowner could do whatever he liked with his land so long as he did not cause a "nuisance" to his neighbor or "trespass" on his neighbor's property.[1] If he did, the neighbor would sue, and the courts would decide the issue. Unless the activity constituted a public nuisance, the municipality never got involved.

But the balance of power shifted dramatically with the spread of formal zoning policies in the Western Hemisphere, starting in the United States. With these policies, governments set limits on how

---

[1]The principle was established long before it was used to decide a landmark 1837 English tort case, which also codified the prudent-man rule that still sets the standard for tort law in the United Kingdom, the United States, and Canada. In that case, the defendant built a hayrick (haystack), with a chimney to deter spontaneous combustion, on the edge of his land abutting the plaintiff's land. The plaintiff repeatedly warned the defendant that his stack was poorly constructed and would catch fire. The defendant ignored the warnings; the stack caught fire; the fire spread to the plaintiff's land and burned down two of his cottages. The defendant argued that he was not negligent, just stupid. In applying the *sic utere* principle, the court held that being stupid is no excuse and that the standard to be applied is what a "man of ordinary prudence" would have done. In this case, the prudent man, having been warned of the danger, would have fixed the haystack chimney before the stack caught fire (*Vaughan v. Menlove*. 3 Bing N.C., 132 E.R. 490 [C.P.] [1837]).

private landowners could use their land, often requiring formal citizen input as part of the process. Zoning as a formal government practice is less than a century old, but European cities practiced forms of ad hoc zoning long ago—forbidding noxious uses in the center of town, for example. As global travel and communication developed, ideas of land use control, environmental protection, and urban planning spread far and wide.

Europeans, whose cities have been teeming with people for centuries, laugh at the concept of a U.S. density issue. The British have greenbelts and enforce them, but the United Kingdom is 94,526 square miles in size—a bit smaller than Oregon—and accommodates 60 million people, or about 637 per square mile. The United States is 3,794,066 square miles in size, about 40 times larger than the United Kingdom, but it has only five times as many people, or about 80 per square mile. When Americans whine about density, Brits politely roll their eyes.

Land use fights are not limited to the United States. All Western-style democracies have land use regulations of one sort or another, and fights over land use can be found in Canada, the United Kingdom, South America, and Europe.

Land Use Regulation in the United States

Adoption of the first zoning ordinance in the United States occurred in New York, where the state legislature passed a statewide zoning-enabling act in 1916. The ordinance was a reaction to the development of skyscrapers in Manhattan and the ensuing complaints from Fifth Avenue merchants that the new buildings blocked light, sunshine, and air from reaching their shops. Adoption of the first zoning ordinance in the United States was thus based on NIMBY opposition to development, and began the long tradition of using zoning as a political tool to benefit one group of property owners at the expense of another.

The use of zoning in the United States began in the midst of the Progressive Era, a period of activism between 1890 and the 1920s that sought various reforms to restore morality and civic purity, including a healthier urban environment. Progressives believed in people's ability to improve their environment, in the duty of government to intervene in economic and social matters, and in the ability of experts to solve society's problems. Although some of the Progressives' experiments proved inauspicious—Prohibition and the income tax, for example—their concern with overcrowding and congestion in the urban environment and their role in poverty, disease, and misery captured the imagination of politicians and millionaires alike. No less a worthy than financier Henry Morgenthau testified before Congress in 1910 that city planning to reduce overcrowding and congestion was essential to America's future.

In the 1920s the U.S. Commerce Department created the Standard State Zoning Enabling Act (SZEA), under which states could allow their municipalities to adopt local zoning regulations. Nearly every state adopted the SZEA, or some version based on it, and it has shown remarkable durability, lasting virtually unchanged in many cases for more than 50 years.

The language in the SZEA is extremely broad. "Health and the general welfare" is a very large area, as are the other sweeping grants of authority under the act. What constitutes "adequate light and air," for example, or "undue concentration of population" is subjective, arguably arbitrary, and certainly debatable. Some people thought the powers far too broad, leading in due course to court challenges. The basis of those challenges was the infringement that zoning imposed on traditional property rights of landowners through the rise of the regulatory state inspired by political Progressives.

Key to the issue of zoning was whether government ought to use its fundamental authority to protect the public—the police power—to limit landowners' rights. Arising from ancient common law, the police power is an elemental, assumed, but often unexpressed power by which government protects the health, safety, security, morality, and general welfare of its citizens.[2] It is the police power that empowers

---

[2] The common-law principle is expressed by courts in Latin: *Salus populi suprema lex est* (The welfare of the people is the supreme law). It is found in Marcus Tullius Cicero's *de Legibus*, among countless other legal tracts.

government to require that children attend school and that they first get vaccinations against communicable diseases.

The landmark case *Euclid v. Ambler* arose in 1926 to determine whether private property rights could be curtailed in the interests of higher public concerns, such as health, welfare, and the prevention of congestion — in other words, whether zoning was legal.[3] Euclid, Ohio, had adopted a zoning ordinance to prevent industrial Cleveland from expanding into the village. The ordinance divided the village into six use classes, three height classes, and four area classes, restricting what might be built in each case. Ambler Realty Company owned 68 acres of vacant land. The new village ordinance divided Ambler's tract into three use classes, as well as differing height and area classes, severely limiting the available uses and substantially reducing the land's value. Ambler argued that the zoning ordinance amounted to an unlawful taking of the land. The court upheld the ordinance, ruling that so long as the zoning ordinance bore a "rational relation to the health and safety of the community," it was a valid exercise of the police power.

Once *Euclid* was decided, "Euclidean" zoning spread throughout the United States and into Canada. At about the same time in Washington, D.C., Progressives were running off copies of the SZEA by the thousands and sending them off to legislatures and municipalities, along with instructions on how to get started. By 1930, 35 of the 48 states had adopted SZEA-based legislation, the kind found in most North American locales even today.

The emergence of the regulatory state also saw the rise of regulatory takings of land, a government imposition that would eventually lead to the rise (or reincarnation) of the property rights movement. While the power of government to take people's land for public uses, the eminent domain power, is contained in the U.S. and state constitutions, it is also limited, requiring a "public use" and "just compensation."[4] Historically, land takings for public purposes had been required for building roads, canals, railroads, and all manner of public works

[3] *Village of Euclid, Ohio v. Ambler Realty Co.*, 272 U.S. 365 (1926).
[4] U.S. Constitution, Fifth Amendment: "nor shall private property be taken for public use, without just compensation."

and public utilities, as well as public facilities—schools, fire stations, hospitals, and public parks. But with the rise of the regulatory state came takings not for direct public use but for economic uses that proponents saw as beneficial to the public, whereby government took land from an owner and turned it over to a new owner for economic development.[5]

Most attentive people in the United States are today aware of the 2005 case of *Kelo v. City of New London, Connecticut* (545 U.S. 469 [2005]), in which the state condemned the working-class homes of Susette Kelo and 14 of her neighbors and took them by eminent domain to accommodate development of a resort hotel, conference center, and other amenities to complement the new Pfizer pharmaceutical research facility nearby. The issue was whether the public use required under the U.S. Constitution includes a public purpose—that is, economic development aimed at strengthening the local economy through urban renewal. The U.S. Supreme Court famously found that it does, but the decision was merely the latest in a long chain of regulatory takings that property rights advocates find infuriating.[6]

Land Use Regulation in Canada

In Canada, agencies and procedures reflect their own culture, political history, and government format, but their mandates are much the same as those in other Western-style democracies: public health and welfare, controlled development, ecological and environmental protection and preservation, and provision of adequate housing, both market rate and affordable. As in the United States, zoning and enforcement are handled at the local level through municipal

---

[5]Because all land in the United Kingdom was essentially nationalized by the 1947 Town and Country Planning Act, the British version of eminent domain, called a compulsory purchase, is available to the government to transfer property from one owner to another for economic development.

[6]For full details, documents, and lawyerly debate on *Kelo*, see Dwight H. Merriam and Mary Massaro Ross, *Eminent Domain Use and Abuse: Kelo in Context* (Chicago: American Bar Association Press, 2006).

boards of officials who hold citizen input meetings, draft plans and bylaws, and are subject to political influence from citizens who, like their U.S. neighbors, feel empowered to express their views and seek redress of their grievances. At the local level, public officials respond to this direct democracy, but there are differences as the Canadian version of regional planning comes into play.

In Ontario, by far the fastest-growing region, land use is a highly contentious subject. Canada, which has been changing from a rural to an urban industrial society, faces the impacts that such a transformation brings. Local officials are responsible for preparing official plans (the Canadian equivalent of comprehensive plans in the United States), zoning bylaws, and other planning documents. While citizen input is encouraged, local land use planning programs must follow Ontario's policies, plans, and laws, which are set by the provincial government. This system is somewhat akin to the process used in the United Kingdom, in which the national government up to the ministerial level can sometimes get involved in land use issues. Thus, Canada's system can be thought of as a sort of cross between the U.S. and the U.K. approaches, with elements tailored to Canadian needs.

Canada has a population of roughly 33 million people. With 9.9 million square kilometers (3.8 million square miles), it is the second largest country, by area, in the world (after Russia) and the largest in the Western Hemisphere. "Over the next 20 years, the Great Lakes Basin is expected to account for one-half of total population growth in Canada," at a growth rate of 22 percent.[7] Most of this growth is expected to occur at the western end of Lake Ontario in an area known as the Golden Horseshoe region (Niagara Falls to Oshawa). It is this kind of rapid growth—along with increasing multicultural issues[8]—that the rapidly urbanizing Province of Ontario will face, and at which much of the planning and zoning effort is focused.

---

[7]"Canada's Response to the Recommendations in the Tenth Biennial Report of the International Joint Commission," Land Use Section, http://www.on.ec.gc.ca/laws/tenth-ijc -response/land_use-e.html.

[8]Canada has two official languages, English and French, and eight recognized regional languages spoken by the First Nations, Inuit, and Métis aboriginal peoples. Ontario faces additional issues in absorbing a heavy influx of immigrants.

The Ontario Municipal Board

Because of the nation's history as a French colony (1604–1763), then as a British colony (1764–1867), then as a dominion, and now as a voluntary member of the British Commonwealth of Nations, Canada's legal establishment and institutions have received much from French and British law and practice. In Ontario, as in the United Kingdom, the process of appeal goes through an appointed agency called the Ontario Municipal Board (OMB), rather than directly to the court system as elsewhere in Canada.

The OMB is an appointed independent administrative tribunal that hears appeals on land use, zoning, subdivisions, official plans, minor variances, land compensation matters, and various other municipal issues. Its power over municipal matters has expanded over the years as various statutes have delegated authority to it, including authority over municipal finance, development, planning, and zoning, among others, and it operates under different ministries depending on the statute involved. It hears evidence on environmental, social, and economic issues; provincial legislation and policy statements; municipal planning documents, including official plans and zoning bylaws; the rights of individuals; and the best interests of the whole community—a broad mandate by anyone's standards.

The lieutenant governor of Ontario, who is appointed by the governor general, determines the number of OMB members, appoints them, designates one member as chair, and may designate one or more vice chairs. Presumably, the appointees to this important, well-paid, and powerful board are politically connected.

OMB hearings are less formal than judicial proceedings, but witnesses do testify under oath, and parties are allowed to cross-examine, submit evidence, and call experts. Although the OMB hearing is designated as an appeal, it actually is held de novo. This means that the case must be presented from scratch, but in the past it has also meant that the OMB has completely ignored the local decision-making process. The OMB seldom reviews its decisions, and even more rarely changes a decision.

The OMB has been subject to great criticism for siding with developers in most cases, despite local opposition from activists and rejection of projects by local boards. As in the United States, this foments resentment among local residents and officials, who don't like provincial government interference. The broad mandate given the OMB and the liberal manner in which it interprets its authority have led to demands that it be disbanded, particularly as urbanization in Ontario continues apace. Recent amendments to Ontario's Planning Act now require the OMB to take note of the local council's decision in deciding appeals. This might present a problem to local politicians, who have been able blame the OMB for decisions their constituents don't like and who often refuse politically sensitive planning applications, forcing the OMB to become the villain. To what extent having regard for municipal decisions will alter the political landscape of land use permitting remains to be seen. Antidevelopment activists and their adherents in environmental, ecological, historical, and preservationist circles would prefer that the OMB disappear in favor of empowering local authority. But such a broadly democratic change is not going to happen.

Land Use Regulation in the United Kingdom

People in the United Kingdom have shared many of the concerns of their cousins in the United States. Worries over industrialization, urbanization, and the attendant pollution and sprawl built through the first half of the twentieth century. Modern development control began in the United Kingdom in 1947 with passage of the Town and Country Planning Act, which essentially nationalized the right to develop land and established a system whereby local government regulates land use and new development. Since then, all development proposals (with a few minor exceptions) have been required to obtain planning permission from the local planning authority (LPA), which generally means the local elected Borough Council or District Council.

When the act was passed in the immediate postwar years, swaths of London were still in ruins from Hitler's bombs, and it was presumed that most new construction would be developed by public sector agencies, which would simply grant themselves planning permission. The planning control system was intended to govern the small number of private development proposals that might appear. In fact, it quickly became clear that the private sector would be far more vigorous in rebuilding the nation and its economy, and a private development boom, begun in the 1950s, remains robust to the present day.

The act—which did not adopt formal zoning as did the United States and Canada—requires the local planning authority to develop a local plan for development of the community, indicating what type of development will be allowed where, and setting forth use classes and regulations for adoption of local plans. Counties are charged with the duty of developing structure plans, setting goals for the wider county area. The act sets forth the rules (and use classes for buildings and land) by which the local plan must be designed, thereby allowing the national government to use planning as a tool to achieve its own goals, including some relating to the environment, housing, and sprawl. Planning policies address a wide range of issues, including energy efficiency, highways and safety, open space, and preserving historical sites.

The local planning authority is expected to hear planning permission applications and make decisions based on how well the development complies with the policies in the local plan, and not whether they are popular with the townspeople. Thus, as planners are anxious to note, planning control is policy-led, rather than influence-led. Still, U.K. citizens, like their counterparts in the United States, feel increasingly empowered and entitled to challenge proposed developments. The Internet is rife with British community organizations, as well as more traditional environmental and protectionist groups. No matter how strictly the planning elite interpret the law, locally elected councilors are sensitive to public pressure and will meet with a delegation of citizens to discuss their concerns.

An applicant whose application is refused has a right of appeal, but project opponents have no right of appeal if planning permission is granted. Appeals are referred to the Planning Inspectorate in England and Wales, and to similar agencies in Scotland and Northern Ireland. An official inspector investigates the case and determines whether to uphold or overturn the local planning authority decision. About 70 percent of planning appeals uphold the original decisions.

Numerous recent amendments intended to streamline the permissions process have not changed the essential nature of the original 1947 act. The local planning authority is still expected to make decisions acting under its local plan (now called a local development framework, or LDF), which is composed of local development documents (LDDs) and supplementary planning documents (SPDs). The authority is still expected to produce and periodically update a plan (now called a local development scheme) and explain the LDDs and SPDs it intends to draft over the following three years, as well as statements of community involvement describing how the authority will encourage participation from the local citizenry. It must also produce a sustainability appraisal (SA) and a strategic environmental assessment (SEA). Not surprisingly, some critics complain that instead of simplifying and speeding up the system, these recent reforms will have the opposite effect, given the increase in the number, type, and length of documents an authority is required to produce, and the sheer number of new acronyms that have been introduced.

CHAPTER 3

■ ■ ■

What Is Land Use Politics?

LAND USE POLITICS is a new discipline in land use permitting that employs sophisticated political campaign strategies and tactics to help ordinary citizens influence public officials' decision-making process in reaching land use decisions. It is not lobbying, and its practitioners do not engage public officials in discussion on the pros and cons of a development proposal. Instead, land use politics practitioners facilitate grassroots activism by organizing and assisting citizens in the effective use of their political rights. These include the right to free speech, the right to petition the government for redress of grievances, and the right to assemble, so that the citizens themselves can urge their public officials to act in a way consistent with their wishes.

Land use politics is based on citizen advocacy, not professional lobbying or presentation. The difference is considerable, and the benefits are many. First, nobody in a community is more credible to public officials or fellow citizens than a local taxpayer and voter who expresses concerns and asks questions about a development proposal. When the voter articulates the reasons for favoring or opposing a project, he will be heard with respect.

The lobbyist, public relations consultant, marketing team, and lawyers will be seen as hired guns whose driving force is money, not community character. Their approach is factual, analytical, academic, or legalistic, not personal or emotional and not driven by what's best for the neighborhood and its residents. The credibility of these professionals is suspect, despite their credentials, experience, and expertise, and their arguments leave plenty of room for doubt. They are paid by the developer, so local citizens might be forgiven for suspecting that they might skew their figures, or liberally interpret the data, or give the greatest weight to data that best help their client's case.

Lawyers, perhaps, as well as architects, engineers, and other professionals might be given a little slack in the credibility department because they have ethical standards that generally prohibit flat-out deceit. People understand that they are necessary to design projects that comply with the building code and to present the resulting proposal to town officials. Still, local officials will listen to the words of a local citizen before they will be moved by paid project advocates, and rightly so. Local citizens can vote to reelect the public officials; the architect cannot. There is another, less cynical reason: local citizens can describe firsthand how the project is likely to affect their lifestyles, property, or families—or at least how they perceive that it will. The architect may have taken great care to make the project unobtrusive, environmentally sensitive, and user-friendly, and may take great personal pride in the design she has created. But the development won't affect her home and family directly and personally every day. No matter how well it is designed, the project is just another commission for her; she will not have to live with the traffic, noise, and disruption it causes in the neighborhood.

Second, local citizens have local memory, including the history and background of the site, the neighborhood, and the town as a whole. They remember people and events that out-of-town consultants, lobbyists, or professionals have no way of knowing. Consultants and professionals can speak from academic, scientific, design, and planning perspectives; local citizens can speak from the heart.

Local citizens also have personal and psychological investments in the community. This means that they are highly unlikely to favor a proposal that they believe is bad for the town, even if they would gain personally, and that they will actively oppose efforts to impose such a development on their community.

Finally, local citizens have local ties; they know their public officials on a personal, neighborly, or family basis, and the public officials share their concerns about the community and the future. In many municipalities, city and town councils are elected by ward or by district; when a vote is taken, other councilors defer to the member who represents the involved district. That district councilor is highly likely to support the view of her constituents, not only because of their power at the ballot box, but also because she knows and respects them—and will have to live with the vote she makes while working in her district on a daily basis.

Land use politics is based on citizen advocacy, pro or con. Citizen advocacy moves political influence out of the shadows and into the light because the citizen speaks directly to public officials about how he believes the development will affect him and his community. It overcomes corrupt machine politics because the citizen speaks publicly for himself, influencing other citizens and organizing them into a political force, while the creaky old political machine is busy pulling levers behind the curtains, trying to trade political favors while disregarding the voting public's wishes.

The job of the land use politics consultant is to find citizens whose support or opposition to a given development concurs with the client's posture, and to help them organize into an effective political force. No doubletalk or arm-twisting is necessary; a practiced political consultant knows how to find people who share a given view and how to track down those who would agree if asked because they are natural advocates of that point of view.

Example: A New School

Who could be expected to support a proposal for a new school? Teachers, certainly, and parents (especially newcomers), as well as members of the school committee under whose authority the school would fall, are likely to support it. Local tradespeople who might benefit from jobs in constructing the school would likely be in favor, and so would vendors of desks and chairs and blackboards and playground equipment. So would local merchants whose businesses attract children or who serve their needs — a convenience store near the school site or a store that sells school supplies. The teachers' union would support the school, but whether other unions, such as those representing police officers and firefighters, would do so depends on their own priorities. It's all well and good to support fellow union brothers and sisters, but not if it means cutbacks in your own department.

Who could be expected to oppose the new school? Elderly and childless taxpayers (especially old-timers) would oppose it because they would gain no direct benefit from the school but would nonetheless pay for it in their taxes. Taxpayer groups could be expected to oppose the school because they dislike big-ticket spending and amortizing huge debt. They will argue that the current school facilities would be adequate if their use were reconfigured somehow. Municipal financial officials — the city auditor, perhaps, or the finance committee — might be opposed because the project is too ambitious, the city's taxpayers can't afford it, and the city has other priorities. They know that the capital cost is just the beginning. A new school means more administrators, teachers, teachers' aides, cafeteria workers, and janitorial staff. Their salaries are paid in current budgets, not amortized like capital expenses, and therefore have an immediate and permanent effect on the local tax rate. The police and fire chiefs might be opposed if development means they will lose out on a new fire truck or squad cars, will have to wait for their own new headquarters buildings to be financed, or will lose momentum in staffing because the money will be diverted to hire school personnel. Opposition can be expected from the landowners in the neighborhood identified as the site of the new school because they will have to tolerate the noise, kids, vandalism, and property value impact of the school for the next 25 years. Although property values are enhanced by being near a school, being next door or across the street reduces values.

Instead of carpet bombing the municipality with flyers or marketing to those who cannot be convinced, the land use politics consultant identifies people and groups who are likely to support the aims he advocates. He works with them to achieve their goals since by doing so he also achieves his client's goals. People's reasons for support or opposition will vary. For example, residents don't want a big-box development because they don't want traffic, noise, and other inconveniences; local merchants don't want to compete with its prices; environmentalists fear it will destroy wildlife habitat and cause pollution. Each has a different impetus, but agreement on one key element—in this case, opposition—is how coalitions are made. How the various members of the coalition arrived there is not important.

Thus, land use politics uses the tools of democracy to achieve political ends, and it is highly effective.

Land Use Decisions Are Political

Land use decisions are really political decisions and are subject to the same rules of play that control political campaigns for office, ballot questions, or passing a bill in the council, legislature, or parliament: plan a campaign, devise strategy, identify leaders, organize field troops, anticipate opposition tactics and plan countermeasures, execute the campaign program, and get out the vote effectively to win.

As noted in Chapter 1, land use decisions are political because the reasons for and against a given decision are subjective and therefore are affected by individuals' own perceptions and agendas. Casting an agenda in lofty moral, nostalgic, or sentimental terms—to save an endangered species, to return to a simpler time, or to encourage walking and biking for good health—does not alter its political nature; it highlights it. For every good land use intention expressed in ethical, nostalgic, or sentimental terms, there is a downside, though the price is not usually paid by the advocate of the high-toned values. Thus, activists' demands to preserve the forest for future generations may mean that the landowner cannot get her land rezoned, cannot engage in logging on her own property, cannot use the land for development, or cannot subdivide and sell it.

Any agenda that seeks to control or influence public decision making is, by definition, political, no matter how morally superior its stated goals. Environmentalists who want to protect the red-bellied turtle and its habitat are no less political than the people who want to reserve the best scenic views for McMansions and zone apartment houses out of existence, even though the former consider themselves objectively right-thinking and above the fray, and believe that their logic and motives are unassailable. Might such people harbor an unexpressed elitism, classism, or racism? Certainly, but the more important fact in land use politics is that they use political tools—the hammer and tongs of campaign strategy and tactics—to achieve their goals. The battle, therefore, is joined; it is a political fight. To win, political techniques are required.

How Will They Vote?

A development application is before the local council for a zoning change. The applicant's development team puts on a thorough presentation and answers all of the board members' questions satisfactorily, and the developer's attorney reminds the board of the many benefits the project will bring in exchange for a simple change in zoning. How will the board vote? Some consultants would analyze an individual board member's voting patterns, public statements, civic organization memberships, employment history, education, personal relationships, and political party in an effort to quantify each aspect of the member's background to arrive at a balanced prediction of the member's likelihood of voting favorably. That's a fine, if formulaic, exercise done in a vacuum, and it ignores the political realities that motivate a politician. It is unreliable.

At the same hearing, the audience is packed with local voters, many known to the council members, all wearing bright pink "Kill the Mall" T-shirts. An ocean of pink fills the hall, leaving standing room only, and spills into the hallway. Now, how do you think the board will vote?

The citizen group leader places a fat petition with hundreds of signatures from registered voters opposing the mall on the council desk. Now, how do you think the council will vote?

One by one, two dozen citizens take the microphone and testify that the mall will destroy their quality of life; bring traffic gridlock; endanger their children; invade their privacy; attract the criminal element; inflict their quiet residential community with noise, litter, fumes, and trespassers; damage the green space; endanger wildlife habitat; and bankrupt small merchants. Now, how will the council vote?

The neighbors testify that the developer has ignored their efforts to set up a meeting (or worse, has treated them rudely at a meeting called to discuss the project). Now, how will the members vote?

The council members' individual backgrounds are relevant, and some analysis is helpful in devising ways to influence a given member's vote. But the key point is that background indicates how a politician will act when other influences are not at work. In the real world, other influences are always at work, and political impacts (such as hearing turnout, crowds of neighbors, and petition drives) have a telling impact on political decision making.

In an era of satellite television and reclining easy chairs, rousing the public to confront the political issue is not always easy. But once inspired (or provoked), citizens can be remarkably determined.

In one case, a developer who was asked to pay the neighbors $100,000 for the impacts of his major project on their neighborhood rejected the request, saying, "You haven't done me $100,000 worth of damage." The neighbors took that insult as a challenge. They brought the project to a screeching halt, and the site remains vacant to this day. They did a good deal more than $100,000 worth of damage.

The Political Motive

Recognizing that land use decisions are political and identifying the political motivations can be difficult; even people motivated by politics sometimes don't realize it themselves. But recognizing the opponent's motivation as political, rather than simply religious, moral, or environmental, for example, is essential to mounting an effective political strategy. If the opponent's motivations are perceived as religious, civic, or moral, they may well be unassailable. Attacking another person's religion is seldom a winning strategy. If the real motives are political, the debate is no longer about right and wrong but about how the issue affects the neighborhood. At that level, campaign tactics will work.

While it might seem otherwise, the issue of whether to grant zoning relief to permit construction of a controversial church building is not a religious decision, but a political one. Consider the motives of the opposing sides of the issue. Parishioners want approval for their personal convenience in attending services, and maybe also as a physical, public affirmation of their faith and rectitude, as a demonstration of their community influence, as evidence of their growing importance, as a monument to encourage others to join up, and as a use that is likely to enhance their community's image. Neighbors of the site oppose the project because they don't want the inconvenience of church traffic, noise, and hubbub resulting from regular services, weddings, funerals, parish events and meetings, fraternal and youth gatherings, and other activities. A busy church, they perceive, is more likely to diminish their property values than enhance them. A few people might be motivated as well by bias against the tenets of the religion involved or the people who practice it, but even if they are, they can't very well oppose the church publicly on that basis. Church proponents will argue that the facility will be an asset to the neighborhood, not only for its architectural presence, but also as a symbol of stability and faith. Opponents will argue that the building's mass will dwarf the neighborhood, and that they don't want the edifice to dominate their lives and sharply change the character of their neighborhood, as it is sure to do. The winner of this debate will be the side that is best organized and that devises and executes the most compelling political campaign.

Similar issues apply in siting a school, which is even more emotional than the church debate because it hits parents squarely in the offspring and childless taxpayers firmly in the wallet. Where a school gets built is rife with sociopolitical ramifications: which kids get assigned to the new facility, which must be bused to attend it, and whether parental choice or geographical location will govern whether a child attends that particular school. Parents who want their child educated nearby will favor the school if they are sure their child will attend it, but they will be furious if a new school is constructed next door (with the attendant adverse impact on property values) and their own child is assigned elsewhere. In such a case, they are forced to tolerate the downside of having a school next door, but receive none of the benefits.

As the eldest baby boomers pass retirement age, they see fewer reasons to support school buildings, budgets, and programs, and an increasing number of reasons to urge frugality where public education is concerned. They argue that fewer children should mean fewer classrooms, not more; that the student-teacher ratio need not equal that of expensive prep schools; that fancy new facilities do not make for better education; and that there are limits to what the taxpayer can bear, given the rising cost of living and the fixed income that senior citizen retirees face. School proponents may well accuse the baby boomers of hypocrisy, since their own offspring were educated in the public school system, and now the boomers want to pull up the ladder on the next generation. As boomers morph from public spending advocates to frugal taxpayers, the less-numerous soccer mom generation will face a real fight.

A final situation bears examination: the broadly unpopular use. Churches and schools are one thing, but what about a porn shop in the business district? Despite often indignant opposition to such uses, they are legal as expressive free speech, even if socially and morally offensive to many. The police power, as we've seen, can be used to protect public health, safety, welfare, and morals. Constitutional rights, however, can trump this motivation. The decision whether to permit a porn shop cannot be based on morality, which is no answer to what is constitutionally or statutorily legal. Moral strictures vary among different religious groups at any rate, and they do not bind those who are not members. In the United States, Canada, and the United Kingdom, pornography at some level (soft-core or hardcore) is legally available to adults. Without delving into the details of how various countries differ in their treatment of porn, the dominant view is that the tenets of free speech in Western republics and current legislation in modern nation-states require that such business uses be tolerated. Communities cannot flatly ban them, and must therefore make some provision to accommodate them.

The battle is predictable: the porn shop merchant proposes a legal use, but lacks political influence. The neighbors argue the adverse impact the store will have on passing children. They are unmoved in their opposition, even though the merchant points out that kids are not allowed in the store, smut is not displayed in the front windows, the signage is discreet, and the decoration is bland. The reason the neighbors will not be moved is that the morality and child protection arguments are often not the real reasons for their opposition. These arguments are used because they raise parental and moral emotions, are perceived as more incisive than the real reasons, and are therefore able to trump any argument that the merchant can offer. They are used politically, for political impact.

The real reasons for opposition are the adverse effects the shop is expected to have on property values and the neighborhood character. A porn shop is perceived as the first step in neighborhood deterioration, in downgrading and polluting the residential character of the area. It will attract an undesirable element, damage the residents' quality of life, reduce livability, and inevitably adversely affect property values. The fact that people consider it morally decadent doesn't help the shop owner's case, but it's legally irrelevant since free speech trumps moral sensibilities.

Who wins this battle? In most cases, the neighbors do. The public officials deciding the case recognize that an organized group of angry voters is more politically dangerous than a disgruntled would-be porn shop owner. Does the porn shop owner appeal to the courts and win? Maybe, if he can afford it and the board's decision is not well couched in legalese. But the politicians are safe: they voted against the porn shop, and if a court overturns their decision, they can rail against activist judges who interfere with the democratic process and legislate their own brand of morality. The case will be remanded to the board for further hearing, and the board will again turn it down or, on advice of counsel, perhaps arrive at some compromise, such as locating the shop in an industrial zone at the edge of town.

Real Reasons Versus Expressed Reasons

There is a stated motivation and a real motivation to every land use opposition battle, and everybody involved has an agenda that may not be reflected in the arguments employed to get their way. Candor may be a virtue, but contenders in a site fight choose arguments for their impact. The profit motive of the developer is generally obvious, and many developers run into trouble when they try to cast their project in high moral tones. But opponents always have stated reasons and real reasons for their opposition. Most often, neighborhood opposition to development arises from opposition to change, and opposition to change is most often driven by self-interest in maintaining (or at least not damaging) property values.

Whatever it is that drives opponents, they will not want to acknowledge their true motives if those motives are shameful, embarrassing, or, worse, likely to turn the crowd and the permitting board against them. If, for example, the real reasons for opposition are selfish, exclusionary, elitist, classist, or racist, the opponents will not use them because they are politically untenable and will not bring the desired vote from the board. Instead, the opponents will substitute socially laudable motives and cast themselves as victims of the greedy developer, so as to provide sympathetic public officials with the ammunition they need to shoot down the project and the cover they need to survive return fire. Whatever the motives (real, imagined, purported, or feigned) of those contending in a land use fight, the land use decision itself is political.

The Right of Advocacy

In Western democracies, anyone and everyone has a right to advocate for a position on an issue. Sometimes, people do it personally in a direct democracy sort of way. Other times, they hire lawyers, accountants, PR consultants, traffic engineers, or lobbyists to present their case. Whatever method they use, the right to advocate a position is a basic right of democracy and free speech, whether the motivation is pure, suspect, or selfish.

Similarly, the right of free enterprise affords anyone the right (in compliance with appropriate laws) to start and nurture a business, develop it, and protect what that business owner has created. This latter point has raised some eyebrows on both sides of the Atlantic, particularly among traditionalists for whom it is ungentlemanly to protect or advance a business by opposing someone else's. In the traditionalists' minds, it just isn't done, or perhaps it just isn't done publicly.

There is no cause for concern, of course, so long as there is enough business to go around or as long as one merchant can specialize in areas that the others don't pursue. Jewelers gather together in one building or on one street in many cities, some specializing in gems, others in gold, and others in watches. They do compete with one another, but not to the death, and sometimes they share profits in a cooperative manner so any sale made in the Jewelers' Building benefits all. Shopping centers are full of clothing stores, each limited by the terms of its lease as to what types of clothing—women's, children's, casual wear, and so forth—it can offer. Each store wants to protect its niche and won't become a tenant if others are selling the same goods. It therefore negotiates exclusivity reservations in its lease, which amount to restrictions in the terms of other tenants' leases, to protect its turf. Likewise, pharmacies and department stores in strip malls are barred from selling certain kinds of food if there is a supermarket anchor in the same shopping center.

Is it ethical to limit a tenant's business so that it doesn't compete with another tenant? Is it proper to oppose another merchant's application to obtain the same government-issued license you have been granted? The issue isn't about ethics, but rather economics. Unless the mall management agrees to protect the anchor tenant, that anchor will not locate in the mall. Unless a merchant is provided with some form of exclusivity or protection for the goods he offers—unless his market share is shielded—he will perceive his situation as untenable. Whether an action is fair or ethical depends in large part on one's point of view.

Even in rural villages, the owner of a liquor store in the center of town will vehemently oppose the granting of a beer and wine license to another merchant, even to a grocery store whose alcohol sales would be a casual sideline, for fear of losing market share. The liquor store owner will try to appear high-minded, arguing that there's no need for another liquor outlet in such a small town, that alcoholics have enough temptation, that another outlet will give teenagers more ways to procure alcohol, that drunk driving will get out of hand, and so forth. His real but unexpressed plea is for market share protection: since he doesn't sell bread, the grocer shouldn't sell beer. He sees this as a fair and equitable posture.

Public officials cannot legally protect one merchant at the expense of another. But their decision about whether to grant another license is discretionary and based on the standard set by the state statute, which generally rests on the board members' determination of whether the "public convenience" (or some similar test) would be best served by granting the license. As with all discretionary land use decisions, both the process and the decision will be political.

The imaginative grocer will ask his customers to sign a petition in favor of the license, and will prevail on some to write letters to the newspaper and the board urging that the license be granted. A few will accuse the liquor store owner of trying to maintain a monopoly. The liquor store owner, in turn, will ask his customers to sign an opposing petition and may recruit influential local traditionalists (a clergyman, the police chief, a retired school principal) to write letters expressing the high-moral-ground arguments. Both sides, if they are wise, will recruit respected citizens to attend the hearing and speak on their behalf. As in all land use political fights, he who devises and executes the most effective political campaign will win.

The nostalgic Victorian image of competing business tycoons enjoying a fraternal glass of sherry while adhering to the highest ethical and moral behavior is not only false, but also never was real. Businesses, like countries, have been protecting their turf for millennia.[1] Today, this means working to block a competitor from building

---

[1]Until the modern era, business regulation laws were scant, so business owners could mostly do whatever they pleased. The ancient Romans did outlaw joint action by monopolies, even those granted by the emperor. King Wenceslas II of Bohemia (whose father stars in the well-known Christmas carol) stopped ore traders from combining to fix prices in the eleventh century. Queen Elizabeth I of England handed out monopoly licenses to her favorites, including one who held the sole right to make playing cards and sued when a competitor crossed the line.

across the street in order to protect one's market share. Publicly, business leaders will say things like "We welcome competition" or "Competition is good for the consumer." Privately, they are acting to protect their businesses in every legal way they can. Only merchants willing to risk destroying their livelihood would welcome a big-box competitor to the neighborhood and do nothing to stop it.

It is this latter effort—working to stop a competitor from locating nearby—that has so provoked the traditional business establishment, no less in the United States and Canada than in the United Kingdom. Working to prevent a competitor from moving into the area, and thereby essentially creating some sort of monopoly, seems unbecoming and distasteful. Even more upsetting to traditionalists is that the perpetrators of this unseemly conduct often carry out their plots surreptitiously, handing out anonymous broadside flyers attacking their adversary and even secretly funding opposition citizen groups that otherwise would not have the resources to impugn the competitor's project.

An opponent who perceives that he is fighting for survival may do things that might be frowned upon in polite society But all land use decisions are political, and the traditionalist business establishment opposes these methods because they are accustomed to winning political fights with a quiet word or two, and they don't like to lose.

Putting the Right to Advocacy to Work

How can people exercise the right of advocacy? The standard answer has been to hire a public relations consultant to advocate for the project using a PR and marketing approach, or to hire a well-wired lawyer or political fixer to advocate for the project with Those Who Count. Neither approach works in a world in which citizens feel empowered, have money, know how to organize, and understand the workings of political pressure.

Since land use decisions are political, the way to use the right to advocacy is political, too; it is not PR-oriented, not legalistic, and not the job of a political fixer. These approaches might still suffice for small, local, noncontroversial projects, but not for large-scale, controversial, politically charged projects. These are impossible to sneak through city hall late on Friday afternoon and are subject to citizen attack, legal appeal, and the many challenges embedded in the broad range of environmental statutes and regulations that opponents can use to stymie development.

The right to advocacy involves both the right to favor a land use decision and the right to oppose one. Organized citizens oppose projects they perceive as undesirable; business competitors and developers have the right to do likewise. When the two assist one another, true land use politics is born.

Perhaps a clearer explanation of this phenomenon is to express it in military terms. When an army seeks to expand its territory, usually by invading another's turf, it is said to be on the offense. When an army is fighting to protect its territory from invasion, it is said to be on defense. Similarly, when a developer seeks to win approval for his development proposal, he is playing offense—seeking to expand his territory or market share. When he works to prevent approval for a competing project, he is playing defense—seeking to protect his market share by blocking proponents of the project from invading his territory.

The rules of engagement differ markedly depending on whether one is engaged in offense or defense; they are discussed in detail in Chapter 7. For now, it is enough to note that in land use politics, both offense and defense campaigns make use of citizen advocates for strategic and political reasons: because of the citizens' inherent credibility and effectiveness.

On the offense side, the effort to get a project approved and permitted organizes natural supporters to carry the issue, works to neutralize or marginalize opponents whose efforts can damage the chances of approval, and stresses the benefits to the community through the citizen advocates organized for the purpose. Those advocates will express their support in their own words and from their own points of view, a much more effective approach than using a canned list of talking points from the PR agency. They will also sway others who know and respect them, deter those who might have reservations about the project but don't want to offend a neighbor or old friend, and dissuade, neutralize, or turn at least some opponents because they clearly speak from their own viewpoints and not as hirelings of the developer.

The challenge for the offense side is that most people who might favor the project are not so rabid in their support that they will miss their favorite television shows to attend hearings and sit for hours at town hall, especially on a weeknight after a hard day's work. There is a good deal of difference between signing a petition in support of a development and getting in the car and driving to town hall. Unless they belong to an organization with its own agenda that can round them up and get them to attend hearings, supporters are difficult to corral and even harder to keep committed.

On the defense side, the effort to block a project from being approved and permitted organizes natural opponents to carry the issue, works to neutralize or marginalize supporters (by attacking their credibility, in most cases), and stresses the risks, costs, and drawbacks to the community from the perspective of the citizens. Those advocates will express their opposition in their own words and from their own points of view, a much more effective approach than reciting a list of bullet points from the competing PR agency.

Since a hefty majority of residents in the community will oppose development of almost any sort—and are particularly hostile to large, controversial uses—locating and recruiting opponents of a project is much easier than finding advocates, and they usually require little in the way of convincing to attend hearings to express their opposition. But opponents also need a good deal more care and attention than supporters do because their personal reasons for opposition, while honest and compelling, are often not sufficient legally or politically for the permitting board to reject the project. Thus, land use consultants make certain that the points the opponents make include sufficient references to sound legal reasons for rejection that the permitting board can rely on in writing its official decision.

Generally, the most strenuous opponents of a project are found in its immediate environs. Neighbors, especially residential neighbors, will oppose any development that promises to bring change, which is to say, any development at all. Add to these the interest groups that have their own agendas, and a coalition is quickly formed.

In general, then, on the offense side, supporters are difficult to find, but the land use consultant can publicly identify the developer and work openly with those who have reason to support the project. On the defense side, opponents are easy to find, but the land use consultant (and the client) must be wary, since it is the credibility of the citizens, not of the anonymous funder of the citizen group, that will carry the day.

CHAPTER 4

■ ■ ■

Common Approaches to Influencing Land Use Decisions (and Why They Don't Work)

IN WESTERN-STYLE DEMOCRACIES, other than in a few holdout areas, the old machine-politics approach to government is extinct where large or controversial development projects are concerned. This is not to say that political influence is dead or that political organizations are kaput, only that tight control and management by the Boss Tweeds of the world are mostly gone when it comes to major development. Modern empowered citizens are not in awe of politicians and are perfectly willing to speak out. Not coincidentally, the power and influence of trade unions have declined as union members vote according to their consciences (or perhaps their pocketbooks) rather than following in lockstep the endorsements of their leadership. This dilutes the ability of union leaders and their favorite political power brokers to deliver an election victory for a candidate.

Moreover, the power and influence of moneyed interests, though far from dead, once again face the kind of suspicion and scrutiny that gave rise to the Progressive Era. Attention at the federal and state levels to corrupt practices has had a hand in discouraging old-fashioned machine politics locally, especially when powerful political figures parade across television screens doing the "perp walk" to prison, while other formerly powerful figures are forced to resign from office. So public officials today are more careful (and perhaps less arrogant). This means that, while a politician may do a constituent a favor, it won't be an indefensible, controversial, or corrupt favor, and it certainly won't be one that could put reelection at risk. It will be a favor that helps the public official's reelection chances, not one that diminishes them.

How does this state of affairs affect land use decisions? It means that neighborhood constituent opposition will have great impact on the politician who, in the old ward-heeler days, might have ignored citizen opponents to get a favor done for a generous developer. Add to that reality the growing hegemony of professional planners in influencing the decisions that public officials make, and the need is clear for a different approach.

Before explaining in detail how and why land use politics is so effective, let's take a closer look at some of the methods that have traditionally been used to get large or controversial projects approved, and their shortcomings in the modern age.

The Public Relations Approach

One standard method seeks to influence public officials by building public popularity, even enthusiasm, for the project. This public relations approach assumes that if people knew the benefits of the project, they would support it, and conversely that the only reason residents could possibly oppose such a beneficial project is ignorance or misunderstanding of its benefits. The public relations method employs direct mail, advertising, press releases, newsletters, and other informational materials, plus outreach efforts in the form of public meetings, to inform and educate poorly informed or misinformed citizens who, once enlightened, are expected to change their minds. Most PR programs also employ some version of the mutual gains approach, a negotiating technique that seeks to answer the question "What's in it for me?" In most cases, though, the PR program poses the question "What's in it for the community?" and then answers the question with a list of purported community benefits.

This approach may seem workable in theory, but it makes many unwarranted assumptions and ignores the realities of modern project opposition. Getting community leaders to buy in (make a political commitment) to a project is an obsolete top-down approach. It assumes people will dismiss their own concerns and will follow the leader, that leaders will dismiss their own concerns about reelection and will buy in, and that people who oppose the project can somehow be educated, charmed, or shepherded into supporting it, or at least dissuaded from opposing it. None of these propositions is true, and nothing is more fleeting than a politician's commitment.

While it is certainly important to inform the public and provide political cover for politicians, the public relations approach offers only a few of the elements that are necessary to win, especially on a large or controversial project proposal. The PR effort assumes that the project is beneficial and that people who are reasonable, intelligent, malleable, judicious, and logical will recognize those benefits and therefore be logically and philosophically unable to oppose it. Like advertising and marketing methods used to sell potato chips, the PR approach assumes that enough repetition of the basic message will eventually win widespread support and, gradually, enthusiasm. It ignores the possibility that opponents could have legitimate reasons for their resistance and disregards their personal (as distinguished from community) concerns. It assumes that opposition arises from ignorance and, conversely, that given enough information, community outreach, and drum-banging from the marketing people (New! Improved!), the project will win public support and approval.

Such is simply not the case in the baby boomer and post-boomer world, where development does not automatically qualify as progress, citizens are not easily led, and intelligent, educated, well-heeled, empowered opponents will not tolerate any disruption of their settled way of life. Educating them with more project information simply gives them more fodder for their opposition arguments. Where the developer's PR agency sees "plenty of free parking," boomers see "lots more traffic."

To kill the project, they will start by hobbling progress, delaying wherever possible, and insisting that the project be rethought and redrawn, substantially reduced in size, and that it feature extensive new mitigation. They will use every argument—traffic, crowding, noise, fumes, safety, strain on public facilities, capacity of the infrastructure, environmental impacts, habitat fragmentation—to stop a project they don't like, which, these days, is every project. Since any project represents change and brings fears and concerns, there aren't many large projects that will not generate substantial opposition. Even churches, hospitals, and schools generate intense opposition.

The Mass Meetings Approach

Another standard approach for convincing the public about the benefits of a development is conducting large public meetings. The usual purpose of these events is to inform the public, answer people's questions, put their fears and concerns to rest, and build support for controversial projects. In fact, the field of battle is littered with the proposals of those who think the answer to a site fight is a public meeting.

To proponents, a large community discussion session creates an opportunity for mature, reasoned talk and explanation, a roundtable for public input, a forum to correct misconceptions, a gathering of community-invested citizens. But modern land use battles are more like street fights than group hugs; project proponents soon discover that there is no "Kumbaya" moment. Rather than creating a medium for reasoned and courteous discussion, a large public event brings together project opponents (who might otherwise not have coalesced) to attack the project, challenge its assumptions, and resolve to organize to defeat it. In the rough-and-tumble of a land use battle, this public relations effort to generate warm feelings actually sows the seeds of defeat. In other words, it focuses opponents' wrath: one objector feeds off the complaints of another, building to a crescendo of unified hostility. The people who attend public meetings are people with an agenda, not the amorphous "general public."

Looked at from a political perspective, who is likely to attend a large public meeting? "Concerned citizens" is the obvious answer, and that is true. Why are they concerned? Do people attend public meetings because they have questions, or because they are opposed? Are they open-minded or suspicious? In either case, the large meeting is a crapshoot for the developer; it exposes him and his project to attacks that may sway people who might otherwise not feel strongly about it. Attendees may learn a few things they like about the project, but opponents will make sure they learn plenty that is unfavorable and will convey the impression that they represent majority opinion. After a display of anger and vituperation from opponents, even a potential project supporter is likely to feel intimidated and keep her mouth shut. She may think the project would be good for the town, or at least not be a derogation, but she's not going to risk being snubbed at church because of it.

The public forum also affords opponents an opportunity to put the developer on the spot: will he promise, here and now, not to file for a property tax abatement? Will he stand by his press releases and require his anchor tenant to close at 11 p.m. each night? Will he guarantee in writing that at least 100 full-time jobs will be created and maintained for five years? Many are the remorseful developers who allowed their PR people to arrange public forums to explain their projects, only to find their own words thrown back in their faces later. And many are the remorseful PR consultants who put their clients at the microphone at large public gatherings only to watch them grow sarcastic, dismissive, intemperate, and profane in front of the whole town.

A damning effect of a large public forum is the self-inflicted wound it can cause for the permitting effort. Public officials who attend the gathering and hear project opponents seethe will no longer be comfortable supporting the project, no matter how enthusiastically they may have responded at first contact. Public officials who do not attend, but read the coverage in the local newspaper or hear about it from people who attended, will be thankful for having had the good fortune not to be present, and they will read the deluge of letters to the editor from project opponents with growing dread. It is usually not necessary for opponents to put too fine a point on citizen influence. Politicians are survivors. They see citizen opposition and get the message immediately: join the winning side.

The Charrette or Consensus-Building Approach

A charrette is an extensive public workshop, often emceed by a developer-friendly planner, held to discuss a project proposal. Worth conducting only for very substantial projects, charrettes can easily cost $500,000 and continue for many weeks or months, a time commitment few ordinary citizens can make. Charrettes are of dubious value: they secure assent only from some of those who are able to attend, who examine every aspect of the project from both a macro and a micro perspective, and discuss at length and in detail every impact and a range of proposed solutions. This is the reason that such mass discussions take so long and the consensus reached is illusory at best. Such protracted meetings, held outside of the approval or public consultation process, are actually attempts to neutralize opposition by achieving acquiescence; what they in fact do is arm opponents with new issues.

Most often, a consensus-building process involves mitigation demands, concessions by the developer, and downsizing of the project. Even then, those attending the meetings do not represent a majority of voters, so there is still nothing to stop disgruntled opponents from finding fault at the public hearing or consultation, deluging public officials with opposition letters, or holding a demonstration at the construction site. The question for the developer is how many opponents did the exercise win over or neutralize, how many undecideds did it move to the support column, and at what cost? If, after a six-week process, 50 opponents were neutralized and 100 neutrals changed to supporters (highly optimistic numbers) and the consensus-building process cost $500,000, the developer spent $3,333.33 per vote switch without having achieved a critical (or even workable) mass of support. He might have done better to buy everybody a flat-screen TV.

Like the public mass meeting, the charrette approach lacks practicality. For all the meetings, vision statements, high-toned community benefits lists, and input that the planner envisions, there remains a missing element: selfishness. What's in it for me, personally, if I support this project? There is no collaborative approach to decision making if you can't get ordinary citizens to the meetings. Because the community involvement is not genuine, holding a charrette certainly doesn't inoculate a project from citizen attack, much as its proponents might wish it did.

The Facilitation Approach

The poor man's quickie charrette, facilitation is actually an open-mike public meeting without the empowered board, sort of a dress rehearsal for the real hearing. It involves less study, preparation, and expense than the consensus-building approach. But it gives opponents just as much opportunity to redesign the project, demand concessions and downsizing, pump up mitigation and linkage demands, and entertain their wildest dreams of what the project should and should not include. Usually, the facilitator-planner has salted the crowd with supportive agents, but unless she has a firm grip on the citizens and can wear them down until they adopt the vision, facilitation produces a creature designed by a committee.

For the developer, the facilitation method shares many of the same disadvantages that the inaptly named consensus-building process presents, because, like the latter, it cannot be done in a vacuum. Facilitation produces no real community consensus. Even if the planner writes up a report of the facilitation meeting and resulting recommendations and presents it to the board, project opponents will still write letters, make phone calls, and turn out at the official meeting to put the lie to the report and the illusion of consensus. A facile response to the opposition—that the opponents who had questions or issues about the project should have attended the facilitation—will not endear elected public officials to their voter-constituents, and intractable opponents will not tolerate such a dismissal. They'll turn first on the planner to critically examine his visionary agenda, and then on the board members, who had no authority to delegate their sworn responsibility to an unofficial tea-and-cakes conclave of elitists. Newspaper reporters and bloggers love such stuff, and they especially relish the opportunity to deflate board members' egos, to portray them as inattentive if not incompetent, and to editorialize on the excessive influence of planning employees over elected public officials.

The Marketing Approach

Often coupled with a PR approach is a marketing effort to sell the "product" politically. The idea is to stress the positive consequences of the project and generate such goodwill and warm feelings that residents will welcome both the developer and the project, much as they would embrace a stranger who saves their puppy from drowning. Again, this approach assumes that citizens will recognize and acknowledge the project benefits, will gladly do what's best for the community to their own disadvantage, and will be unable to resist the compelling case that the marketing people will present. It absurdly assumes that citizens absorb information only from the marketing team, not from antagonistic sources, or at least that the marketing team is held in higher esteem than project opponents and therefore has greater credibility. Neither assumption is true.

Superficial PR thinkers believe that the endorsement of a local celebrity or sports hero will ensure victory by igniting general adulation for the project. No consideration is given to the idea that citizens might be able to think for themselves or might have perfectly good reasons for their opposition. Great effort is therefore expended to recruit local champions thought to be charismatic, but who, if they can be found at all, usually prove less than persuasive. While deference to local big shots and celebrities might make some headway with people who otherwise don't care whether the project proceeds, it's awfully difficult to translate a winning football season into support for a landfill. The celebrity marketing approach will not be effective in convincing those who are likely to organize and lead the opposition: people whose lives, homes, and families are directly and adversely affected.

The fatal flaw in these approaches is that they seek to charm the resolute and convert the intractable. The agenda of the intransigent opponent is to kill the project, not to improve it, adjust it, or cooperate in finding ways to get it built. The true reasons for people's opposition may be based on fact or on misperception, but the difference is a nullity since they believe their perception to be reality. In other words, it will do the developer no good to reassure opponents that the project will not cause a traffic jam, since they believe it will, viscerally and intuitively. No amount of number-crunching proof from a traffic engineer or reassurances from a public official will convince them otherwise. They know better than to trust a politician, and they certainly know better than to believe a developer's hired lackey, particularly when his figures produce counterintuitive results.

The Advisory Panel Approach

Another ill-conceived notion of how to sway public sentiment is the task force or advisory panel, which some consultants pitch as a wonderful exercise in democracy and understanding and a good way to gain buy-in. In this effort, the consultant proposes involving citizens in the process by inviting them to join a developer-sponsored project advisory board. The group can consist of a few citizens, or it can involve dozens of people, with study groups, committees, and subcommittees all managed and coordinated, presumably, by the consultant. The ostensible purpose of the panel is to advise the developer about the project and make suggestions on how it might be better, more attractive, more welcoming. Such an undertaking is expensive and fraught with peril.

From a political and financial perspective, appointing a panel of amateurs who have no financial stake in the project and inviting them to suggest improvements makes no sense unless the developer "owns" the panel members and plans to use the board to somehow influence or shore up the vote on the permitting authority. The difficulty in this approach is that a task force whose members are controlled by the developer will have no credibility with the public, the permitting authority, or the news media, and it will be criticized as the developer's attempt to hoodwink the citizenry and the permitting board. Appointing locals carries a heavy risk, since each member will have a personal agenda, usually unexpressed, and reputational baggage—a spotty past, perhaps, or powerful unforgiving enemies—that the developer may learn about only when it's too late.

Some consultants think that appointing major project opponents to a task force is a good way to silence their complaints, neutralize their opposition, and get them invested in the project plan. The problem is that any authority the developer gives the task force will diminish his own control over the project. Task force members, whose first loyalty will be to their neighborhood, will still suggest ways to downsize the project and add expensive mitigation—only now, they will have the aura of authority the developer has given them and announce their ideas publicly. If the developer gives them no authority, they will resign in a huff at the first disagreement and write angry letters to the editor about the fraud that the developer attempted to perpetrate in appointing citizens to a task force but refusing to listen to them. They will then use every fact they learned about the project to undermine it, a foreseeable revenge that could have easily been avoided by nixing the advisory panel approach in the first place.

The Mediation Approach

Mediation, by its very nature, favors opponents, since the project proponent already has his offer on the table and must negotiate down from there; opponents, with nothing at risk and starting at a build-nothing posture, have nothing to offer except perhaps to moderate their demands. Opponents will clearly never agree to the project as proposed—else why have the meeting? So the proponent cannot win unless he has allowed plenty of wiggle room in designing a viable project. This is generally not the case; banks and other funding sources finance projects based on real designs, not puffery, and take a dim view of being misled. The developer is therefore limited in the extent to which he can economically agree to opponent demands and maintain project feasibility. Project opponents, however, with nothing on the table, are free to offer objections and suggestions, limited only by their imaginations in concocting fresh arguments against the project and in favor of further mitigation and downsizing.

The mediator, who has no decisional power but is determined to bring the parties to agreement, cajoles each side to be reasonable and reduce its demands in exchange for concessions from the other side. Since the opponents in mediation have nothing to lose, the developer, whose project, finances, and future are at risk, is bargaining against himself.

This method is popular with social engineers because it presents the illusion of vigorous participatory democracy. Things usually go like this: the proponent wants to build a 1,000-unit condo project; the opponents want nothing built. Halfway between nothing and 1,000 units is a 500-unit project, which the planner-mediator-facilitator thinks is reasonable. But opponents will also expect 10 acres of mitigation open space donated to the town, plus a new fire truck to offset some of the added infrastructure expense the project will bring. The developer agrees, but opponents insist that the project is still too large for the site, too intense a use, and too demanding on the town water, sewer, and roadway systems, and that it includes too many three-bedroom units that will add children to the schools. Opponents declare that the project needs to be reduced further, perhaps to 300 condos, and the 50 three-bedroom units reduced to 20. The town is also in dire need of a new police cruiser, which opponents believe the developer should provide, since a 300-unit condo complex is sure to generate many disturbance calls. And so it goes until the developer reaches the point that he cannot economically build the project, or the opponents decide they have enough loot.

The Lawsuit Approach

In their anger and frustration, hard-charging developers sometimes resort to suing project opponents. They generally fail legally, and they always fail politically. A developer who expects to win the votes of local public officials by suing their constituents understands neither the workings of politics nor the thirst of the news media for a David and Goliath story. He will have wasted his time and money suing the opponents and will lose whatever goodwill he might otherwise have built with town officials. The local news media, firmly protected by the First Amendment, take a dim view of developers who sue local citizens, and they are not afraid to say so.

The developer will be depicted as an ogre, if not a thug, and a creative editor will send reporters to scour court records and public filings to gather mud to fling. The resulting newspaper clippings and editorials will soon appear on the Internet for the entire world to see, and will prove especially handy for opponents of future projects to download whenever the developer seeks zoning relief elsewhere.

The Court Appeals Approach

Once the local board has denied the application, appeals are seldom successful. Even if the developer can show standing and grounds for appeal, courts generally defer to the decisions of local boards whose members heard the evidence firsthand and are the local arbiters whose decisions ought not to be second-guessed without good reason. The common standard of proof—that the board acted in an arbitrary and capricious manner—usually proves insurmountable because the board did not, in fact, act that way. Even in the rare instance that the court does find that the board acted in an arbitrary and capricious manner, the developer wins the battle only to lose the war: the court will not order the requested relief or rezoning, but will simply remand the case to the local board for rehearing.

A developer who thinks that a humiliated and resentful town board, now under even greater pressure from citizens, is more likely to grant relief the second time around lives in a fantasy world. The board will definitely be more careful the second time around in setting forth the reasons for rejection on rehearing, so as not to give grounds for another appeal. Once burned, board members will ask the city solicitor to write the decision, making sure each required element is fully covered and the decision is legally sound and ironclad, as appeal-proof as possible. The upshot is that the developer has wasted lots of time and money and is no better off after 18 months than when she started.

Sometimes, a particularly incensed developer will file suit in federal court based on some academic or arcane constitutional theory, alleging that his equal protection, due process, or other civil rights were violated, or that the board's actions essentially confiscated his property. While such litigation presents a challenging mental exercise for lawyers on both sides, instigates massive multiple-lawyer research, and generates a lot of legal brainstorming and detailed brief writing, the result for the developer is usually far less than optimal. In any case, a lawsuit is expensive and doesn't get the project built.

The Building-at-Risk Approach

A developer who undertakes construction before appeal periods expire or while litigation is pending is said to be building at risk. Sometimes taken in the United States by self-financed developers convinced of the virtue of their case, the building-at-risk approach is extremely perilous, since a loss in court can generate an order to demolish the newly completed project. Although some developers, exasperated or arrogant (or both), seem to think that such a draconian outcome is improbable and that a spirit of compromise will somehow triumph, many have learned to their dismay that this is not the case and that it sometimes leads to bankruptcy. As a practical matter, only an exceptionally well-funded corporate sponsor, sure of its ground, can afford to build while a project is in litigation, and then only rarely: if things go badly, the board of directors, to say nothing of the stockholders, will want a good explanation, and Wall Street will punish the stock if profits suffer as a result of management machismo.

The Political Fixer Approach

Local PR is rife with political fixers because many retired and ousted politicians do public relations as a follow-up career. They enjoy basking in the admiration of younger pols who call on them for help, advice, and contacts. If the ex-pol is also a lawyer, he strives to be the go-to guy on sticky political matters, including controversial land use proposals.

For the developer, the fixer's story is attractive (three-term former mayor, pillar of the church, leading light of some fraternal order, widely respected, or something similar), and the temptation to engage his services on behalf of the project may seem overwhelming. He is, by definition, politically connected, and doubtless knows where many political bodies are buried. He can arrange lunch with the mayor or city council president, motivate the chamber of commerce, get the city Democratic or Republican club on the right heading, convince other leading citizens to listen, whisper in the right ears, promote the project behind closed doors, and help work out a political strategy that leaves everyone with heads held high. He knows how and when to trade political chits, and with whom. He has experience, institutional knowledge, and political gravitas. The local fixer can influence public officials and introduce to them the advantages that the project will bring and the tactics by which the current administration, or key members of it, can take credit for bringing its benefits to the community in the form of jobs, taxes, much-needed housing, expanded shopping opportunities, redevelopment of eyesores, and so forth. He can also help orchestrate the public perception (conveyed through friendly coverage in the local news media) that current public officials fought hard to wring concessions from the developer, who reluctantly agreed to them under great political pressure in order to get the project approved.

The inherent problem with the fixer's approach is that it thrives in darkness at a time of openness and sunlight in government. The old machine boss could shut the door, light a cigar, and tell the mayor what he wanted done. These days, smoking is banned at city hall, and there just might be an FBI microphone in the mayor's potted plant. And even if politicians operate at the highest moral plane, their idea of what land use best serves the community is likely to conflict with the opinions of property owners and residents who, these days, will not be quiet about it. Granted that the city needs a new sewage treatment plant, neighbors of the site are not going to want it nearby or upwind of their homes or businesses, and they will organize to resist any such siting.

The fixer may want the plant sited on the developer's locus. Or he may represent unions whose members would work in building the plant or get jobs operating the facility. He may represent propertied interests whose own land values would rise if the new plant were built, if the municipal sewer system replaced their old septic systems, or if the sewer line were extended to run past their undeveloped tracts. Often, there are dueling fixers plotting one against the other in a contest of political one-upmanship to achieve their respective clients' goals.

But modern political realities have greatly diminished the fixer's power and influence because citizens—assertive, empowered, well-educated, well-heeled, politically sophisticated citizens—will not tolerate intrusions on their lives, and public officials can no longer ignore them or act in defiance of their concerns. Worse, the modern citizen deeply resents the political fixer, his top-down approach, and his sneaky tactics. Citizens want transparency and responsiveness to their needs and wishes. The fixer deals in the shadows and cares nothing for citizen issues beyond his own agenda.

The expanding influence of professional planners in land use decision making also limits the fixer's ability to deliver because the planner will point to the city's vision statement, master plan, and data cache to pronounce a site unsuitable. The developer who locks up a location before making sure it will get planner approval has not done his homework. The fixer will not be able to take the professional planner into the back room for a quiet chat and change her mind because the planner is morally certain that she is correct. A fixer's effort to supersede planner influence when both the planner and the citizenry are opposed is doomed.

There are additional solid reasons why the old-fashioned political fixer approach is obsolete in twenty-first-century land use battles. The local political fixer, by her nature, has local ties, strings, and agendas, as well as other projects to promote. In most cases, the client will have no idea, or only a vague idea, of what those other obligations may entail, and no means by which to judge whether they are inconsistent with the client's own goal. Whether the fixer has conflicting projects on her plate or not, it cannot be denied that she does have a political agenda of her own. Whether that agenda involves staging her own political comeback, becoming kingmaker for the next mayor, or forming a consortium to buy up all the industrially zoned land and rezone it as commercial, personal goals are always in the fixer's mind. Her every move on behalf of the client will be tinted (and may be hobbled) by the effect that move might have on her own plans.

Furthermore, fixers, no matter how popular and respected, are politicians, usually former public officials, who carry political baggage. Such people are repeatedly required to pick one side over the other and do not go through life without acquiring enemies. City officials are particularly prone to losing support in public service agencies—police, fire, and public works departments, for example—because they are required to be firm in labor negotiations. This is not to say that off-duty firefighters will turn out to oppose the developer's project. But it does mean that residents who also happen to be off-duty firefighters or sewer department foremen will not be swayed to favor the project because of loyalty to the ex-mayor and might look for ways to sink it just to teach their old adversary a lesson.

Fixers also have devoted political enemies, including those they ran against in the past, those they should have supported but didn't, and those they double-crossed, smeared, or refused to help in a pinch. The level of enmity a fixer inspires will vary with the situation. Prospective clients who do their homework should find out not only who respects the fixer, but also who despises him. This includes the fixer's personal enemies, who may be harder to detect but whose animosity is no less real.

A further, and perhaps the most serious, concern is that the fixer cannot afford to offend the sources of his influence. Since the fixer's essential sphere of influence extends to the current city administration, he will be able to approach them and quietly discuss his client's proposal, but he cannot get tough with them, embarrass them, or issue an ultimatum. He needs to maintain their goodwill. After the project wins or loses and the client moves on to another community, the fixer will still need to work with the local officials. He still has other projects and clients to promote and an agenda to pursue. He therefore cannot, and will not, burn any bridges in getting the client's project approved. Thus, his options in dealing with officialdom are limited, and his skein of tactics is compromised, even before he starts.

The Do-It-Yourself Approach

Occasionally, a developer working on his first large project will wonder aloud why he can't handle the outreach himself. He soon learns why. After deploying ineffective political amateurs from his office staff to soften up the citizenry, he still finds himself abused and accused of all manner of development turpitude when he appears at public gatherings to sell his proposal. Ordinarily, the failure of such an approach can be chalked up to inexperience, and the developer quickly engages professionals to handle matters. The trouble is that the professionals first have to clean up the mess that the developer and his well-meaning staffers have unwittingly made, reversing the damage, undoing the misunderstandings, clarifying the project parameters and goals, patching up relationships, and smoothing ruffled political feathers. This makes success more difficult and presents an additional and unwelcome expense to the developer, as well as a likely delay in meeting his desired deadlines.

Much the same result arises when the developer decides that his in-house public relations person or ad director can smooth public opposition to the project and build support, thereby saving both time and money. But developers' in-house staff members are singularly ineffective when employed for large or controversial development, particularly when complex political issues and fractious relationships are involved and quick decision making is required. This is not to denigrate those who, in their proper sphere, do a fine job. But an in-house PR person, accustomed to juggling speaking engagements for the boss and producing press releases touting the firm's latest charitable contributions, or an in-house ad director, versed in brochures and media buys that promote the company's products, is simply not equipped experientially or professionally to engage the enemy on the street, any more than she could suddenly take over as company auditor. To expect salutary results from such an assignment is both unrealistic politically and unfair to the employee so burdened, especially if a lengthy corporate approval process makes every action an ordeal.

CHAPTER 5

■　■　■

Land Use Politics Is
a Different Discipline

LAND USE POLITICS is a completely new discipline, different from the old-fashioned ward-heeler fixer regime. While it might use public relations elements, it is a far cry from the sort of press release approach to project approval that PR employs. Land use political consultants make no effort to peddle influence or to waste time trying to educate people who resolutely oppose a project. They do not treat the public as a market to whom they sell the project, and they do not harp on the developer's vision of the benefits that the project will bring the community.

Instead, practitioners of land use politics practice politics—the process by which citizens decide who gets what. Although most people understand politics as the system by which we select public officials to speak for us at City Hall, the State House, Congress, or Parliament, true politics doesn't stop at formal elections. Everything a government does, every decision it makes at any level, is steeped in politics, because in the process, the government decides who gets what.

In a representative form of government, officials are empowered to act on behalf of their constituents. There has long been a spirited debate between those who see representative democracy as a mere extension of pure democracy and those who think it is a new animal

altogether. On one side are people who believe that elected representatives should vote as their constituents want because they speak on
the constituents' behalf—that their actions should reflect the will of
the people. On the other side are people who think that elected public officials owe a duty to do what's best, in their judgment, for their
constituents, even if that decision is unpopular at the moment.

At higher levels of government, this debate is largely academic,
since a public official who represents 50,000 people, or 500,000, or
5,000,000 hardly needs to worry if a few hundred or even a few thou-
sand strongly disagree with his decision on a particular issue. The
vast majority of them will agree with him on other issues, and his
politically astute staff will be certain to put the best possible spin on
his controversial votes and decisions to limit their adverse impact. He
may lose the votes of a few diehards on a "third-rail" issue, but most
of those voters will return to the fold when they consider the incumbent's history of public service against the credentials and campaign
platforms of challengers.

At the local level, however, the elected officials and the voters
who elect and reelect them are so close and personal, and the numbers so small, that representative government can be influenced, even
controlled, through application of direct democracy by a relatively
few voters. A small crowd of angry voters, even if they are not necessarily perceived as representing a majority view, can be effective if the
public official believes that other voters would agree with the protestors if goaded into action and might endanger his reelection. In the
case of development proposals, change is usually perceived as bad, so
building nothing is politically safer than building something. The
status quo is usually best for reelection, so voting against a project is
generally easier than voting for one.

Advantages of the Political Approach

The political approach to project approval gives both the proposal and the developer credibility and a degree of popular support
because it employs citizen-soldiers to carry the message. Once they

are psychologically committed to the cause, these citizens will influence others and bring them aboard. The organization and management of citizen support groups is the key to land use politics because it creates an aura of popularity and approval. It also undermines and helps short-circuit opposition efforts to treat the developer as an unwelcome outsider inflicting a monstrosity on the town. If this effort is properly handled, opponents will find themselves unable to establish a convincing local chauvinism—us against them—since the "them" contingent includes their own neighbors.

The political approach also helps equalize the battle by providing a voice to citizens who might otherwise be intimidated into silence by the attitude or bullying of people who take a contrary view of the issues. Giving voice to the minority view—which can be built into the perception of being the majority or consensus view—establishes legitimacy in the minds of local officials. Politicians realize that there are two sides to the matter and that they cannot simply adopt the view of the squeakiest wheel.

The political approach is also focused on what is important and avoids what is not. For example, the political approach focuses on how we can get the votes we need for approval (or rejection). The community consensus approach generates issues by asking citizens for their ideas, criticisms, and suggestions for improving the project proposal. The public relations approach assumes that people need more information and fills their mailboxes, but does nothing to galvanize action. At best, it neutralizes people who didn't care very much in the first place. And the marketing approach treats citizens as customers or buyers, to be sold on project benefits but not spurred into any kind of action to encourage project approval.

The political approach also provides a setting in which the development team can succeed. Instead of walking into a hornet's nest of vilification at the public hearing, the team finds friendly faces and hears friendly voices testifying in favor of the project. Although opponents have a voice as well, the perception of a balanced crowd will make the board members reluctant to dismiss the project out of hand, and where the developer's land use consultant has packed the hall with supporters, the development team might be seen as speaking for the majority of citizens, the consensus, in the community. The mere presence of support to offset the customary antidevelopment sentiment of crowds at public hearings will surprise and unnerve opponents and get the attention of the public officials. This affords the development team a chance to make its presentation in a professional and compelling manner, rather than under the censorious groans and exclamations of a clearly hostile crowd.

The political approach also has significant political value. Because it organizes citizens and rouses them to express their views, it is politically effective in putting politicians on the hot seat—creating the predicament of voting against their constituents' expressed wishes. Because it uses a political campaign approach that organizes public support, generates an inference of consensus, and identifies and addresses issues, it is effective in providing public officials with validation, or political cover, to justify their votes in favor of approval. This political cover is highly valuable, even essential, on several levels: it provides the politician with shelter from opponent attacks; it provides a shield for use in the run-up to the next election; it provides an opportunity to take credit if the project succeeds and proves popular; and it provides an excuse to blame implementation if the project fails or proves unpopular.

The political approach also avoids litigation, a very expensive, time-consuming, and usually unsuccessful method of resolving permitting problems. The legal appeals process, for example, requires the complaining (appealing) party to exhaust all administrative remedies before filing a legal action. This means first appealing within the permitting system, applying for administrative review, passing through each level of the government hierarchy, dealing with agencies and bureaucracies and their agenda-driven staffers, and meeting all of the various filing and deadline requirements at each level and with each entity. This costly and protracted process is exacerbated where environmental issues are involved because they invoke an entirely different panoply of agencies, statutes, and regulatory schemes, each with its own requirements.

Professional Management Versus
Good Intentions

In a day of instant experts, it is perhaps worthwhile to distinguish real land use political consultants from wannabes. Just as everybody with a computer and printer is a publisher, advertising expert, or public relations maven, so too can anyone who has ever passed out flyers in a political campaign cast himself as a campaign manager, highlight it in his résumé, and nail up a shingle. Results from such an instant consultant are unlikely to be stellar since, in politics as in many other fields, experience counts. The developer of a large, controversial project no more wants an inexperienced political consultant than a cancer patient wants a surgeon trying out her scalpel for the first time.

The discipline of land use politics, like other professional disciplines, requires knowledge and experience at each level but, above all, practical expertise in understanding political tactics, crafting a campaign plan, managing the foot soldiers (citizens) who will build critical mass, and implementing the plan. An inexperienced political campaign manager who runs a land use political campaign is like an inexperienced scientist who cobbles together an atom bomb, and with the same result. There is nothing wrong with academic credentials: a political management degree from George Washington University, for example, can be extremely valuable. But academic education should augment practical experience, not the other way around. Site fights are a lot like street fights: it doesn't matter if you're well-educated if you don't know how to throw a punch.

That's why a land use political practitioner's credentials should include substantial political campaigns that he managed (really managed): a campaign for governor or Congress, for example. To be selected to manage a congressional campaign, the individual must first have worked his way up through the political ranks by building practical, personal, essential experience; learning the trade; honing his technique; and developing a political sense. He's done all the dirty jobs, stayed up all night licking envelopes, stood on street corners in the rain holding a candidate's sign, knocked on thousands of doors handing out flyers, and spent weeks in a political boiler room dialing phone numbers to urge voters to the polls. Moreover, he's worked on developing campaign strategy and tactics, managed a budget, observed how more experienced political hands get things done, and learned that a manager must be flexible, nimble, imaginative, and paranoid to win in politics.

The reason that all of this experience is necessary in a land use political manager is that street-level politics (as distinguished from the ivory-tower kind) cannot be taught; it's impossible to teach a person to have imagination, creativity, and perspicacity. Academic settings can use the case study method to explore examples of how others managed election campaigns, but trouble in campaigns arises from unpredictable turns, not from well-worn paths. If political campaign tactics were set pieces, predictable and regular, there would be no need for campaigns; everyone would know the winner the minute she announced the candidacy, and everybody could vote and go home. But how often in electoral politics do pundits' predictions prove ludicrously wrong, do January's front-runners lose by a landslide in November, do has-beens surge back and snatch victory from the jaws of defeat? If the favorite always won, we wouldn't need horse races. Land use political campaigns are no less unpredictable, and often more so, since there is usually a lot of money, time, and professional expertise involved, and the financial consequences of losing may be serious for the contestants. If a candidate loses his bid for Congress, he's sad but not ruined, and some premier law firm or consulting organization will hire him as a rainmaker while he writes his memoirs. But if a developer has invested heavily in a project, has banks breathing down her neck, and faces opponents who create delays and obstacles at every turn, the result of losing can be financial ruin.

The Land Use Politics Approach

We've seen how public relations experts, marketers, and political fixers approach a land use problem. How does a land use political consultant's approach differ?

Citizen-Soldiers

The land use political consultant essentially designs and runs a political campaign aimed at achieving his client's goal the same way a political campaign manager in electoral politics plans and executes a campaign to get her candidate elected. The difference in land use politics is that the manager uses the passions and influence of those with the greatest credibility and impact—local citizens—to make the case, rather than rabid Democrats or Republicans (or Tories or Laborites or Conservatives or New Democrats). The difference is significant. The foot soldiers in an election campaign believe in the candidate, or the platform, or the party. The citizen-soldiers involved in land use politics act from their own dispositions and concerns: they want (or don't want) a new supermarket because it does (or does not) provide shopping opportunities that will (or will not) enhance their lives, and they are willing (or are not willing) to tolerate the traffic, noise, and other problems that the new development might bring.

These citizens are not duped into supporting or opposing a project. They decide for themselves whether they like or dislike the proposal. The land use political manager seeks out natural supporters or opponents (those who share his client's position for or against a project, albeit for their own reasons) to form a citizen group, and to arrange coalitions with other groups, each with its own agenda and reasons for supporting or opposing the project.

If modern-day citizen-activists are so sophisticated, empowered, and aggressive, why do developers need to hire land use political managers to guide them? The goals of the land use manager's client and the goals of citizens, while consistent as far as the project is concerned, doubtless diverge in other areas. The land use political manager prevents the citizens from straying off target and running after irrelevant (or even damaging) issues, and nudges them to stay on message largely by controlling the message. Citizen group leaders enjoy the title and the recognition but aren't ready to alienate their neighbors, even disagreeable ones, by arguing over policy or strategy with the neighborhood know-it-all. The professional land use political manager can offer her experience as the reason things ought to be done one way rather than another, and when the citizens see the strategy work, they are less likely to question future decisions. Besides, the manager, as an outsider, isn't too worried about miffed feelings, since she can capture the know-it-all's support by lavishing praise on him for offering ideas (regardless of whether the group ever uses any of them). Managing middle-class activists is like herding cats, and a professional hand is needed.

The citizens, though feeling entitled and aggressive, are also busy. Soccer moms and dads may know how to organize but don't have time to do it, what with Junior's lacrosse practice and Sarah's ballet lessons, not to mention Dad's softball league and Mom's reading club. Even if they organize and have a clue how to manage a group of self-assured, assertive people, they likely don't have the time or the inclination to undertake the time-consuming research and grunt work needed to assemble the arguments and make the political case, nor do they have the skills to formulate and execute a strategy that will assure a crowd of assertive voters attends the crucial hearing. A land use professional is needed to keep the organization together, committed, and focused, and a political professional is needed to build the critical mass, galvanize the troops, and launch the onslaught. The land use politics practitioner fills these roles, and several others.

Being sophisticated is not the same as being knowledgeable. The citizens will likely not be aware of political campaign law, land use law, or strategies and tactics that an experienced political practitioner would employ. Although a citizen could arguably read up on politics or land use law, that doesn't make him an expert any more than reading a book on medicine makes him a surgeon. Citizens are interested in the project, but they aren't going to have the experience and expertise needed to catch a fatal flaw in the opposition's arguments or evidence. That's what the manager does. An inexperienced civilian, no matter how sharp her native intelligence or how extensive her education, is simply not up to the task.

Even if the citizens were able to stay on message, they don't know how to craft the message effectively or express it to its optimum effect. Left to their own devices, citizens will argue about the wording for weeks, discussing whether the campaign literature should be a letter or a flyer, and spend time passing drafts back and forth while the window for effective action slams shut. The professional political manager cuts to the chase, identifies the issues, formulates the message, writes the copy, and gets it promptly into the hands of people who matter.

The crux of land use politics practice lies in the ability to identify citizens and groups of a similar mind, organize them into an effective political force, coordinate their efforts, and then assist them in exercising their rights of free speech, petition, and so forth, making them far more effective than they otherwise might have been.

The Campaign Plan

The land use political consultant designs and runs a political campaign aimed at achieving the client's goals, the same way a political campaign manager plans a campaign to get the candidate elected. This means that the land use consultant uses political campaign methods, tactics, and strategies. He analyzes the situation, identifies key issues, and prepares strategies to turn the public perception of those issues to his client's favor. He studies the locus, the ordinances, and the political requirements needed to achieve the goal. He devises methods of advancing the client's agenda, choosing forums carefully and orchestrating events. He analyzes the local political situation and the actors who will be instrumental in arriving at the desired goal. He identifies key opponents and prepares tactics to neutralize or marginalize them. And he anticipates opponents' activity and devises preemptive countermeasures.

The land use political manager has learned through experience that the key defensive tool in politics is the fast response: any accusation hurled, any rumor circulated, any obstacle encountered must be addressed immediately, before it takes root in the public mind not as a mere accusation or suspicion but as a fact. Does anyone remember that Lizzie Borden was acquitted, or do they just rely on the rhyme for their belief that "Lizzie Borden took an axe, and gave her father 40 whacks"? Failure to respond promptly and convincingly risks being "swift-boated" to defeat.

Backup Plans

Experienced political professionals and strategists know that perception is reality in politics; the objective truth is far less important than the public's perception of the truth, and the public is easily led astray. For that reason, the land use political manager devises a variety of scenarios and backup plans so that he is ready to handle a fluid political situation at a moment's notice. What if the opponents stage a rally and invite the mayor? What if they boycott the proposed anchor tenant? What if they blanket the town with signs and bumper stickers against the project? What if they bombard the newspaper with nasty letters? What if they threaten to close all their accounts at the bank financing the project and notify the news media? What if they hold a candlelight vigil in front of city hall, led by a local clergyman, on the evening of the vote? What if the developer's site foreman gets in a fistfight with a neighbor? What if opponents discover damaging comments from citizens or officials in towns where the client previously developed a project, and feed the comments to the press? What if opponents display photos of overflowing Dumpsters and poorly maintained buildings at the client's earlier project? What if the developer's son is arrested for drunk driving? What if the IRS records a tax lien against the developer and opponents discover the public record?

A shrewd land use political manager will be prepared for all kinds of surprise attacks, direct and collateral, because his experience tells him that opponents use sniper fire—an embarrassing revelation, a "gotcha"—whenever they can to catch their victim off-guard, and that a facile, dismissive response is not adequate to deflect the punch. He will know that an immediate, convincing, and well-executed response is essential and must include steps the developer will take to rectify any fault situation. He will know that vituperation aimed against the opponents will be counterproductive, seen either as shooting the messenger or as a sad display of sour grapes. He will also know that finding a diversion to distract the press and public can be enormously helpful, and he will have stowed away a couple of such grenades in his campaign satchel.

Lawyers, PR, and Money

A further way to distinguish the land use political consultant is that he is a real political campaign manager, not a person who manages a land use campaign on Monday, supervises the grand opening of a hair salon on Tuesday, and issues press releases for a used car dealer on Friday. He is a specialist, a professional who knows how to focus on the matter at hand, undeterred by conflicting roles or loyalties, and he concentrates on deploying the available resources to the greatest effect for his client.

In this, he is certainly distinguished from the PR consultant but also from most land use lawyers, who often seem to come in two flavors: the local lawyer and the big-city-firm attorney. The local lawyer (whether or not she's also a fixer) generally sees her role as a peacemaker, compromiser, and worker of deals. When she manages a land use project, her goal is to mediate, settle, and reach common ground, using the logic that something is better than nothing, and she is mindful of her own agenda, including a few political apple carts that she does not want to upset. Many local lawyers assume that the developer has built plenty of fat into the project and can afford to lose a good chunk of its density and still make money, a result that enhances their popularity with the locals. Finally, the local lawyer works under an inherent conflict, having to live and work in the community long after the developer is gone; she will stick out her neck only so far on the project's behalf.

The stereotypical big-firm lawyer comes to town in a pinstriped suit, full of wisdom, and presumes he can get the project built if he can just charm and schmooze the neighbors, reason with them (or bully them, or threaten expensive litigation, depending on his style), and arrive at an understanding. He's extremely busy and doesn't return phone calls. The big-city lawyer evokes instant distrust in local citizens, who usually don't like lawyers in the first place and are particularly suspicious of big-time out-of-town ones. When his charm offensive inevitably fails, his proposed solutions for the client turn to litigation, an approach that allows the big firm to immediately assign three lawyers and two interns to begin preparing the case. What the big-firm lawyer might achieve in court in a years-long lawsuit, the political manager seeks to accomplish at city hall in a months-long campaign.

For the land use political manager, the assignment is to win. The land use consultant has no agenda other than the client's agenda. Unlike the local lawyer, he does not seek settlement at the project's expense, and unlike the big-firm lawyer, he does not see litigation as the answer. He is not above the fray; he's knee deep in it and will do everything in his power to bring home a victory, just as he learned to do in electoral campaign politics. In the throes of battle, he eats, sleeps, and obsesses about the site fight and how to win it. It is not his job to convince his client to take less than she needs, nor is it his job to instruct the client on what's best. In a land use fight, the client determines the parameters, knows what's best for her business, decides what constitutes victory, and determines whether and where there is wiggle room. If the land use consultant employs that wiggle room at all, it is at the optimum moment, not prematurely, because he knows that once a mitigation proposal or compromise is announced, it becomes the opponents' starting point for downsizing and mitigation, not the conclusion.

The political reality is that an uncompromising position is the only way to achieve the client's goal, whether the land use consultant is promoting or opposing a project. If the client needs a given density, it is not the consultant's job to talk her down to a lower number. On the defense side, if the client wants absolutely nothing built on the site, then 200 condos is no better than 400. The land use consultant's position in that case needs to be that the site is unsuitable, not that the project needs trimming.

Qualities to Look for in a Land Use Political Consultant

The land use political consultant is essentially a political campaign manager and strategist with some knowledge (sometimes detailed knowledge) of land use law. Although real-world experience in the political sphere is essential to winning a land use political fight, the requirements of land use law can be readily learned. Since enabling statutes vary with each state and zoning ordinances vary with each community, it's necessary for the land use political consultant to familiarize himself with the rules and parameters. He will recognize those elements as political tools that offer opportunities to win: the devil in land use law is often in the details. But unless he has the requisite political expertise, he will not see the opportunities or understand how to use them to his client's advantage. In other words, it's far more important that a land use battle be entrusted to a political expert who knows a little zoning law than that it be put in the hands of a zoning expert who knows a little politics. There may be zoning, planning, environmental, and legalistic sideshows, and the land use consultant will educate himself on the state statutes, local ordinances, bylaws, regulations, and practices during the preparation or "scope" period, before actually drafting the campaign plan. But the main event, in the center ring, is political.

A successful land use political manager is creative, imaginative, and a problem solver. As a political campaign manager, he has learned the importance of deadlines and the need to get problems solved quickly and effectively. He has learned to consider the consequences before taking or recommending a course of action, and he will have a backup plan with ready alternatives to use when surprises crop up. He will not tell his client, "There's nothing we can do," both because he would never paint his client into a corner and because he knows that there is always something he can do.

Here's an example of project manager creativity from the Saint Consulting Group's case files. Saint was working with a client who planned to build a supermarket. It was clear that residents of a senior citizen housing complex would support the client's proposal and help overcome opposition from a residential neighborhood near the project site. But the hearing was scheduled to begin at 8 p.m., and it promised to last at least a couple of hours, well past the seniors' bedtimes. It was December, and some seniors would find driving in the dark difficult and might be reluctant to attend or stay at the hearing. Rather than risk their absence or have them leave in the middle of the hearing, the project manager arranged bus transportation and a night out, which included dinner at 6 p.m., followed by a tour of Christmas light and crèche displays in the area and arrival at town hall right on time for the hearing. With two dozen senior citizens appearing at the hearing in favor, the board approved the project.

Sometimes, town hall bureaucrats create obstacles that require the political manager's creativity to overcome. In one defense case, the entire town political establishment favored the project that Saint's client was opposing. Every time the project manager asked the town clerk for a public record, the uncooperative clerk would be unable to find it and would report the conversation to the aldermen. In a similar case, the town clerk's office lost the zoning bylaw language that Saint's project manager submitted three separate times to keep it from coming up at the town meeting. In the former case, a Freedom of Information Act request through the state's attorney general produced the records; in the latter, a deft application of *Robert's Rules of Order* substituted the client's preferred language for the wording that town officials proposed.

A land use political manager should be able to size people up quickly, read body language, see through masks and misdirection, and deduce an individual's reliability. This is not to ascribe the powers of a seer or mind reader to the consultant. It is only to say that, based on her experience and the subtle signals people convey to those who notice (and maybe the sixth sense that grows from dealing with political doubletalk for years), the land use political consultant is able to evaluate people quickly. This is an important ability in recruiting potential supporters, identifying opponents, and selecting a committed and reliable citizen group leader to serve as the face and voice of the citizen group. Some may think this ability belies a suspicious nature, and they would be correct: a healthy dose of paranoia inhabits every successful political campaign manager. It makes her wary of people who are not quite real, too good to be true, perhaps seeking entrée into the group in order to spy or undermine the effort. It also enables her to read opponents carefully in word, deed, approach, and determination, to know the enemy and what drives them. Are they unsure of their facts? Do they temporize and equivocate when they speak? Do they hesitate to take a firm stand? Do they deviate in their stories? Is their real agenda the same as their stated agenda? Do they seem to have multiple leaders who are at odds with one another? All these measures help tell the land use political manager what her client is up against, and provide valuable insight into the most effective tactics to use in winning the battle.[1]

The experienced political manager is able to elicit information, both directly and indirectly, from the multiple sources she'll use to monitor the political situation. She will have the talent (and sometimes the instincts) of a good newspaper reporter in getting people to provide information without realizing they are doing so. She will notice not only what they say, but how they say it—with conviction, or with hesitation and doubt. She will notice how they refer to others in the group, including group leaders—respectfully or derisively, by first name or last, amiably or more formally.

Finally, the successful manager will be adept at understanding and anticipating the consequences of every action and reaction, not only to what she does, but to what others do as well. If the other side is self-destructing, it may need no help in doing so, or perhaps a little shove would move things along. Her ability to anticipate and evaluate, arising from her experience in electoral politics, helps her decide among alternatives. What will be the consequences of taking Step A, as distinguished from launching Step B? What will be the upshot if the opposition reacts to Step A with Action C? Through an assortment of possible actions and a field of possible reactions, the manager weighs the implications, both short range and long range, and determines which combination of actions will best advance the client's agenda. A professional political campaign manager does not barge into a situation or act precipitously; and she certainly doesn't bungle and blunder her way through a politically sensitive land use fight. Where others wield a cleaver, she inserts a scalpel.

---

[1]Identifying an opponent's weaknesses is key to plotting victory, as noted in Sun Tzu's *The Art of War* (Chap. 6), Machiavelli's *The Art of War* (Bk. 6, 7), and von Clausewitz's *On War* (General Principles of Offense [12]), among many others.

Using Political Campaign Techniques

A land use battle is a lot like any political fight: contenders try to convince the decision makers that one argument is superior to the other, or that one argument represents the majority view. Generally, there is a date certain on which a decision will be made, a concept less easy to pin down in the throes of meetings and hearings on zoning relief than the certainty of election day. Still, at some point there will be a vote, and the back-and-forth battle will become more intense the closer it gets to the decision day.

It is therefore essential that the land use political campaign manager be agile in thought and nimble in response, creative in selecting his political tools and imaginative in employing them. No matter how expert or how experienced the manager, it is seldom possible to know exactly when and how the other side will act, or whether the permitting board will postpone a key hearing after the manager has gone to great lengths to make sure the developer's adherents will pack the hall. The manager must therefore use his head at all times, anticipating problems and preparing solutions and countermeasures. To do this effectively, he must think in a free-form creative manner. No formulaic, cookie-cutter approach will do in handling a fluid, unpredictable, ever-sloshing political situation.

How the Land Use Political Manager Wins

How does the land use political manager win the fight? She designs and works through a flexible political campaign that builds a support base by attracting people with a common interest in the project, including natural supporters, those who can be convinced, and those who would support the program if they understood what is in it for them. The land use politics approach uses true grassroots organizing: citizens organize, carry out a campaign, and bring the case to the public officials, to whom they speak on their own behalf, not as agents of the client. They achieve the goal by the influence of their forceful presentation and sheer numbers.

The land use political consultant assists in this effort by scoping the issues, designing the campaign, preparing strategies, organizing the citizens into an effective and cohesive force, and managing the citizen organization to make certain the members stay committed and focused and that the work gets done. Citizens might oppose a project but have no idea what to do about it. They may be willing to speak in public but have no idea of what to say or how to say it. They may be willing to write a letter to the editor but have no writing skills. Or they may want to hold a rally but not know how to attract a crowd, make signs and banners, force the mayor to attend, or secure press coverage.

In all these aspects, the land use political consultant assists by nurturing, writing scripts and speeches, teaching telephone technique, rehearsing the nervous, and reassuring the doubtful. Her experience really shows when it comes time for a quiet, unassuming local merchant to stand up to the big-box lawyers; it's equally vital in keeping group members committed. Keeping them active and interested reduces the risk of their losing interest or becoming frustrated and going back to their daily lives. But it's quite a challenge when development approvals can take many hearings and months to decide and modern citizens live at a hectic pace.

Besides building support, the land use political manager must deal with the opposition, winning over opponents where she can, neutralizing them with arguments that cast the project in a different light or calm their fears, or marginalizing them by demonstrating to public officials that they are simply unreasonable people who will never be satisfied with any solution. This is delicate work and requires the deft hand of experience to achieve the end without destructive, perhaps fatal, backlash.

In this, as in all other aspects of land use politics, it is street smarts—not theoretical knowledge—that wins the day. For example, "as-of-right permitting" is a reassuring phrase to those who believe it, but a street-smart political strategy can easily raise so many issues that as-of-right permitting is mostly a nonstarter for a controversial project. In one campaign in the eastern United States run by a Saint Consulting project manager, the client's opponent had built a big-box store and had as-of-right status (including correct zoning and sufficient land) to add a large addition to expand it even further. The project manager was able to organize citizens and raise so many issues that the addition was delayed for years, giving the client time to build the market share he needed to survive. Did the effort stop the addition? No; but victory is defined by the client, and he was very happy. He needed 18 months and got three years. (This example is reported in more detail as Defense Case 12 in Chapter 9.)

Client Confidentiality and Security

One of the benefits of engaging a professional for any task is the practitioner's ability to keep a secret. Whether dealing with a doctor, a lawyer, or an accountant, clients expect their private information to remain private and their papers secure. In the case of land use politics, it may be vitally important to keep a client's involvement in a defense case under wraps to avoid detection as the funding source or sponsor of a grassroots citizen group. A seasoned political campaign manager is well practiced in keeping secrets, having submerged the foibles of his candidates and their families over many years, and having handled many tricky, delicate, and embarrassing situations. He makes a habit of operating sotto voce (speaking softly so others don't overhear) and sub rosa (keeping secrets so opponents don't divine strategy or the client's identity).

Amateurs not only do not understand the importance of keeping client confidentiality sacred, they don't know how to do it. Horror tales of amateurish handling of important information abound in land use politics, with misdirected faxes, sloppy phone calls, smoking-gun documents left in saloons, and briefcases lost on the bus. In Texas a developer's PR person, unaware that city officials' e-mail messages are considered public records subject to Freedom of Information Act disclosure, bragged in an e-mail to a city councilor about his work in killing a Wal-Mart store, only to find the story in the newspaper. In Massachusetts a big-box retailer tried to hide its identity by listing its architect as the applicant, but the architect included the client's name on the plans he filed at town hall. Land use politics is rife with such perfectly avoidable missteps. A professional political campaign manager is careful, paranoid, and self-protective. He does not keep files that he does not need, and he does not carry documents that are not relevant to the meeting at hand. He does not leave files on buses and does not fax to wrong numbers. He earns his client's trust by making client confidentiality and security a hallmark of his practice.

This attention to client confidentiality and privacy carries over into the campaign process. A veteran campaign manager knows how to operate behind the scenes, form grassroots organizations, and select citizen-leaders who do not know and do not care who is funding their efforts, or why. This is a benefit of recruiting and organizing natural friends (or enemies) of a project: they not only speak honestly about their feelings (they can't get caught in a lie if they don't lie in the first place), but they also have their own reasons for favoring (or opposing) the project. This gives them credibility and impact on the public officials they seek to influence. The client's identity and reasons are not relevant to them. Would they be relevant to the opponents? Yes, for two reasons: first, to destroy the citizens' credibility by painting them as dupes or hirelings of the developer, and second, to embarrass the developer by leaking the news to the media.

CHAPTER 6

■ ■ ■

Why Use a Land Use Politics Approach?

CHAPTER 5 EXPLAINED why old-fashioned approaches don't work in the modern world and how the land use politics approach differs from the public relations, marketing, mass meetings, political fixer, and other approaches. Land use politics requires engaging a campaign consultant and manager, and it is therefore more expensive than, say, sending a mass mailing to every home in town reinforced with a full-page ad in the local newspaper. Why use a more expensive method?

The short answer is because it works. A developer who spends two years going through an approval process only to be voted down in the end has wasted both his time and money, and has only two choices: start over or walk away. To throw good money after bad after trying and failing with one or more of the obsolete approaches to project approval seems ill-advised, if not foolish, particularly when a more politically effective method is available. Although a land use political campaign may require "boots-on-the-ground" management for several months, it is actually more cost-effective than either the consensus or legalistic approach.

Why Hire a Land Use Political Consultant?

The reasons for engaging a land use political consultant are the reasons for hiring any professional: knowledge, experience, and effectiveness. Managing a land use political campaign is no job for amateurs; developers are often their own worst enemy because they are constitutionally unable to act in a disinterested and diplomatic manner when the project under attack is their "baby." Developers need not be tyrants or buffoons to alienate citizens who already mistrust their motives and deny their credibility. Political and diplomatic skills are needed. How much worse things can get is quickly revealed when the developer is pressed to make generous promises, is embarrassed publicly over a previous project or sticky episode, or loses his temper in public and tells the crowd exactly what he thinks of them. The reasons people are unwise to represent themselves in court are the same reasons developers should not attempt to represent themselves in securing project approvals.

The crux is that political campaign management, especially as applied to land use, is not a commonsense undertaking: political experience and expertise are required for success. Lawyers sometimes assume that a law degree equips them to manage political battles, an assumption that is not borne out by the facts. For one thing, most lawyers get hung up on the potential legal ramifications of each possible action, essentially paralyzing what needs to be a nimble, creative, quick-response organization. Lawyers who try Machiavellian strategy usually get caught doing it, damaging the client's credibility. Second, lawyers don't know how to shape or deliver a political message. Third, they cannot do community outreach: ordinary people typically don't like or trust them, and because they are advocates for the developer, they lack credibility. Last, whatever other skills they may have, lawyers lack the time and staff for the boots-on-the-ground campaigning that is essential to recruiting, organizing, training, and managing the citizen-soldiers necessary to implement the campaign.

The list of those ill-equipped to manage a land use political campaign also includes number crunchers who believe that land use, citizen preferences, and every human response can be reduced to a formula, and that simply assigning values to each variable will yield the answers to every issue. This approach is all about collecting and manipulating data to predict response and acting on the assumption that the prediction is accurate—a dubious notion at best, given the potential for wide swings in public opinion and the broad range of assumptions that crunchers make. Crunchers assume that people's opinions, emotions, responses, and politics are static and perfectly predictable, that variables are knowable and explicable, and that human interaction is mathematically quantifiable. They are not, of course, but a social engineer armed with a spreadsheet can prove anything, including her inductive conclusion that her assumptions and biases represent consensus, and that the measured population is archetypical. Various software programs and mathematical modelers are involved in this chase for the grail, but the fact is that land use politics is more an art than a science, and no amount of data shuffling can trump a well-wrought political campaign. Land use politics works on large, complex, and controversial projects because it is infinitely scalable and limited only by the imagination and creativity of the manager in crafting a customized political campaign designed to achieve a client's goal. No formula and no cookie-cutter routine will suffice.

This does not mean that land use political managers don't use opinion polling; the opposite is true. But they use the results to identify issues and trends, and they understand that public opinion is fickle and easily swayed. Sometimes they use polls to learn public opinion; sometimes they use them to shift public opinion; and sometimes they use them to create the impression of public opinion and thereby influence votes. To them, a survey is a tool to be used in planning strategy; it does not dictate strategy.

What to Expect from a Scoping Study

Once the land use consultant is ready to begin preparing for the project assignment, his first step is to familiarize himself with the locus of the project and the political pulse of the community. To accomplish this, he begins with a scope study to evaluate the political, social, demographic, geographic, and other aspects of the community as well as to identify site-specific issues. The scope investigation begins with online research, reading the community's official website, checking websites of local newspapers and publications, looking up population and demographic figures, and generally gathering intelligence on the community, its leaders, and its background. The manager will then travel to the community (in a car with local plates so as not to call attention to himself) and view the site, looking for potential issues and usable political ammunition, such as

- the size and location of the site; accessibility relative to major traffic arteries; types of land uses on surrounding and nearby parcels; especially sensitive uses such as schools, playgrounds, or senior citizen facilities; proximity of residential development; nearest similar land use; whether the area is built up commercially or industrially; height and mass of nearby uses; availability of public transportation; distance from the nearest major population center; whether the locus appears to be in a flight path of an airport or military base; and whether runoff from or to the site may be an issue, among many other considerations;

- the current evident uses of the site, with a description of improvements such as buildings, outbuildings, offices, parking areas, parked or stored vehicles, and green space; whether there appear to be utilities and infrastructure facilities serving the site; impressions on whether the current use emits fumes, noxious odors, noise, smoke, or other undesirable externality elements; and an educated guess whether traffic to and from the site might be an issue; and

- geographic features and condition of the site, including whether it is forested; whether wetlands, waterways, or vernal pools are present; whether the site is flat and buildable; whether the site appears to be a pristine greenfield or a contaminated brownfield; whether any easement or right of way appears to impinge on the site; whether it appears to be a wildlife habitat; whether it has significant environmental or ecological elements; and first impressions on whether it appears to have historic, architectural, archaeological, or preservation value.

The consultant will then do some discreet reconnoitering, starting with a drive through town, gathering a general impression, and paying a visit to the public library's newspaper archives, followed by research at city hall and record-checking at the assessor's office, planning board, zoning board, and building commissioner's office.

Conducting defense research operations at the local level can be unnerving for the uninitiated, since gaining information from public employees often involves satisfying their curiosity about why the individual wants the information, the better to feed the gossip grapevine that snakes through all city operations. If the consultant is publicly representing the developer on an offense project and is able to disclose that information, the town employees will take little interest in him or his research, but they are unlikely to be forthcoming with extra help or suggestions unless they personally approve of the project. Where the consultant is doing confidential research or conducting a defense campaign, things get trickier. He does not want to disclose his own information, let alone the client's, but risks losing all cooperation from the rebuffed gossip if he refuses to say anything at all. An experienced land use consultant will know that seekers of public records are not required to explain themselves, much less produce a driver's license or photo ID. But he also knows that curious town municipal employees may not be cooperative unless their thirst for gossip is slaked. The land use consultant evaluates the situation and acts to elicit more information than he gives.[1] He might tell the nosy employee that he heard a big-box store is planned for the site, thereby tacitly inviting the employee to tell what she knows. He might say

---

[1]In performing confidential research, a consultant may employ an alias to help maintain both his privacy and the client's. The use of an alias is legal so long as there is no intent to defraud, in a legal sense. Since the consultant is seeking information—not money or property—there is no legal intent to defraud. This also has the benefit of curtailing the efforts of nosy journalists and the client's competitors.

he's thinking of moving to the neighborhood but wants to know what is going to be built on the nearby site. Or he might say he's doing research for a lawyer and doesn't know anything beyond the site address. Sometimes, the consultant will want to engage in some small talk and turn on the charm. Other times, the visit will be strictly business, straightforward and as brief as possible. Sometimes, in highly contentious situations, the consultant will sense trouble in advance and will ask a company lawyer to call ahead and advise the appropriate town official managing the office that he is sending in a researcher on legal business to look at public records and would appreciate the town employees' cooperation and assistance.

After recording his notes and impressions of the town, the site, and the city hall research, the consultant will try to find a spot — usually a diner, barber shop, or saloon — where locals gather and socialize. If he can insinuate himself into a conversation with some townies, he is likely to gain valuable insight and get a handle on local attitudes, issues, and prejudices, all of which will be useful in drafting the campaign plan. He will evaluate the situation and decide what to tell the locals, being careful not to contradict the story he gave at city hall, keeping it simple and not embellishing. Once he has satisfied the locals' curiosity about who he is and why he's there, he can become a "regular" and win a measure of trust.

Preparing the Campaign Plan

Once the land use consultant has gathered all of the information he needs to thoroughly understand the situation and the local laws and regulations applicable to the client's goals, he begins drafting a campaign plan. The plan is designed to advance the client's interests by organizing local citizens to influence their public officials to act the way the citizens want them to act, which is also the way the client wants them to act, though usually for different reasons.

Campaign plans are as unique as the situations that require them and the people who write them. The expertise and professionalism of the land use consultant tells him what political tactics would be useful, what strategies will be most effective, what public officials are empowered to provide the vote desired, and what groups and organizations may be relied on to take up the banner. Like the manager of an election campaign, the land use political consultant must understand the political lay of the land, the parties involved, and the forces at work. From all of these sources, he draws on his knowledge and experience to fashion a winning campaign strategy.

Are there existing groups the consultant can graft onto in building strength? Is the municipality likely to conduct multiple complicated hearings? Will the developer be expected to make presentations to local business and taxpayer groups? Does the status or history of the site present problems? Are there people near the project who would be particularly vulnerable to its impacts because of age, health, or condition (for example, children at a daycare center or nursing home residents) and who might need protection and reassurance? Does the zoning allow uses even more objectionable than the proposed use? Will mailings be an important factor, and, if so, how will they be printed and mailed and at what estimated costs? Should the citizen organization be designed to qualify for charitable status so it can conveniently raise money and appear independent? Will the organization need legal counsel at the outset, and, if so, how much money should be included in the budget for that purpose?

In preparing the plan, the manager will apply principles of politics and human nature learned through experience. He knows, for example, that a door-to-door neighborhood campaign is far more effective than a mass meeting, and not just because it demonstrates respect and deference for the residents and gives them an opportunity to air their concerns quietly. It also provides a measure of bonding: it's difficult to publicly attack someone who has enjoyed coffee and polite conversation at your kitchen table. He also knows that people will act in what they perceive to be their own best interests, so he formulates a campaign strategy to emphasize those interests and focus citizens' perception to nurture support (or opposition) in the coming land use battle. And he knows that campaigns are not won without a political organization, so he will craft the campaign plan to build a strong grassroots organization to carry the message and change minds.

High on the list of elements in the campaign plan is the role of the citizen organization and related coalitions that the land use political manager will create, nurture, educate, and manage. The hub of the land use politics universe is the influence and credibility of local citizens exercising their constitutional rights and thereby influencing their local officials.

Finding Natural Supporters and Opponents

Natural supporters and opponents are people with innate or personal reasons for supporting or opposing a project. They don't need to be sold either way, but they might not come forward and take a position if the political manager doesn't reach out and encourage them.

Natural Supporters
The natural supporters of a project are those who believe they will benefit by or through it, directly or indirectly. Let's take a look at a few so-called interest groups and see why they might be natural supporters.

- Parents and teachers support projects that they perceive will generate more revenue for schools: parents for the books, playground equipment, or additional teachers the money can provide, thereby reducing class sizes; and teachers for pay raises or extra help in the form of teacher's aides. There are limits. Neither parents nor teachers will support a project they think will have a detrimental effect on the children or the schools; no amount of tax revenue will make them support a pig farm next to the elementary school. But they will seriously consider supporting other controversial projects (shopping centers, big-box stores, casinos, and power plants, to name a few), provided the projects don't undermine their influence in town. Because developers of these kinds of projects know that tax revenues are important to many local constituencies (police, fire, and public works employees, to name three), they emphasize the volume of taxes the projects will produce.

- Building trades workers, such as electricians, plumbers, and sheet metal workers, support just about any development project for the construction jobs it will generate—provided, if they are union members, that the subcontracting jobs will be bid at union rates for union workers. This distinction is more important in some states than in others; trade unions are stronger in the Northeast and West Coast than they are in the South. But where they are important, unions can quickly become adversaries to developers who insist on right-to-work (nonunion) standards and rates, and their locally based members can become leaders of the opposition. In states where unions are strong, politicians are far more likely to side with the trades than with the developer, since union members vote.

- Service trade union workers support projects that will provide union jobs, such as operations personnel at unionized supermarkets: checkout clerks, shelf stockers, meat cutters, and so forth. Many of these positions are held by twentysomethings and retired people, who often need goading from their shop steward to get involved, but they generally favor development that expands job opportunities or that may improve their lives, such as affordable housing.

- Town employees support projects that they believe will provide money for pay raises or other opportunities for income, or that will improve their quality of life. For example, a police officer knows that a project that creates a lot of traffic will need to hire off-duty police officers to direct traffic. A firefighter knows that a large project can be expected to offer enhancements to the fire department to demonstrate good citizenship. Town employees know that a project with high labor demands will offer part-time work that some of them might use to enhance their household income. There are limits to their support: they will support a big-box store, but on the other side of town—not in their backyard.

- Business and taxpayer groups support projects that they perceive will help spread the tax burden and provide jobs. Business owners also support projects that they think will benefit their businesses: commercial developments that may do business with local merchants, offer them sales opportunities, or draw customer traffic to the neighborhood; or housing that may generate customers. The local newspaper and radio station are businesses that may benefit from new development in the form of advertising; they should not be overlooked when rounding up support. Business and taxpayer groups especially like light industrial development because it's usually located at the edge of town and provides jobs and taxes without bringing additional traffic to the downtown. It's also usually clean and quiet. Public officials also like light industrial development because it's often welcomed, and it gives politicians an opportunity to take credit for bringing new jobs and taxes to town.

- Senior citizens generally support shopping centers because they have plenty of time on their hands and like to walk around enclosed malls, even if they don't buy much. For the same reasons, they support projects that offer plenty of green space but not too much traffic, such as office and industrial parks. They also typically support senior citizen housing, assisted living complexes, nursing homes, and the like, for obvious reasons.

- Young marrieds and low-paid residents— including many municipal employees, people in food service, personal services (tailors, hairdressers, and barbers), and other service businesses—support affordable housing because their income limits their ability to live in town unless affordable housing opportunities are made available. Parents of such workers support such housing not only out of loyalty to their children, but also because they want to have their grandchildren handy for spoiling. They believe that their children should have the right and opportunity to live in the hometown in which they were raised and in which their friends live.

Natural Opponents

The obverse of natural support is natural opposition. The natural opponents of a project are those who believe they will be harmed by or through it, directly or indirectly. Let's take a look at a few candidates and the projects they probably won't like.

- Neighbors and abutters of a project, especially residential neighbors, are the foremost opponents because they are most directly impacted and bear the brunt of the downsides that projects bring: traffic, noise, fumes, light trespass, and so forth. They are also the most determined and strident; they see no reason why they should tolerate intrusion or why development should occur at the expense of their quality of life. Since they want no change at all in the neighborhood, they are usually not receptive to mitigation ideas unless the project is an improvement of an existing use (and the user has been a good neighbor) or the proposal involves a project that they would favor if it weren't next door. Sometimes, these neighbors can be convinced (or bribed) to curb their opposition, but not often.

- Old townies (who may or may not also be senior citizens) are opposed to projects that threaten to "ruin" the town's character, which sometimes means the way the town looked in 1955, or 1975, or whatever year fits their nostalgic memories. A subset of the old townie group is made up of historic preservationists, who are also opposed but are more specific about it. They not only oppose change, but they also want to preserve buildings, forests, meadows, viewscapes, and other town features that they perceive as being of historic or scenic importance. What differentiates townies from the historic preservationists is that the latter often have the law on their side, as do other preservationist interest groups concerned with historic architecture, ancient burial grounds, archaeology, and so forth.

- In contrast to their support of shopping centers and senior citizen care facilities, senior citizen homeowners usually oppose public spending on buildings, infrastructure, or anything else that threatens to raise their property taxes. They see no need for such wasteful spending and needless tax increases, particularly if they are surviving on fixed incomes. Unless senior homeowners have grandchildren in the public schools, they will oppose new schools, and they also oppose new police and fire stations, and even senior citizen activity centers.

- Young professionals who have purchased a large home in a nice neighborhood and have (or want to have) kids and build a life are understandably opposed to any project they perceive will interfere with that dream. Unlike people in low-paying, relatively menial jobs, these well-educated and relatively well-heeled young people see themselves as on the way up. They feel empowered and entitled, and they see no reason to compromise their comfort or enjoyment by tolerating unwelcome land uses. Since they have a stake in the public school system, and since nothing is too good for their children, these "soccer moms and dads" support school spending and tend to be activists.

- Environmentalists and ecologists will oppose any kind of development if they believe the project will adversely affect their area of interest or interfere with their goals. If the project might have adverse environmental consequences, directly or indirectly, for people or animals and plants, environmentalists and ecologists will oppose it. Environmental activists are true believers in their cause, and they take particular umbrage when the object of their concern comes under attack right in their own hometown.

Organizing and Managing a Citizen Group

Once the consultant has identified natural friends (or enemies) of the project, his task is to show them that they can act on their concerns effectively if they organize and work cooperatively with one another and enter into alliances and coalitions with other groups whose members share their concerns.

Once again, the land use political consultant's experience comes into play as he determines how to best make contact with the concerned citizens and groups he has identified, and how to earn their trust so they will feel comfortable talking openly with him and listening to his suggestions. Sometimes, the initial contact may arise from chats with local residents in local gathering places. The consultant needs only one or two local residents to say they love (or hate) the project to begin the recruitment process. Do their neighbors, friends, coworkers, or relatives feel the same way? Is anyone organizing them to make their concerns public and to push public officials to address these concerns? What are the reasons for their opposition, and who else might share these concerns? Sometimes, there is a preexisting activist, neighborhood, taxpayer, or citizen group that the land use consultant can adopt (or that adopts him). If so, the consultant can use its existing leadership structure to treat the land use campaign as a project the group undertakes, provided he can get past the suspicion and cynicism that invariably greets the interloper.

Early in this conversation, the local residents are going to want to know why the consultant cares. Because this question is certain to arise, and because it is vitally important to building a relationship with the local people, the consultant will have thought the matter through and have a ready answer. Usually, on an offense project, he can simply say he works with the owner or developer and would like to build local support to offset anticipated opposition from naysayers and to show municipal officials and the local news media that there is real support for the proposal. On the defense side, things are more delicate because the consultant is obligated to protect the client's confidentiality, as well as his own, and cannot expect local citizens to keep the secret.

In considering what to tell the local citizens, the consultant realizes that whatever he says will define how he is identified going forward. It is important that he not be seen as a liar and not have told different stories to different people: hence, the need for caution in making initial contact with employees at city hall. The consultant must be seen as trustworthy, but also as resourceful, competent, and effective. Local residents are willing to follow his lead and are more than happy to have someone else do the work and pay the bills, but only if they have confidence that he can and will do the job and will not embarrass them or get them sued.

Quite often in the defense case, the cynical and worldly members of the local citizen opposition have already begun organizing and are thrilled at the prospect of getting help, administrative as well as financial. In such cases, the land use consultant can often simply state the truth: that he works with some local business interests who need to remain anonymous for political and business reasons, but who are willing to assist the citizen group financially and provide it with legal counsel, if necessary, to oppose the project that all agree would be bad for the community.[2] What the consultant is saying is true. While citizens might assume they know the identity of the business interests involved, the consultant has preserved the client's confidentiality. Sometimes, however, the consultant needs to be somewhat less forthcoming to protect the client and the citizens: citizens who know the identity of the client must disclose that information when questioned under oath, thereby potentially opening themselves and their neighbors to liability as codefendants in whatever plot the plaintiff alleges. Citizens who don't know can truthfully say under oath that they don't know. In such cases, the consultant will put discretion first, explaining that various interests—environmental, ecological, commercial, preservationist—assist local citizens in their opposition to undesirable projects, and he represents one or more of such groups, who must remain anonymous. With such a reasonable (if vague) explanation, the citizens are usually ready to listen to what might be done to effectively stop the development.

Having talked with some citizens and collected some names, the consultant is ready to arrange an informal meeting, perhaps in someone's living room, where similarly minded people can discuss the project privately. Such chats should not take place in a public setting,

---

[2] The business interests could be a coalition of interests who compete with one another but share opposition to the project. Thus, two competitors might jointly fund opposition to a third competitor's project, or an employer and a union might join forces, often through a joint labor–management committee, to block an antiunion competitor from building. This joint activity is fully protected under the Noerr-Pennington line of cases. See Chapter 8.

such as a restaurant, where the risks of being overheard are much too great, especially in a small town. Besides, people are more comfortable and more likely to speak their minds openly in a private residential setting. It's also far easier to outline what might be done and whip up enthusiasm if the group members feel secure and comfortable and are not on public display.

Usually, supporters are people who want the money or jobs the project will bring, rather than the project itself. For some of these people, the project is a necessary evil to be endured in order to get the jobs and tax revenues; for others, the project is a benefit to the community, but it is still the money that counts. The problem with project supporters in general is that they lack the enthusiasm, determination, and zest that drive project opponents and are therefore difficult to keep committed. The difference is that opponents really do oppose the project, have a visceral dislike for it, view it as a threat to their quality of life, and do not care about whatever promises the developer makes regarding jobs and tax revenues. Without close supervision, opponents will sometimes take matters into their own hands, engaging in activities, such as vandalism, that are counterproductive, especially when the news media identify the culprit as a leader of the opposition group. Supporters, then, need constant attention to keep them busy, while opponents need constant attention to keep them from getting too busy. For this reason, citizen group handling differs markedly, depending on whether the assignment involves an offense or defense campaign. The differences between offense and defense campaigns will be discussed in Chapter 7.

The land use political consultant has three goals for the first in-home meeting with citizens: (1) get them interested and enthused about the chances of effectively influencing the political process; (2) select a leader or at least identify someone with leadership abilities; and (3) begin getting firm commitments from members of the group to make sure they remain occupied and don't drift away. It's also wise to remember that people who belong to other groups, or those in a preexisting citizen group, may have conflicted loyalties, even though they join the land use battle with good intentions. The land use political consultant will make sure to know about these potential conflicts and avoid putting such members in an uncomfortable position.

Goal 1: Get Them Interested and Enthused

The formative stages of the citizen group are the most important in setting the tone, especially if the land use consultant is organizing the group from scratch. An ad hoc group can be the most effective kind because it carries no past baggage, isn't stuck with world-weary existing leadership, can focus on the problem rather than adding it to an existing list of issues, and has the enthusiasm of newness. Still, it lacks the automatic influence that well-established local groups often enjoy, lacks institutional memory, and amounts to a "dead lift" for the land use political manager, who must create all of the elements of group governance and dynamics from scratch.

Whether the group is new or preexisting, the land use political consultant's immediate task is to convince the members that they can effectively influence the progress and outcome of the land use battle. Usually, an outline of potential activities that the group might undertake—a petition drive, a rally, a letter-writing campaign, bumper stickers, a fundraising event—begins to get members' juices flowing as the manager explains how citizen activism affects the attitude of elected public officials and the news media, and how activism builds on itself as more and more citizens realize that they share the group's goals and want to take part. A few war stories demonstrating the effectiveness of citizen groups (and the competence of the manager) are usually enough to pave the way for discussion of the project approval timeline, likely stumbling blocks along the way, the attitude of the permit-granting board toward such a project, and immediate steps the group can take to get started.

Goal 2: Select a Leader

At this point, the manager should have a good idea which group members seem to have the leadership ability and talent to chair the organization. The manager knows she can expect to do the lion's share of the work herself. What the group really needs is someone who can serve as the face of the group, someone who is articulate, knowledgeable, and, if possible, mildly photogenic and is not likely to embark on a control-freak ego trip that will drive members to quit and discourage new ones from joining.

The land use consultant needs to be especially careful at this point, selecting the leader but not being seen as imposing the leadership on the group. She needs to avoid a nomination-and-election process, which leaves hard feelings and often produces an egotist who didn't really want the job beyond saying that he holds it, and who won't do the work or be dependable. The land use manager, as emcee of the meeting, leader of the discussion, and facilitator of the process, has considerable sway with the group, particularly after just introducing it to the world of political activism and citizen influence. She is, essentially, the leader at this point, and can therefore ask her choice to "coordinate" some activity or "be in charge" of something without actually pronouncing the individual leader. The advantage of this approach is that such a leader is easily replaced if he turns out to be a dud.

Goal 3: Get Them Committed

Maintaining a citizen group is far more difficult than organizing one. Citizens high on the prospect of having some control over their destiny are enthusiastic at first; but in the obligations and routine of everyday life, citizens find their drive wilting and have difficulty finding time to devote to another project, a problem exacerbated if they are also bored because nothing is happening. This is standard for any new volunteer organization—there are doers, there are talkers, and there are no-shows. The no-show contingent grows as job and family responsibilities supersede the needs of the group and people peel off to live their lives. The problem is especially troublesome in managing a citizen group working on a land use battle because the lags between actionable events can be long and unpredictable. Approvals on a major project can take many months, as any developer of such a project well knows: hearings may be weeks apart; environmental impact documents take months to prepare and review; bureaucratic processing can be tedious. Worse is the series of false alarms that inevitably plague a major land use battle: the planning board schedules a hearing; the citizens go on alert, galvanize their forces, prepare for battle, polish their arguments, clear their schedules; and then the hearing is postponed, usually on the day it was scheduled to take place. Too many false alarms result in battle fatigue, making it difficult for the manager to get the troops enthused again when the skirmish is rescheduled. (Crafty land use managers on the offense side deliberately use hearing postponements to wear down the opposition and thereby demoralize their enthusiasm, increase attrition in their ranks, and reduce their turnout.)

Political junkies enjoy electoral politics because of the urgency, the constant crisis atmosphere, the sense that there is much to do and too little time, the continual need for decision making and problem solving, with no time for rumination. It's not possible to maintain a constant crisis atmosphere in a land use fight because of the delays. In addition, there is a playbill of multiple actors, the dramatis personae, each with a role, an agenda, a process, and a pace of getting things done: the developer, the developer's lawyer, the planning board, the city planning staff, the zoning board. There may also be the building commissioner, the city council, the city legal department, the county or regional planning agency, the state environmental agency, and sometimes federal agencies such as the Environmental Protection Agency or the Army Corps of Engineers, as well as assorted public officials at all levels who will intervene and posture if they see an opportunity to advance their agenda or enhance their reelectability.

Maintaining a state of continuous agitation, crisis, and chaos is not possible. But since the strength and influence of the citizen organization depends on its perceived membership and activism, the manager must keep the group together and engage a stop-loss program to curb attrition. The manager maintains a continuous flow of activities and projects aimed at keeping as many members as possible aboard and sustaining the perception that the organization is both activist and formidable. The means of doing so include meetings (but not too many), e-mails, a Web site, a blog, and a phone tree, among other things. Most important are the duties and activities that the manager and group leader ask members to perform, since most people try to do what they have promised to do (especially when goaded). In other words, keeping members busy is the way to keep them committed.

This requires the manager to maintain and augment a revolving list of things that need to be done, so that once a member completes one mission, the manager is ready with another task to assign—even if he knows that he will wind up doing it over because the citizen will not do an especially thorough job. Most citizen groups, like most social organizations, have a very small core of actual workers and a good many hangers-on, and the land use manager will do most of the work. The citizens in the group (especially the leader) will perceive themselves as doing a good deal more and working a good deal harder than they actually are doing and working, and they will take credit for anything the manager does. It's all part of politics, and the professional land use manager knows that his job is to do whatever is necessary to move ever closer to achieving the client's goal.

The citizens must not see the tasks assigned them as make-work, so the manager must take pains to explain the importance of the task and the vital need for the information or activity the citizen will undertake. In some cases, assigning duties is easy: someone has to be in constant charge of maintaining and updating the website; someone needs to organize and coordinate the fundraising barbecue and will need help from a drinks organizer and a potato salad coordinator; someone needs to arrange a list of vehicles and drivers to bring senior citizens to the hearing and set up a schedule for pickups and drop-offs; someone needs to get bids for the T-shirt silk screening and then coordinate with the printer; someone needs to check the planning board twice a week for new or amended filings; someone needs to draw maps; others need to do research and gather information; someone needs to coordinate letters to the editor, making sure they get written and mailed; someone needs to run the blog and insert comments in existing community blogs; someone needs to write, edit, and publish the group's newsletter; and so forth. Sometimes, of course, it's difficult to think of things for people to do when there is a hiatus in battle activity; a resourceful political campaign manager will find a way to do so because the alternative is to lose the edge as the group falls from formidable to paper-tiger status.

Focus on Security

Because clients accept their land use political consultant in the inner circle and share proprietary or sensitive project information, they are understandably concerned about confidentiality and security. A professional land use political consultant who can't keep a secret or who develops a reputation for double-dealing will not last long in the business. The good reputation of the land use political consultant is therefore the client's best protection against disclosure. Although a client can request a written confidentiality agreement, it is unwise to rely on such a document for protection because filing a lawsuit to enforce it would ensure that the confidential information the client is trying to protect gets into the newspaper. It's far better to limit the list of people who have the information to those who truly need to know, and to remind them that the information is confidential. Experience has shown that leaks usually come either from wannabe consultants who don't appreciate the importance of sensitive information or from the client's own in-house team. True industrial espionage is rare in the development business: the cause of the problem is usually to be found in the developer's own nest.

A professional land use political consultant treats client information, as well as project information, as highly confidential. This applies as well to campaign plans and strategies, since opponents who have access to the developer's war plans can easily devise countermeasures. Experience has shown that most project strategy documents eventually wind up in the wrong hands, leading to the First Rule of Inevitability: never put in writing anything that you don't want opponents to know. In political circles, this method of inscrutability is known as "the nod and the wink": never write when you can speak, never speak when you can nod, never nod when you can wink.

Melodramatic as that may seem, many clients want to keep their business (and their involvement in some aspects of some projects) quiet. That is why, in dealing with a client, a professional land use political consultant will generally work at the "C" level: chief executive officer (CEO), chief operating officer (COO), or chief financial officer (CFO).

A professional land use political consulting firm will go even further to maintain security. For example, the Saint Consulting Group's invoices tend to be deliberately vague. A client who wants to see detailed bills to be certain that the consultants are actually on the job can have a detailed invoice faxed to the CEO to review (and shred if so inclined), while the less-detailed version is e-mailed to the accounts payable clerk. This approach is not intended to imply that the accounts payable clerk can't be trusted, but does the client know the clerk's friends or their affiliations? Does the client know whether the clerk's sister works for the competition? Or is married to the vice president of the opponent? Would the clerk be able to distinguish between an innocent remark about work and disclosure of confidential information? He won't have to if he's not told. Why insert a needlessly detailed invoice into the client's permanent corporate records, where it is discoverable should litigation eventually ensue, when it would be eminently useful to an opposing attorney to bludgeon the CEO on the witness stand?

Security procedures can be extensive, but they should go only as far as the client wants or needs them to go. Faxing materials to the CEO's home, rather than to the office, is a common safeguard. So is a separate e-mail address through Yahoo, EarthLink, or some other provider outside the corporate network, so that every e-mail to and from the client does not wind up in a permanent corporate file. There is nothing untoward in such practices; they are a first line of defense against snoops and those who would engage in corporate espionage. A government agency with a right to the information, or a plaintiff's lawyer engaged in court-sanctioned discovery procedures, could easily secure the information if the need arose. But the world is full of busybodies and troublemakers with axes to grind; these procedures make it a little harder for them.

Defense clients are generally more concerned with confidentiality than are offense clients. They know that a leak at the wrong time can damage the citizen support group's credibility and may encourage the competitor to launch nuisance litigation. Because of these dangers, defense campaigns are conducted sotto voce, with careful attention to detail. Keeping the identity of a client confidential even from the citizen group, making use of disposable cell phones, driving locally registered rental cars, staying in motels a few towns away, and being judiciously vague about the backgrounds of project managers are useful safeguards against prying reporters who would smell a story and nosy project opponents who would like nothing better than to embarrass the client and derail the project.

A citizen group has members who may not appreciate the consequences of idle chatter; it may include members who are spies for opponents or the client's competitor. The less confidential information they know, the better. A citizen group also includes people who should not be burdened with information they will have to expose if ever asked under oath. Although the Noerr-Pennington line of legal cases holds that the funding source of project opposition is irrelevant (Chapter 8 explains the legal underpinnings of land use politics defensive tactics in detail), the opponent's lawyer can still ask the question and require a straight answer. It is best for the client if the answer is "I don't know."

What Makes an Effective Campaign Manager?

The land use political campaign manager must wear a lot of hats and do the drudge work as well as management; but above all, he must never lose sight of the goal. Everything he plans, every maneuver, every liaison with another group, every discussion and meeting must further the client's desired outcome.

On the offense side, besides organizing a support group of citizens, he must form alliances and coalitions with other groups to augment and build strength. His campaign plan must include tactics to educate the public, showing how the project affects them personally, giving them reasons to support it, and then reinforcing that perception. He must conduct door-to-door outreach sessions in the affected neighborhood, reassuring the residents, asking for their input, and developing a program of neighbor-to-neighbor convincing. He must circulate a petition to gather signatures that demonstrate lack of opposition, if not support. He must anticipate opposition tactics and devise countermeasures, preemptive where possible. He must protect supporters from intimidation by opponents, and keep opponents off balance. He must select speakers from among the citizen supporters to speak at hearings, assign each a specific topic, write the scripts for them, and rehearse them so they address key issues intelligently. He must make sure their speeches and the evidence they submit not only assist the developer's lawyer in making his presentation, but also help create a record useful to the lawyer in further proceedings. He must ensure turnout at the hearing, making sure to get his troops to the hearing room early so they can take all of the best seats in front, filling the room if possible, thereby forcing opponents to stand outside in the hall to listen. Finally, he must provide political cover to public officials so they can grant approval without committing political suicide.

In all of this, his professional experience and training are indispensable. Novice political operatives think that simply inviting people to a hearing will produce turnout. A seasoned political campaign manager knows that mobilizing citizens requires a lot more than that. Even with an organized citizen group, turnout results only after you invite the members, remind them, pin them down, remind them again, pick them up in a vehicle, and drive them to the hearing.

Clumsy Amateurs

An additional point, and an important one, is that land use politics methods work only for those who know how to use them. Many is the public relations operative who thought he knew how politics works, who barged into town full of ideas and threw his weight around, only to dash his client's hopes. And many are the clients (and their corporate lawyers) who erroneously think they know how to attract and keep project support. For example, one corporate lawyer insisted that the way to turn out favorable crowds was to hire clowns with balloons. He was serious and insistent. His client lost. Another big-firm lawyer spent so much effort trying to figure out the identity of Saint's campaign manager that Saint killed his client's project while the lawyer bumbled around playing Sherlock Holmes.

Clumsy amateurs create a mess, poison the well for future attempts, and destroy the proponent's credibility. Since they don't foresee the consequences of their actions, they will use a blunderbuss where a feather would have done nicely. They hold contentious public meetings in auditoriums when a small friendly gathering over coffee in a neighbor's kitchen would have been far more effective in curbing opposition. Their inept efforts and statements reflect on the project and the developer. Amateurs destroy the developer's credibility by making promises the developer can't keep and by inaccurately describing project details that are vitally important to neighbors. When the neighbors discover that the parking lot is twice the size described, they will never trust the developer again. Even if the developer withdraws the plans and tries to refile later, the damage has been done: people decide that the project is bad, and no amount of tinkering with the site plan will change their minds.

Amateurs also make enemies because they don't understand the nature of politics. They burn bridges needlessly, force compromises that no one wants, and push their agenda to the detriment of the project and the client. In contrast, professional land use practitioners are agile and surgical in their approach. In one case, a Saint project manager was able to organize coalitions of citizens to support the client's supermarket proposal and get it approved while making sure that the same citizens vehemently opposed a competitor's proposal for a rival supermarket nearby. He completed his work and faded out of town unnoticed, like the Lone Ranger. In another case, a client needed help developing a site. Saint was in the midst of executing a successful strategy when the client advised the firm that he had a falling-out with the contractor and Saint's assignment was now to kill the project. The team shifted gears, and the project was dead in a week. Because the managers in both these projects were professionals, expert in the delicacies of political maneuvering, each was able to respond effectively to the rapidly changing circumstances without missing a beat and delivered results for the client promptly and in full.

In another case, Saint's customary review of legal notices regarding a client's competitor's project uncovered a procedural error that delayed the hearing, forced the developer to readvertise, and gave the Saint team time to convince city council members to switch their votes from supporting the project to opposing it. The project was voted down. In another case, a newly vetted Saint campaign manager beat an expansion of a big-box store, protecting three of the client's stores, by finding a silver bullet: a procedural error in the proponent's request for a parking variance that neglected to set forth the "hardship" required. Because Saint's managers in both these projects knew the local regulations and were attentive to detail, the client's interests were protected.

One final case is worth mentioning: a Saint client telephoned one of the firm's principals at home on a Saturday afternoon to report that he had just learned that a competitor was applying for zoning variances to build a competing supermarket across the street from his very profitable store. The hearing was scheduled for Monday. The client wanted the project killed, of course, knowing that he would inevitably lose a percentage of his customer base to a new store in a business that operates on 1 percent profit margins. Saint quickly organized an opposition citizen group to call town officials at home over the weekend, galvanized the subject neighborhood, and rounded up a large crowd of citizen opponents to appear at the hearing. The local newspaper reported "widespread opposition" at the hearing, and even though the proponent was represented by the go-to zoning lawyer in the area, the zoning board unanimously rejected the application. Saint had killed the project in 48 hours.

Before Selecting a Land Use Political Consultant

The developer, his development team, and his lawyers need to ask themselves a number of questions in advance of engaging a land use consultant. The answers will affect how the consultant will approach the project, including fashioning and executing the scope study and campaign plan. A competent land use political consultant needs to know and is sure to ask questions about the property ownership, financing plans, and other factors. Before talking to a land use political consultant, the development team should already have considered

- whether to buy the land, take an option, or make other arrangements;

- whether title should be in a new entity;

- what financing arrangements will be involved;

- whether to attempt a tax increment financing (TIF) approach; and

- whether there are easements, restrictions, or rights-of-way on the land.

The development team should also know

- whether the use involved is nonconforming and grandfathered;

- what zoning and other relief is needed and what local, state, and federal agencies will be involved;

- whether there are listed species, wetlands, vernal pools, or habitat issues;

- whether there are geographical or geological issues; and

- whether there are historic or archaeological issues.

Regarding the campaign strategy, the land use political consultant will need to know answers to these questions:

- How tight is the project's timing? Will the financing source be patient in case of delay?

- Can the project withstand a lengthy court appeal?

- Is the developer able and willing to buy out residential abutters?

- How much wiggle room does the developer have on the plans, the timing, and the acreage?

- How many units or square feet is the developer willing to concede?

- How much density can the project surrender and still be viable?

- How much is the developer willing and able to spend on mitigation or linkage fees?

The land use political consultant asks these questions to determine what the client believes would be a successful outcome, as this affects strategy. If the client wants victory with no compromise, no downsizing, and no added mitigation, the consultant will plan a strategy to achieve that goal. If, however, the client is ready to concede substantial density or double mitigation, the strategy and tactics the consultant devises will be quite different, and the campaign implementation will take a different tack. If the client needs quick approval, the campaign approach will be decidedly different than it would be if the client were prepared for the long run. The process being political, the road to victory will have unavoidable twists and turns. But it's important for the campaign manager to know what the client wants, so he can work to achieve it.

It is also helpful to advise the consultant what the client foresees as the major obstacles to project approval, including whether the client suspects competitor involvement driving the opposition and whether personal animosities—between the developer and local civic leaders, for example—may cause trouble. True, the campaign manager can do the research and find the obstacles, but the client often has insights, experience in the community, or personal knowledge that may not be easily discovered, and it's much more efficient to alert the manager at the outset so she can plan and act accordingly. When the doctor asks where it hurts, it's not because he can't eventually find the difficulty.

Interviewing Candidates

Interviewing land use consultant candidates should be a straightforward affair. Ask each candidate what kinds of land use battles he has won, how many of each, and what tactics he has used. If he cannot answer those questions satisfactorily, he's probably a wannabe or a novice, not an experienced professional.

Once past the threshold questions, the process is a matter of being satisfied that the candidate is worthy of trust and confidence:

- Ask to see his résumé. Does the consultant list substantial political campaigns he has managed? Did he win? Are land use campaigns listed? How many? Did he win? If not, why not?

- Ask to see newspaper and magazine clippings, if appropriate, and recommendation letters from prior or current clients. Ask for a sample of something the candidate has written, such as a magazine article or a detailed campaign plan. An experienced professional will have these readily at hand, properly redacted to protect the client whose project was involved. Ask what past or current clients can be telephoned to discuss their experience with the consultant and what political figures can confirm his role in their campaigns.

- Observe whether the candidate seems knowledgeable and articulate. Does he seem genuinely experienced, or has he padded his résumé and exalted the roles he played in campaigns? Is he ill at ease in discussing his background, experience, or success rate? Does he have deep organizational support from his employer, so that the campaign resources he will need (research, support personnel, graphic arts, production, survey execution, staffing) can be provided in an expeditious and efficient manner?

Finally, the client should be satisfied that the consultant understands

- his needs and expectations;
- his level of determination to win;
- his need and level of confidentiality; and
- his tolerance for public criticism and possible embarrassment from opponents.

The Gofer Error

A land use political consultant is not a gofer, but rather is an experienced professional whose advice and counsel are valuable. Occasionally, clients (apparently confident of their own political abilities) treat project managers as gofers whose job is to await instructions, jump when the phone rings, and perform whatever menial tasks are assigned, no matter how ill-advised, shortsighted, or self-defeating. This is a wasteful and expensive way to do business with a land use consultant. The consultant is being paid for his expertise and political acumen, not his talent at picking up the developer's dry cleaning. Real gofers are far cheaper, and a developer who wants to run the land use political campaign himself should probably go ahead and do so. From the perspective of the consulting firm, which has a reputation to uphold and a record for winning to preserve and expand, such an arrangement is not acceptable.

CHAPTER 7

■ ■ ■

The Differences Between Offense and Defense Land Use Politics Campaigns

A LAND USE POLITICS offense campaign is a political campaign that empowers and invigorates local citizens to support a project they favor in ways that effectively influence land use decisions by their local officials. A land use politics defense campaign is a political campaign that empowers and invigorates local citizens to oppose a project they disfavor in ways that effectively influence land use decisions by local officials. While these two definitions may seem the same, except that citizens provide support in one campaign and opposition in the other, the political campaign techniques employed in offense and defense campaigns are not the same. This chapter discusses the distinct approaches that the Saint Consulting Group uses for offense and defense campaigns.

One thing is true of both offense and defense campaigns: the first principle of land use politics is that preparation is indispensable. It bears repeating that learning about the community and its political and demographic makeup, town history, government, civic leaders, local issues, and attitudes toward development are all vital elements in the campaign manager's preparation for developing a successful political campaign strategy.

110

Preparing an Offense Campaign

For an offense campaign, self-education on the project site is vital: its history, background, and abutting and surrounding land uses; its geography and prior uses; environmental and neighborhood issues; and less obvious matters that could become issues. Does the parcel have historic, nostalgic, emotional, or symbolic importance in the community? Do neighbors use the site for community activities or sports, or does it serve as a shortcut for walkers or motorists, or a spillover parking lot for the local church? Do the neighbors have flooded yards because the site discharges runoff? Does the site serve as a buffer between the residential neighbors and a nearby noisy or noxious use?

Only a firsthand site inspection and chats with neighbors and other locals can bring these kinds of issues to the surface early on, so they can be addressed at the outset and not at some later crucial moment. Similarly, only an investigation at town hall will reveal the zoning district, applicable overlay districts, nature of zoning relief that may be needed, tax category and status, as well as proximity of infrastructure services such as water and sewer and information on previous attempts to develop the site and why they failed. And only an effort to reach out to local citizens and neighbors will give a hint of political obstacles, challenges, and issues that might arise unseen.

Saint Consulting management considers this preparatory stage so important that it employs an extensive scope report form that requires project managers to fill in answers to dozens of questions not only concerning their observations and investigation, but also their impressions and suspicions. It forces project managers to stay alert and think critically and in specific detail about the political campaigns ahead and the elements that will be needed for success.

Everyone has an agenda, whether they realize it or not, and in the modern age, everyone is a stakeholder, whether they have legal standing or not. Gently extracting information from civic leaders, citizens, abutters, and stakeholders will help the campaign manager learn what truly motivates supporters and opponents of the project and what might be their true agendas. It also provides hints of the issues or strategies that might change minds or influence public and official opinion.

Writing the Offense Campaign Plan

Once the research is completed, the project manager writes his scope report, including all of the information and impressions he gathered in his study and recorded on his scope report form, and begins fashioning a rough campaign strategy. Important at this stage is his understanding of the client's timeline, goals, budget, and other matters outlined earlier, since these will influence the approach he takes and the campaign elements, strategies, and tactics he recommends.

Writing the report is excellent preparation for writing the campaign plan. It focuses the mind on the issues and problems that the research identified, and it allows the manager to analyze problems and begin considering strategies and tactics to address them. Plans, backup plans, alternatives, and options all go into the scope report, together with the project manager's recommended strategies and tactics for each problem, issue, and obstacle, and his reasoning for selecting those options. This exercise is well worth the effort because the resulting detailed report will serve as the scaffolding for the campaign plan. It will also give the client a preview of the political problems and issues to be faced, and methods to effectively neutralize or reverse them.

Before finalizing the scope report, the project manager submits it to his regional manager for a vetting, and to Saint's chief communications director for any needed editing. Everybody at an operations management level at Saint started out as a project manager, so the more senior a manager, the deeper the experience and streetwise advice he or she can provide, and the better able he or she is to judge the quality of the scope report and proposed strategies. The vetting process allows senior managers to make sure the client is getting what he needs, as well as affording them an opportunity to fine-tune the approach. Once the vetting is complete, the project manager has a strong sense of the proper direction and is ready to draft his campaign plan. The client, meanwhile, receives a copy of the final scope report so he has an opportunity to discuss it, comment on problems or issues he considers pressing, and provide insight into any special information or intelligence he may have received.

The campaign plan is as detailed and comprehensive a political campaign program as is possible at this stage. It includes strategies, contingency plans, and tactics; identifies resource needs and a timeline; and presents a clear program of action, together with time commitments, budgets, and expense estimates.

The campaign scoping and budget process may seem like a long, convoluted affair that might take weeks or months of preparation. But through long experience and efficient management, Saint is able to perform the scope investigation; get the scope report written, vetted, and submitted; and construct a campaign program of exceptional quality and effectiveness in just a few days. Once the client has given the okay to proceed, the project team is usually on the ground in the community within 24 hours.

Saint managers have learned from personal experience that immediate and reliable support from headquarters can make all the difference in avoiding a campaign disaster. So the company maintains a robust research and support department that can get answers and produce results instantly for operatives in the field. This backup, which includes the ability to produce color maps and charts—such as red-dot maps showing where in a politician's district project supporters live (see figure on page 114)—as well as reports and documents, is a powerful tool when the going gets rough. It also avoids showing the client's hand at the local Kinko's, where the kid running the printer probably lives in town and is likely to be curious, if nothing else, about what the documents and flyers mean, why the maps show all the red dots, and who is planning the big development.

Timing Is Vital

Timing is vital in an offense campaign, not only to meet the client's desired schedule, but also because local political feathers can easily get ruffled at this early stage. Political preparation, organization, and initial forays into the community are important at this juncture, and so is discretion. Political sensibilities come into play early, and so do ingrained animosities among politicians and civic leaders.

Red Dot Map

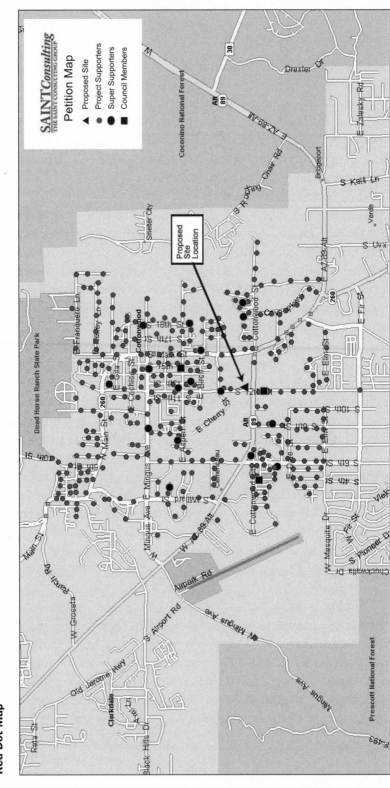

Petition Map

▲ Proposed Site
• Project Supporters
● Super Supporters
■ Council Members

Proposed Site Location

It's important that the client's project not become a pawn in some political game of get-even, and certainly it must not become an issue in a pending political election campaign. Saint managers usually advise clients who plan to file their projects during the local political campaign season to wait until after the election. If they do not, they risk becoming an issue—perhaps the key issue—in the election and suffering relentless criticism and second-guessing during the campaign and after the election, whether or not a project supporter wins.

It's important at the outset of an offense campaign to respect political authority and to inform people about the project in the correct order: public officials, followed by neighbors of the project, followed by the news media. Public officials are told first because they expect deference and hold political power. They will be insulted if they first learn about the project on the street or, worse yet, read about it in the newspaper. Giving them prompt notice also works in the developer's favor because they will often offer insights and useful comments, and may even provide help if they believe the project is a good one for their community. The principle of timing correctly is important because disclosure too early gives the opposition time and incentive to organize, while disclosure too late annoys opinion makers and abutters, who may carry grudges throughout the process because they were not respected.

What is the proper time to disclose the project to politicians and neighbors? As with all else in politics, it depends. Once the project application is filed, the project is a matter of public record, and city hall gossips will be busily feeding the grapevine. Disclosure to key political figures before the filing may have a salutary effect because it makes the politicians feel that they have inside information. Their ability to maintain confidentiality is put to the test here, but that may be a necessary risk, and can be minimized by very carefully selecting the politicians to be entrusted with information.

The issue of when to disclose also demonstrates the value of the in-depth scope study, which has already identified likely project opponents among local politicians and civic leaders. The campaign manager will want to make sure he has his preliminary work done and his support network organized before giving opponents a chance to attack the project. More important, he will want to make sure he has informed the news media before opponents learn of the project, because they will try to define the project and characterize it as bad for the community at the earliest opportunity. Most news organizations will afford the project proponent one clear, uncritical opportunity to present the project and outline its benefits and features before opening the floodgates for criticism.

Divulging project information can be a dicey business, since politicians are notoriously unable to keep secrets, and neighbors have no reason to do so. Disclosure must be planned carefully, perhaps with an explanation to the public officials that the project and the promised benefits will evaporate if word leaks out prematurely, and the project will go elsewhere.

It usually also makes sense in proposing a controversial project to let the mayor appear to wring concessions from the developer, thereby creating political cover for officials to grant project approval. This involves a preexisting sotto voce agreement on what the developer will provide, followed by a public demand in the newspaper from the mayor that the developer provide it. After an orchestrated closed-door meeting at which the mayor ostensibly lectures the developer on the project's shortcomings, the developer sheepishly emerges and reluctantly agrees to the mayor's demands, to the applause of the citizenry and local news media. While everyone is feeling warm and vindicated, the project is quickly approved. Once again, timing is essential: an announcement of the concession too far ahead of the approval vote will give project opponents time to think of other sacrifices to demand; an announcement just before the vote will have a smell of a political fix and sour the mayor's victory.

The timing issue points once again to the value of the scope study and report. In some campaigns, slow and quiet may be the best way to build support; in others, intense and loud is the best method; in still others, a multipronged approach, using some coalition members to make noise and others to keep their counsel, is most effective. The strategies and tactics tailored for the client's campaign will dictate how, when, and to whom disclosure about the project is made, all subject to the goals to be achieved, the deadlines to be met, and the vagaries of the political winds.

Once the project has been announced, deliberate speed in managing supporters and building a critical mass is vital. Delays give opponents time to call for a moratorium or to rewrite the applicable ordinance. The opposition will try to derail the project by forcing withdrawal of the application so that the protection afforded pending projects no longer applies, or by rezoning the parcel or surrounding parcels so that the project proposal is no longer appropriate for the site. Anticipating opposition efforts to derail the project and devising countermeasures involve political actions as well as legal ones, and are part of the campaign manager's responsibility. If opponents start a petition drive against the project, the manager may want to launch a counter-drive, or he may want to find community leaders willing to bring the petitioners' motives or methods into disrepute, thereby reducing the chances that "nice" people will sign. Meanwhile, the developer's attorney will be involved in responding legally to the opponents' efforts to force withdrawal or deprive the client of legal protections.

Saint Consulting has had some success with video petitioning, in which a citizen identifies herself on camera and states her reasons for favoring (or opposing) the project. This can have quite an impact on local officials, particularly when a number of video clips are combined to create a citizen testimonial presentation. This approach also avoids the problems that can arise when a citizen signs a petition, then is pressured to deny having done so or to claim the signature is a forgery or to assert that she was duped into signing.[1] A video clip in which a signatory states her reasons for supporting the development is difficult to deny, and although she can always say she later changed her mind, she can't claim fraud. Saint field personnel make sure to get a citizen's support in writing first, just in case she turns out to be camera shy.

---

[1] It is for this reason that Saint never allows anyone to sign on behalf of someone else, even if that person is a spouse or sibling. It's much cleaner to make sure each person signs for him- or herself, thereby protecting the firm from entanglement in a family dispute.

Beware the Planners

Planners are not necessarily even-handed processors of land use applications. The influential planner will have written some, if not all, of the use restrictions in the local zoning code, will have influence over the elected board empowered to decide the case, and, like everybody else, has an agenda. The planner's recommendation for or against a project can be decisive, so understanding his motives is important in crafting strategy. Although most professional planners have learned to assume poker faces when dealing with disagreeable projects, the political campaign manager will have developed a sense of where the planning staff is likely to stand on the project and how the elected officials are likely to treat the matter. Both evaluations will be included in the scope report. Because a joint assault on the project by the planning staff and project opponents can easily be made to look like community consensus, it's important that the campaign manager's organization and management of citizen supporters of the project be effective to influence the elected officials who will make the decision. Before they will approve the project, those officials may need to be convinced to reject the recommendations of their own planning staff, a reversal that may well require the campaign manager to produce a political revelation and conversion.

Project opponents in the modern world are astute at delaying progress; they know that delays can render a project infeasible. Perhaps the carrying costs become too much. Maybe the option runs out, and the landowner, tired of waiting, signs with someone else. Maybe the anchor tenant gets a better offer and goes elsewhere. Whatever the reasons, delays are not good for developers, and opponents know it. They call for community meetings; engage in discussion, debate, analysis, and studies; and negotiate trade-offs, preferences, and compromises because doing so serves their goal: delays that prevent the applicant from building anything. Groups whose members want nothing built are not going to collaborate with the applicant to improve the proposal and help get the project built; they are going to go through the motions, but only so they can raise one issue after another to block, delay, and increase costs until the applicant finally gives up and leaves town. Status quo ante—no change—is the goal.

When planners speak of collaboration and input, beware: the entire process is skewed toward the planning staff. Who determines who the stakeholders should be and rounds them up? Who decides what issues are important? Who selects what compromises are relevant? Who settles the value of vague concepts like appropriateness? Who drafts the agenda, manages the discussion, facilitates the topics, and makes the recommendations to the board? In every case, it's the planning staff.

The campaign manager, aware of all this, will plan strategies and tactics to counter any effort to sink the project based on planners' orchestrating of public opinion or efforts to skew input from stakeholders. Sometimes a public opinion poll might be in order; other times, packing the planners' public meeting with project supporters might be sensible; or changing the subject and riveting public attention on the tax burden or the jobless rate, both of which the development would help alleviate, might be prudent. Whatever combination of strategies and tactics is employed, the important point is that the land use professional recognizes the problems and addresses them. In addition, making certain that the client's side is well represented and effective at the hearing before the permit-issuing board is an essential art that a professional land use campaign manager will have mastered in his past life in getting out the vote for his candidate on election day.

Special Offense Cases: Buying Off the Neighbors

While it is perfectly legal for a developer to make private compensatory arrangements with neighbors, it must be done with discretion and finesse lest it produce adverse publicity and destroy the neighbors' credibility, as well as wreck any chance of project approval. Such arrangements differ from the practice of buying neighbors' homes as part of assembling a site, or even buying homes the project doesn't require in order to avoid confrontation with neighbors—both tried-and-true techniques for quieting opposition and reducing the number of people with legal standing to appeal. Those acquisitions are plainly business deals that should not carry any ethical or moral censure in the community. But where a compensation agreement might make sense, the land use campaign manager needs to study and weigh the implications to make sure there are no slipups and no adverse impacts on the project permitting campaign plan.

One method involves making what are nicely called "private agreements" with neighbors who are likely to appear at the zoning hearing to either speak in favor or stay home. Public disclosure of such an arrangement would damage the neighbors' credibility with the board, the press, and the community at large, and it is also likely to generate fury from neighbors who were left out of the deal and adversely impact the developer paying the "bribes." Such an approach is certainly not uncommon, but it must be handled with care and diplomacy, and cast in morally (and legally) unassailable terms. Careful, but full, disclosure needs to be made so the truth doesn't leak out at a critical moment. Making the neighbors sign a nondisclosure agreement is unenforceable in a practical sense. Once the word is out, what would be the point in suing the leaker and reminding everybody of the embarrassing facts? The developer is much better off simply stating that the neighbors have been compensated (or reimbursed) fairly for the costs and inconvenience that the project may cause as part of the mitigation program, which also includes items A, B, and C for the benefit of the entire community, and that the neighbors consent to the project's approval.

For particularly large projects, there may be too many neighbors to make individual compensation practical and creative mitigation may be required. Installing lights or bleachers at the youth baseball field, for example, has proven popular in some communities. Donating land for open space or a park also takes the edge off development, although a fiscally alert town manager will insist that the developer keep ownership of the parcel to assure that he continues to pay taxes on it. Communities in dire financial straits are sometimes responsive to offers to buy a police cruiser or fire apparatus for the town, while others may have pet projects that need a financial boost. The political campaign manager will have developed a good sense of what options would be both affordable and effective, and will devise a way to allow the necessary politicians to take credit for the mitigation, thereby welding their support in place.

Nonresidential development provides benefits to a community and may put the developer in a position of asking for concessions, rather than providing them. If the developer is in a strong negotiating position because the project will bring jobs to the community, generate badly needed revenue, clean up an eyesore, or bring some other boon, he may be in a position to get help from town officials with zoning issues and exact concessions in the form of tax abatements, tax incentive financing deals, or reduced water and sewer charges, for example. If the town has a municipal electric plant and the project will have large power demands, limiting or capping the electric bill can be discussed. If the development will require infrastructure improvements — road widening, turning lanes, off-site drainage improvements, and so forth — those, too, may be in play.

Special Offense Cases: Dealing with Labor Unions

Labor unions are much more prevalent in some areas than in others, and much more powerful in cities than in rural areas. Where they exist, and where they are not captive agents of the employer, their help and their members' activity can make a difference in a land use site fight.

Like all membership organizations, labor unions seek to do what's best for their members; and labor leaders, like all politicians, will do what will best enhance their chances of reelection. No matter what trade, business, or profession the union members represent, the labor organization is a political one, and the principles of politics apply. Labor unions are much more influential in some areas than in others, and some are far more powerful than others. It is the duty of the land use campaign manager to know whether a union is worth pursuing from a project permitting perspective, and what issues might arise as a result of such a pursuit, since the developer may be expected to provide concessions in return for the union's help.

Where a labor union is a natural supporter of a project — such as where members of a trade union of electricians, sheet metal workers, or painters will get construction or finish work — it usually doesn't take too much urging to get the local shop steward or president to support the project. He'll sign a letter and perhaps make a few calls. But a seasoned political campaign manager knows that if a more active role is needed from union members, it takes hard work to make that happen. For one thing, like most large organizations, a quick and nimble response from a union is usually not possible, even though quick and nimble is what is desperately needed. It does no good to win official union support a week after the project has been rejected, so going through union signoff channels, one sluggish level at a time, is usually a waste of time. Although some union leaders are more adept than others in convincing members to get involved in a land use fight, in most cases, working at the local union level—not the state, national, or even district level—and dealing informally with actual union members who have a personal stake in the outcome, rather than just a presumed philosophical impetus, is the most effective way to get active participation. A union member who lives in the neighborhood has more reason to get involved than one who doesn't, and he is more likely to urge his union colleagues to involve themselves as a personal favor to him.

Special Offense Cases: Affordable Housing

Affordable housing development can be a prickly problem. Citizens and officials pay politically correct lip service to the dire need, while subversively opposing such development as a danger to property values, even where it's only a segment of a mixed-use development.

As in any political fight, it doesn't matter whether the developer makes logical sense; she needs to make emotional sense to overcome opposition. An argument that affordable housing will be an asset to the town usually brings no response. An argument that it's the right thing to do brings unanimous nods of agreement, followed by no action. An argument that affordable housing is needed in the community generates clucks of concern and public hand-wringing, but continued opposition from those who imagine the neighborhood overrun with junk cars, screaming children, and drug pushers.

The argument that does gain traction with local citizens is that their own children will not be able to afford housing in their hometown when they marry and have kids, and that grandma will have to travel many miles to see her grandchildren, all because the town refused to allow housing that the nice young couple could afford. Even if they don't marry, grown children won't be nearby to help their aging parents if they are forced to move elsewhere; elderly homeowners will have to sell their houses and move to an assisted living or nursing home environment. Properly injected into public debate, this sort of argument will bring a response. Now the need for affordable housing is a wake-up call, a vision of the future. It opens minds to the potential downsides of not having affordable housing in town. It changes people's perception of the issue: no longer is it about poor people with junk cars. Now, it's about the citizens' children and grandchildren being able to live near their parents and grandparents. Now, it's about help with groceries and medical appointments when old age brings frailty and forgetfulness. With this argument, citizens have an answer to the selfishness question heard so often: what's in it for me?

Although appeals to the generalized need or propriety of affordable housing are usually ineffective, the argument can be fine-tuned in some vacation communities and resort towns to a song local citizens and business owners can hear: if we don't have affordable places for our service employees to live, they can't work for us, and the local economy will suffer. Larger resort destinations often build dormitory-style housing for their help, especially for seasonal workers, either on-site or nearby. But these places aren't suitable for permanent employees with families, and in smaller, less-organized vacation towns and quaint villages, where small business abounds, it's usually not economically feasible for the employer to provide housing (or enough housing) to meet the need. These businesspeople will listen to the argument that the community government should encourage and help developers to build such housing, whether for rental or purchase, and will actively support the idea, having answered the question: what's in it for me?

Preparing a Defense Campaign

Most modern-day citizens are automatically opposed to nearly any development in their community; they fear the unknown, oppose change, and worry about property values. Since elected officials listen to citizens, one might expect opposition to a development proposal to be a simple and straightforward affair of alerting officials to public sentiment and expecting them to vote accordingly. But because some public officials—and most planners—think they know better than the general public, and because ineffective opposition is perceived as arising from a small minority who can safely be disregarded, there are often leadership issues in which the official or planner is determined to have his way and will recommend or vote for what's best in his opinion, rather than for what people want. Add to this the fact that most project opponents, left to themselves, will grumble but stay home unless they are spurred to action, and the need to organize and manage development opposition becomes clear.

In communities where activist citizens hold sway, rounding up opponents and bombarding the developer and the officials who support the project has become standard. But where a business interest concludes that defense against unwarranted market intrusion is necessary to defend market share, protect investment, or protect major tenants—or to keep current or prospective tenants from migrating—citizens are hardly likely to pour into the streets to protect the business, and a ready-made opposition group is unlikely to be available. Even if it were, the group's motivations would not match that of the business interest: citizens will oppose that business's efforts to expand just as eagerly as they will fight a competing business, using a scorched-earth policy against any development whatsoever. An adept land use political manager, with careful organizing and focusing of citizen attention on limited goals, can surgically remove a threat without crippling the patient.

The campaign research, investigation, preparation, and planning necessary for offense campaigns—including the need for a detailed scope study and report—apply to defense campaigns as well, though the methods used to implement the defense campaign require a different set of talents. Professional land use consultants are much more circumspect about revealing the client's identity in a defense campaign, and they will be looking for opposition ammunition to fire at the project and developer, rather than preparing countermeasures to such attacks as they would in an offense campaign. But the initial stages—researching the community, the site, and the political landscape—remain pretty much the same. Like an offense campaign, the

Defense Threat Map

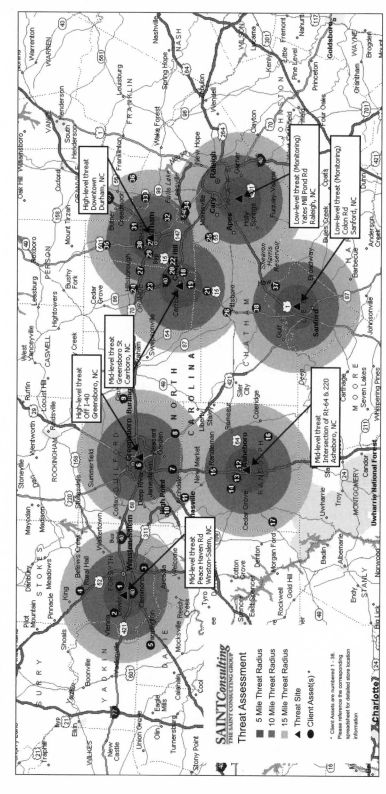

Low-level threat (Monitoring)
Yates Mill Pond Rd
Raleigh, NC

Low-level threat (Monitoring)
Colon Rd
Sanford, NC

High-level threat
Downtown
Durham, NC

High-level threat
Off I-40
Greensboro, NC

Mid-level threat
Greensboro St
Carrboro, NC

Mid-level threat
Intersection of Rt-64 & 220
Asheboro, NC

Mid-level threat
Peace Haven Rd
Winston-Salem, NC

SAINT Consulting
THE SAINT CONSULTING GROUP

Threat Assessment

■ 5 Mile Threat Radius
■ 10 Mile Threat Radius
■ 15 Mile Threat Radius

▲ Threat Site
● Client Asset(s) *

* Client Assets are numbered 1 - 38.
Please reference the corresponding
spreadsheet for detailed store location
information

defense campaign plan will utilize citizens, but defense is much less a commonsense affair than an offense campaign. Diversion tactics tend to be convoluted, so the manager needs to break down each gambit into simple steps that citizen group members can readily understand and implement. It is here that the care the manager used in selecting group members, and the trust he has built with them, bears fruit.

The first major difference between offense and defense campaigning lies in recruiting members of the opposition citizen group that the manager organizes, educates, and manages. While citizen supporters on the offense side tend to be people who will benefit somehow from the project, project opponents come in every stripe, from those with real, worrisome concerns, to those with NIMBY reasons, to conspiracy theorists who smell a plot in every chance remark, to lonely figures who join for the social contact.

The first and foremost caveat in recruiting opponents is that they cannot be crazy, violent, lecherous, foul-mouthed, or foul-tempered or have issues with personal hygiene. Amateurs forming citizen groups usually welcome anyone who turns up as a member, and consider themselves lucky. They put everyone to work right away without screening for shortcomings or character flaws, and later they have difficulty unhitching the undesirable member or finding activities in the back room to keep him occupied. The professional land use campaign manager cannot be so cavalier in organizing her group. Consider the consequences of having people with such drawbacks as the public face of the opposition. Their actions, language, and reputation will characterize the opposition in the minds of many, making it easier for project proponents to dismiss opponents as marginal, and destroying respect from the public officials and boards that will make the land use decisions. Furthermore, managing a member who (for want of a better term) has issues consumes valuable (and irreplaceable) time: the manager and citizen group leader always have to worry whether Crazy Henry is going to act up, or spend time apologizing, explaining, and undoing. Exiling such a local citizen raises a whole new array of problems, not the least of which is the potential for revenge and sabotage. Obviously, the manager cannot psychoanalyze every potential opponent, but being aware of the possibility of difficulty alerts the manager, as well as those she relies upon, to employ a modicum of caution and discretion.

In recruiting opposition citizens, project managers find that natural opponents are the best prospects. Abutters and other neighbors of the project locus, especially residential neighbors, are extremely valuable, not just because they can point to proximity and direct impacts, but also because they have legal standing. Not only can they effectively insist on reviews and studies that nonabutter opponents cannot, but they have the right to be directly notified of every action, meeting, and hearing that the government body schedules, and they have standing to sue the developer, the town, or both and appeal any decision. They also have a certain moral sway and a claim on community empathy that less-affected opponents do not: their neighborhood, families, and children will bear the brunt of the development, and but for happenstance any citizen might be in the same unenviable situation, seeking the support of fellow citizens.

Other residents whom the development might impact will oppose the project once they are made aware of the threat and given reasons to be opposed (which the manager will be ready to supply), and interest group opponents will clamber aboard once they are alerted and galvanized to join in a coalition with the opposition citizens, a job the manager is experienced and expert in undertaking.

Beware of Loose Cannons

The desirable traits for citizen group leaders are pretty much the same whether the group is on offense or defense: the individual must be intelligent, articulate, presentable, and unflappable and have leadership qualities. But on the defense side, the campaign manager and citizen leader must also be on the lookout for loose-cannon members who get a bright idea on how to annoy the proponents and act on it without clearing the scheme first. This sort of activity is much more common on the defense side than on offense for several reasons, not the least of which is that project supporters tend to be more staid and less given to pranks and destructive behavior than opponents, who sometimes let their frustrations cloud their judgment. To the agitated project opponent, the faceless corporate entity seeking to profiteer at the neighborhood's expense deserves retribution, and he is perfectly willing to deliver the message in a pointed and creative manner. He does not see beyond his single-minded objective, or appreciate the consequences that may ensue, including police involvement, litigation, bad publicity for the cause, loss of credibility, and a shift in public sentiment toward sympathy for the project proponent. The experienced manager will make clear to members of the opposition group that off-message mischief is counterproductive; can damage the group's credibility, reputation, and effectiveness; and is not to be attempted.

Creative Campaigning

This is not to say that creative methods of conducting an opposition campaign are not productive. They are often the most productive elements because they bring attention to the cause that ordinary campaign methods could not achieve. In one of the cases presented in Chapter 9, a Saint campaign manager published a public official's home phone number in the newspaper along with the message that the official was the only thing stopping development of a badly needed grocery store. The citizens' irate phone calls to the alderman's home brought the desired result: he voted in favor of the project. Had that campaign manager been squeamish about calling an alderman at home — or had the manager been deterred by the alderman's bluster that he would not tolerate calls to his home — the overwhelming weight of public pressure would not have forced the politician to change his mind. The manager's job is to do what works to win (within the bounds of law). If that involves staging a vigil on the mayor's front lawn, handing out flyers outside a church, renting a billboard, sending a plane or hot-air balloon aloft to display a message banner, holding a rally at the project site, or creating a public spectacle, then so be it.

In all of this, knowing when and how to use the press is vitally important to success. Public perception of the issues will be driven in part by the attitude that the press conveys. This does not mean relying on the press to do the job, the way a public relations approach might work; it means using the media's thirst for news to the client's advantage. An astute campaign manager in a defense campaign will not let any attack in the press go unanswered; nor will the manager fail to take every opportunity to present the opponents' arguments in the media through letters, op-ed pieces, and comments from the citizen group leader in news stories covering the proposed project.

It's also important to know when and how to go around the press and take the message directly to the public, particularly in communities where the media pay homage to city hall or the chamber of commerce and follow the party line on development. Receiving fair coverage in news media controlled by the establishment or the developer is not possible; but the media no longer control public perception, and alternative methods are available to counter adverse journalism. Newsletters that look like newspapers can be effective, as can the Internet, where an opponent website and chat room can provide citizens with an accessible and insulated forum to critique the project without media bias. Going around the media also includes citizen action—making use of the citizen-soldiers that the campaign manager has so painstakingly recruited and trained. Unleashing their enthusiasm by suggesting that everyone call the mayor (or the newspaper editor) at home is one example of this approach.

Organizing Protests and Rallies

In staging a public opposition meeting, it is essential to invite the developer, thereby placing him in an unwinnable situation. If he refuses to attend, he can be cast as having something to hide or being unspeakably arrogant, unwilling to hear constructive criticism, deaf to the cries of the families he is hurting, or uncaring about the environmental damage he is causing, proving that the fix is in at city hall. Opponents can use his absence productively by bashing the developer and the project for the benefit of the audience and the news media. If the developer does attend the meeting, he can be cornered, asked embarrassing questions, forced to make concessions, confronted by neighborhood opponents, put on the defensive, made to look devious or contentious, or both, and roundly vilified for his attitude. If he can be goaded into losing his temper, so much the better. It is also vital to invite public officials to witness the developer's doubletalk and tantrum, and the news media to report on it. If public officials are present, accusing the developer of dirty politics is usually helpful in prodding them to distance themselves from the mud; denouncing the developer's past failed developments in other communities, together with a list of unkept promises and outright lies, is always a crowd-pleaser and is sure to get attention from the news media.

Attending Charrettes

A defense campaign relies on a continuous flow of information, gossip, and actionable intelligence in order to remain politically fresh and effective. The easiest way to gather and maintain the flow of data is to make certain that knowledgeable members of the opposition group attend every meeting, hearing, gathering, and charrette to gather information, recruit new members, and challenge the developer's every assertion.

But can't the proponent demand that all objections be raised at once? Sure, she can demand that—but there's no law requiring it, and it's doubtful that an elected local board would so muzzle the voting public. Even if the board does so rule, the opponent can always come in later with more issues cast as newly recognized or newly discovered evidence, which would have been raised earlier if the developer had been more forthcoming in disclosing the impacts of the project. A neighborhood group can always fall back on the argument that its members are simple nonexpert citizens, working nights and weekends to protect their community, without the massive resources of the out-of-town developer; they are just striving as volunteers to preserve their neighborhood way of life. An elected local board will certainly listen to that argument. The neighbors can also feed the issues to the press, and let the reporters ask the board for answers.

With this approach, and constant pressure, opponents can cause delay after delay, challenging the traffic study as covering an inadequate study area, thereby forcing it to be done over; pointing out holes in the environmental impact statement and forcing expensive and time-consuming supplements; challenging the adequacy of the conservation order of conditions and appealing to state authorities—each element adding time and expense to an already protracted process.

The Art of Traffic Studies

Traffic studies, which purport to be authoritative, are no less political than any other aspect of land use permitting. Traffic engineering is an example of an art posing as a science: it depends entirely on the assumptions the engineer makes, rather than (as most people assume) on the traffic counts. Traffic counts are considered an important measure of how heavy traffic is in the area at different times of day. The traffic engineer uses this information to project how heavy the traffic will be once her client's project is developed and all of the infrastructure mitigation is in place. It is here that science turns into political art. What traffic engineering category is she going to apply to the project?[2] What pass-by rate is she going to assume? What pending or partially built projects in the area has she included in the assumptions? What future highway improvement is she assuming will be completed? Even the "science" of traffic engineering is an art because the engineer can easily skew the results by what she includes and excludes from the study area she selects and the time period she picks to conduct the study: a small study conducted at a ski resort in August is not going to record much traffic.

Usually, the traffic engineer can justify her choices one way or another, but those choices are assailable and debatable. One useful way of undermining the credibility of a traffic study is to station citizen group members to conduct their own study, using a study area and time period intended to maximize traffic counts. Citizens can make assumptions just as well as engineers can, and a competing traffic study will force the permitting board to focus on the traffic issue and not simply accept the developer's study as gospel.

---

[2]The Institute of Transportation Engineers (ITE), formerly the Institute of Traffic Engineers, publishes the ITE handbook, *Trip Generation*, a manual listing project categories, estimates of the amount of traffic they will generate, and pass-by rates that may be assumed. The problem is that the data lag behind for several years because studies must be collected and new land uses may not be included. For years, for example, the manual did not include a category for "supermarket" or "superstore" or "supercenter," which meant that traffic engineers for clients building 75,000-square-foot supermarkets or 250,000-square-foot Wal-Mart Supercenters simply used the obsolescent grocery store category as the next closest thing, a choice that woefully underestimated traffic impacts. ITE members are active in 92 countries, so the manual's influence is considerable.

A traffic engineer's results are suspect and can be brought into question because (1) the engineer is selected, retained, and paid by the developer; (2) the engineer must not annoy the developer if he expects to receive further work; and (3) traffic studies are pretty malleable contrivances, with countless adjustable variables and arguable conclusions. Absurd as it may seem, traffic counts are sometimes done on New Year's Day, when almost no one is on the road, and survey crews sometimes measure peak summer traffic in October. There is a good deal of fudge room in analyzing 300 pages of traffic data print-outs, and all of the conclusions are based on assumptions the engineer chooses to make, and the various ways he chooses to manipulate and interpret the data. Traffic engineering is an art, and forecasting traffic growth is a guess.

An effective defense method of handling developer traffic studies is to insist that the town select its own independent traffic engineer to perform a separate, broader study, either paid for or reimbursed by the proponent. This produces two benefits: data are more likely to support opponents, and delay is likely in the permitting process. The trick here is for the opponents to find an engineer who dislikes, mistrusts, or feels contempt for the developer's engineer, and who can be relied on to look on the developer's engineer's numbers with skepticism. Although there is a general sense of professional courtesy and collegiality among traffic engineers, they are also in competition, vying for the same clients and subject to the same umbrage and retaliatory feelings that affect any profession or business. A little digging will usually locate someone who has a grudge, wound, bias, or resentment against the developer's chosen firm, or who at least considers himself far superior to the chosen outfit. Savvy opponents will always come armed with a name or two to suggest to the board the minute it votes to have an independent study performed.

Other Compliance Issues

In focusing on the local permitting procedure, the campaign manager must never lose sight of other arrows in his quiver: permits and certificates from agencies at the county, state, or federal level verifying compliance. There are countless potential obstacles for the developer, many allowing citizen comment, testimony, or submission of evidence. Filing with these agencies prevents them from rubber-stamping approval and encourages them to take a second, longer look at the applicant's submission.

Whether the contest is in the United States, Canada, or the United Kingdom, environmental laws and regulations must be satisfied, studies completed, and appropriate permits secured. But there are also wetlands regulations, rules governing curb cuts into public highways, coastal zone management and water-dependent use statutes, air quality requirements, noise limits, "light trespass" regulations, "dark sky" standards to control the "stadium effect," height regulations for buildings near airports, design requirements under the various disabilities rights acts, environmental remediation standards for contaminated brownfield sites, and laws and regulations governing historic, archaeological, and sacred burial ground sites. Tax liens and regulations may come into play if the developer is not fully compliant. Finally, there is always the potential for a public land taking if the citizenry and public officials think the site would make a better skateboard park than it would a shopping center.

Decisive Techniques

Besides all the options project opponents have to stop a project within the permitting process, determined opponents can take decisive measures under the tutelage of a land use politics professional to send a project to oblivion:

- Rezone the land to disqualify the proposed use.

- Amend the zoning ordinance to delete or restrict the proposed use.

- Amend the ordinances to require large mitigation, linkage fees, and exactions.

- Force application withdrawal over some flaw, and then amend the ordinance.

- Prevent annexation.

- Block infrastructure.

- Require a referendum vote on rezoning the parcel.

- Amend ordinances while the decision is pending to allow public official recall.

One particularly effective tool is a building moratorium, imposed ostensibly to halt the building frenzy and provide quiet time to study and update the comprehensive plan, the zoning code, or both. A moratorium seems perfectly sensible to people in a community where zoning hasn't been updated in decades, or where a frenetic building boom is making citizens uneasy. Courts and statutes limit a moratorium to a "reasonable" length of time, generally considered 18 months or less, but extenuating circumstances can come into play. While a committee of community leaders studies the issues and prepares recommendations, the question for the developer is whether he can wait 18 months to begin the process of land use permitting, considering that there is no guarantee that the proposed use will still be allowed on the site, or that the new ordinance won't ban projects with the bulk and density he needs. If his financing dries up in the interim, so be it.

Buying Standing

If all else fails and it's clear that the project proponent is going to get approval, the question is whether to appeal and, if so, how. If the opposition campaign has developed a determined group of citizens ready to go the distance, filing the appeal in the names of those with legal standing—usually, abutters or abutters of abutters within some statutorily prescribed distance—is preferred, since they are real citizens with personal reasons for opposing the project. They will be asked during the proponent's informational fishing expedition who is funding the appeal, even though courts have ruled this information irrelevant, so it's particularly beneficial if they neither know nor care and can therefore say just that under oath.

Still, citizens sometimes lose courage and determination after a few months in a lawsuit, and they begin to think of ways to withdraw from the litigation and get on with their lives. Litigation is intrusive and stressful, especially for laymen. Even where they are competently represented by counsel, citizens' commitment may wane, despite a campaign manager's reassurances and continued reminders of how important the case is to their own families. This is especially true when the developer contacts citizen plaintiffs with offers to buy their land or otherwise compensate them for quitting the appeal, and works to pick them off, one by one. Without the support of fellow neighbors, few appellants will stand alone.

In such cases, a forward-looking campaign manager will have suggested to a determined client early on that it would be wise to acquire some small parcel in the area that will, by its location, afford legal standing to the owner. Standing not only gives the client (or his nominee) legal status to sue; it also affords other benefits, such as the right to be notified by registered or certified mail of any hearing, and the political benefit of receiving special deference from the board as a most-affected neighbor. Besides, the client (or nominee) can always sell the land later—maybe even to the competitor in exchange for concessions elsewhere.

Obviously, neither the client nor the client's real estate agent should hold title to the property if the idea is to maintain credibility, though some clients simply don't care if their identity is known because they intend to use their legal standing as a means of forcing the project proponent to the negotiating table. This approach should be taken advisedly, perhaps only where there are strong grounds for appeal or where delay is a significant factor, since courts eventually uphold the permit-granting authority in most cases. Creative campaign managers also sometimes use a land purchase where the idea is straightforward blocking: the client buys the land because the project proponent needs it to assemble the site, or for egress, green space, or detention ponds, and cannot build without it.

Usually, clients in defense campaigns do not want their identities disclosed because it opens them to adverse publicity and the potential for lawsuits. The adverse publicity may not play well in the subject community, which can present a real problem if the client is seeking some sort of discretionary zoning relief in the same town. It also can present an unsavory corporate image that the client's opponents in other communities will use to the client's disadvantage. And there is a practical financial consequence: if the citizen landowner knows that the deep-pocketed corporate client is interested in buying the land, the price will skyrocket.

To avoid such complications and risks, campaign managers sometimes instruct counsel to establish a trust in a convenient jurisdiction that requires only the name of the trustee to be disclosed, not the name of the beneficiary. The manager then secures the services of an attorney whose name is not associated with the client to serve as trustee and counsel to the trust. The client is protected because the beneficial interest, which may go through multiple layers and interlocking trusts, need not be disclosed, and because the principle of attorney–client privilege will prevent the project proponent's lawyer from forcing the trustee-lawyer to divulge the client's name.

Given this sort of arrangement, the political campaign manager can scan the area for likely target properties, trying to find one already on the market, or perhaps one in danger of going into tax title or mortgagee auction, or a run-down place whose owners have died and whose out-of-state heirs are anxious to sell. The trustee can then contact a local real estate agent to make an offer on the property, set the pricing parameters, and handle the details. Once the land is in proper ownership, the principles of land use politics will help the campaign manager decide whether to install a project consultant to live on-site, perhaps to breathe new life into the opposition and lead the ongoing fight against the unwanted project as an irate abutter.

Chapter 9 presents a series of case studies that show how the Saint Consulting Group has applied political offense and defense campaign tactics to prevail in a variety of real-life land use politics battles.

CHAPTER 8

■ ■ ■

Legal Foundations
for Defensive Actions

ALTHOUGH SOME PEOPLE may view working secretly to derail an opponent's project as unethical, such activity is not illegal. In fact, it is clearly protected in the United States by federal law. Recognizing the importance of preserving personal liberties, the U.S. Supreme Court has ruled in a series of cases that free speech, the right of petition, the right of assembly, and other provisions of the Bill of Rights supersede legislative enactments that might otherwise curtail a business owner's efforts to protect his market share by opposing his competition. And state legislatures have enacted laws to protect project opponents (including competitors) against strategic litigation intended to intimidate them into silence.

Particularly important is the Noerr-Pennington doctrine. Noerr-Pennington, which was developed from two U.S. Supreme Court cases in the 1960s[1] and was expanded in the following decades,[2] solidly protects the First Amendment right to petition the government for redress of grievances. Although the definition seems pedestrian and peripheral to land use law, the reach of this doctrine is great.

---

[1]*Eastern Railroad Presidents Conference v. Noerr Motor Freight, Inc.*, 365 U.S. 127 (1961) and *United Mine Workers v. Pennington*, 381 U.S. 657 (1965).
[2]*California Motor Transport Co. v. Trucking Unlimited*, 404 U.S. 508 (1972).

137

The *Noerr* case pitted railroad companies against the burgeoning trucking industry in what the court called "a 'no-holds-barred fight' between two industries both . . . seeking control of a profitable source of income,"[3] long-distance freight hauling. Each side accused the other of using malicious tactics in their opposing efforts to lobby the government for legislation and regulations that would injure the competitor, and each engaged in a public relations assault on the other. The truckers sued under the Sherman Antitrust Act, alleging that the railroads conspired to restrain trade and monopolize the industry, and the railroads filed a counterclaim alleging much the same thing against the truckers. The U.S. Supreme Court held that the parties were immune from antitrust scrutiny because the right to petition the government is protected, even if the motive is to eliminate competition and the tactics used are unsavory.

In the *Pennington* case, the coal miners' union and large coal mining companies entered into a collective bargaining agreement that effectively set an industry-wide minimum wage that smaller coal mine operators could not afford to pay, and convinced the federal secretary of labor to require the higher wage standard for contractors selling coal to the Tennessee Valley Authority. The goal was to eliminate the smaller companies so the large firms could dominate the market. Under the reasoning of the *Noerr* case, the Supreme Court held against the small coal mine operators, ruling that "joint efforts to influence public officials do not violate the antitrust laws even though intended to eliminate competition."[4]

Thus, Noerr-Pennington started out as a pair of antitrust cases holding that an effort to influence government decision making is an exercise of the constitutional right to petition and cannot therefore be a violation of the Sherman Antitrust Act, even if the petitioner's purpose is to gain an anticompetitive advantage. But the doctrine has been expanded far beyond that limited scope to enshrine personal constitutional rights with immunity from lawsuits.

---

[3] *Eastern Railroad Presidents Conference v. Noerr Motor Freight, Inc.*, 365 U.S. 127 at 144 (1961).
[4] *United Mine Workers v. Pennington*, 381 U.S. 657 at 670 (1965).

Where once an aggrieved party would have slapped a project opponent with a hefty lawsuit, today the Noerr-Pennington doctrine protects individual freedoms by essentially granting immunity from various common-law and civil tort claims, including unfair competition, tortious interference, and abuse of process. Noerr-Pennington is applicable to all branches of government (executive, legislative, and judicial) at all levels (federal, state, regional, county, and municipal). So political shenanigans at the local zoning board are just as protected as those in the halls of Congress, and a business owner has the right to oppose a competitor's expansion plans without necessarily identifying himself as the source of opposition and to fund opposition groups secretly and anonymously.

An instructive case is *Alfred Weissman Real Estate, Inc. v. Big V Supermarkets, Inc. et al.,*[5] decided in the Appellate Division of the New York Supreme Court. Briefly, Weissman Real Estate bought a former Saks Fifth Avenue distribution center in Yonkers, New York, intending to develop it into a shopping center that included a supermarket. To do so, the company needed the zoning changed from commercial to retail. Big V Supermarkets, which operated a ShopRite supermarket store a half-mile away, sought to become Weissman's supermarket tenant, but the two sides could not agree on terms, and Weissman entered an agreement with a competing supermarket. Weissman then submitted its zoning change application to the Yonkers City Council and started the required environmental review under New York's State Environmental Quality Review Act (SEQRA).

At some point during the process, Big V hired Matthew D. Rudikoff Associates Inc., a planning and engineering firm. Weissman charged that Big V and Rudikoff formed a corporate shell company intended to provide legal standing to oppose the project and created two purported citizen groups to oppose the project by disseminating misleading and disparaging information. Rudikoff's job, Weissman asserted, was to "derail" the rezoning.

---

[5]*Alfred Weissman Real Estate, Inc. v. Big V Supermarkets, Inc.,* N.Y. Sup. Ct., App. Div., Case No. 0931B, Argued Sept. 28, 1999. Decision No. 1998-11026, Index No. 010739-1998.

Rudikoff subsequently notified the city council president that it was conducting an independent review of the project on behalf of one of the citizen groups, the Association for the Preservation of Tuckahoe Road (a group allegedly headed by the Big V store manager), citing traffic, congestion, air quality, and other issues. Eight months later, Rudikoff submitted adverse comments on Weissman's environmental impact statement (EIS) and thereafter submitted several additional letters. Nearly two and a half years after Weissman first filed its zoning change application, the planning board voted 4 to 3 to reject Weissman's application, even though the board members noted that it was "handled extremely well and extremely professionally." Weissman responded with an amended proposal offering $3 million in traffic improvements to alleviate perceived traffic impacts, but while this was pending, the city council rejected Weissman's final EIS as incomplete.

Weissman sued Big V, Rudikoff, and others, alleging that they acted to prevent competition with the Big V store, acted in retaliation because Weissman refused to lease to Big V, and used deception, misrepresentation, and misinformation to further their campaign. As causes of action, Weissman asserted tortious interference with a contract, tortious interference with prospective economic advantage, prima facie tort, and deceptive trade practices in violation of New York's General Business Law, and asked the court to enjoin the defendants from any further participation in the SEQRA process or hearings on its zoning change. The defendants moved to dismiss, responding that their participation in the public review of Weissman's project was protected free speech under the First Amendment and within the Noerr-Pennington doctrine. The trial court upheld most of Weissman's claims, but the appeals court found that, while the defendants' actions might have been devious, underhanded, or objectionable to those of higher ethical standards, this was irrelevant under Noerr-Pennington.

Among other telling statements, the appellate court said that "the fact that the effort to influence government is part of a broader scheme does not make the conduct illegal," and that "courts have upheld the application of the doctrine even when the petitioning activity included the use of questionable or underhanded activity." The court flatly rejected Weissman's ethical argument that the Noerr-Pennington doctrine ought to be applicable only in disputes between competitors or "to groups who are motivated by 'higher civic principles' and who disclose their true identity." It pointed out that "the defendants have the right to engage in petitioning activities under an assumed name or without disclosing their true identity."

Noerr-Pennington protects speech and petitioning activity, and there is no requirement that those enjoying its protection be pure of heart, honest, forthright, or candid. In dismissing all claims, the court summed up the situation succinctly: "The plaintiffs do not possess cognizable causes of action for what amounts to the defendants' mastery of the local political process to protect their legitimate business interests."

The defendants' "mastery of the local political process" amounted to the Machiavellian use of feints and tactics to bring about the desired end, protecting Big V's "legitimate business interests," which is to say, protecting its store's market share against competition by preventing a nearby supermarket from getting built. To do so, Big V adopted strategies and tactics that might merit a caning in a Victorian boys' school but that are common (if not acknowledged) in the twenty-first century.

The Sham Exception

It is important to note that the U.S. Supreme Court has carved out a "sham" exception to the Noerr-Pennington doctrine, by which those who are not really exercising the right to petition are not protected. At first glance, this might seem to undermine the doctrine, since on one hand it condones less-than-candid behavior, but on the other it seems to require that one be honest about being devious. Such is not the case.

The sham exception applies only to intent, not methods: is the individual serious about stopping the competition, or is he just out to annoy the competitor? In most cases, this is not an issue; stopping competitors is usually the real goal. It is important to understand that the sham is not about whether one uses trickery to harm an opponent but rather about why one is really trying to influence government officials to act in a certain way. In the Big V case, the exception did not apply because the defendants were genuinely trying to keep Weissman from getting his land rezoned. Note, however, that if one is genuinely trying to stop a competitor, the fact that one fails to do so does not render the effort frivolous. In other words, there's no harm in trying.

The sham exception does apply where the purpose is to harass the competitor or drive up the competitor's cost of doing business without an accompanying intent to gain government action. A party who files objections with government officials seeking to prevent his competitor from developing land receives Noerr-Pennington protection; a party whose real goal is merely to delay his competitor's construction or drive up his costs by filing frivolous objections does not.

The Supreme Court has designed a two-pronged test to determine whether a set of circumstances amounts to a sham under the doctrine. In the case of a lawsuit, for example, the first prong of the test asks whether the lawsuit is frivolous — "objectively baseless" such that "no reasonable litigant could realistically expect success on the merits." If the answer is yes, the court moves to the second prong: whether the party's true motivation in filing the frivolous lawsuit was merely to interfere with the competitor's business. If that answer, too, is yes, Noerr-Pennington does not apply. Note that it is not enough that the lawsuit be frivolous; the motivation also must be unprotected.

Attempts to raise the sham exception are rarely successful, since most competitors genuinely want to stop their rivals, not merely to annoy them. Note in particular that whether an action is frivolous does not depend on whether it is successful. By definition, a successful activity, such as blocking a competitor's development plan, cannot be objectively baseless. But even an unsuccessful activity is not objectively baseless unless it can be fairly said that "no reasonable litigant could realistically expect success."

Surreptitiously funding citizens in their fights against development is clearly protected activity, and the political reasons for doing it are obvious: competitors lack the credibility that citizens have in opposing a project. If local citizens have high credibility but lack the financial resources to effectively oppose a project they dislike, and a competitor has the resources but lacks the credibility to wage an effective opposition campaign, the melding of the two would seem efficacious. Whether the competitor discloses its true identity or, indeed, whether the citizens know or care who is funding their campaign is legally irrelevant.

In Europe, Canada, and elsewhere, antitrust law is called competition law, and it outlaws the same evils: monopolies, price-fixing, and restraint of trade. Does that mean that other countries have a version of the Noerr-Pennington doctrine? No. It took the strange interplay of the U.S. Sherman Antitrust Act and the Bill of Rights in judicial minds to develop the Noerr-Pennington doctrine. Given that, it seems unlikely that it will be adopted elsewhere.

SLAPP Lawsuits

A discussion of the right to advocacy would not be complete without including developer efforts to intimidate critics into silence by suing them. This approach is known as a strategic lawsuit against public participation (SLAPP), a term coined by two University of Denver professors, Penelope Canan and George W. Pring, who did a nationwide survey and found thousands of examples of SLAPPs.[6] In the classic case, neighbors opposed to a developer's proposal make critical remarks about it, or about the developer, or both. The developer then sues the critics for a frightening sum, alleging a menu of common law torts: defamation of character, tortious interference, conspiracy, abuse of process, malicious prosecution, trespass, nuisance, invasion

[6]George W. Pring and Penelope Canan, *SLAPPs: Getting Sued for Speaking Out* (Philadelphia: Temple University Press, 1996). ISBN 1-56639-369-8.

of privacy, and so forth. The purpose of the lawsuit is to intimidate the neighbors into silence and to burden them with the cost of defending the lawsuit and the worry about losing their homes if they have to pay huge damages. This aggressive approach has proven effective not only in silencing critics, but also in dissuading others from commenting unfavorably on a project. Sometimes, the mere threat of a lawsuit in a lawyer's stern cease-and-desist letter is enough.

SLAPP lawsuits were originally used in retaliation for critics' action in submitting adverse testimony and comments to public agencies that were considering development applications. The idea was to keep adverse information out of the public record and to prevent neighbors from influencing the board members' votes. SLAPPs were also sometimes used to deter citizens from reporting violations of environmental laws to regulatory agencies.

But don't the clauses in the Bill of Rights guaranteeing free speech, assembly, and the right to petition protect these SLAPP defendants? Doesn't Noerr-Pennington apply to them as well as to business competitors? Aren't they petitioning the government when they ask the zoning board to turn down a developer's variance application? The short answers are yes, yes, and yes. But the purpose of filing a SLAPP lawsuit is not to win; it's to intimidate and silence the opposition. Will the defendants in a SLAPP case get it thrown out by the court? Yes, eventually. But the wheels of justice grind exceedingly slowly, and while the neighbors spend many anxious months waiting for an outcome—responding to interrogatories, answering notices to admit facts, preparing for their depositions—they remain silent about the development. They make no more appearances at the zoning board hearings; they submit no more letters to the editor; they attend no more meetings of concerned neighbors; they make no further statements. The litigation costs the developer money, but he is much better suited to handle the cost and knows that if he doesn't sue, the opponents will delay his project and may be able to kill it. For him, it's a worthwhile cost of doing business.

SLAPP suits have been such a powerful tool that a few developers grew SLAPP-happy, filing lawsuits to silence dissent at every opportunity. But the effectiveness of the SLAPP approach may be waning, at least in the United States. In response to SLAPP suits and the delays in getting them dismissed, many states (24 at last count) have adopted anti-SLAPP legislation designed to expedite the dismissal process and award attorney's fees and costs (and sometimes punitive damages) to SLAPP victims.[7] Under these laws, statements to public officials and agencies relating to a matter under review are protected. Courts are pushed to determine early in the proceedings whether petitioning activity was involved and, if so, to dismiss the case and often award attorney's fees and costs. In some jurisdictions, any speech to anyone regarding a matter under review is covered. In others, it must be to the proper agency. In still others, it must be made in a public place or forum. In some, knowingly false statements are not protected at all. In many, a special motion to dismiss is filed, and an expedited hearing is held, while discovery procedures (interrogatories and depositions, for example) are suspended while the dismissal is considered; the burden shifts to the plaintiff to prove that the defendant was not engaged in petitioning activity or did not act in good faith.

The anti-SLAPP statutes and publicity seem to have been effective. A dozen Web sites now provide SLAPP information and advice. Free speech organizations, including the Electronic Freedom Foundation and the American Civil Liberties Union, have taken up the cause. Most SLAPP suits today in the United States are dismissed, and as lawyers become more aware of anti-SLAPP statutes and decisions, the volume of such cases seems destined to decline. After all, what developer's lawyer wants to inform his client that his lawsuit has been dismissed and that he has to pay not only his own lawyer's fees, but also the attorney's fees and costs of the citizens he sued?

Internationally, using litigation to intimidate opponents seems common and expected. In Canada, the British Columbia Supreme Court threw out the 1999 claim of a hospital director after holding

---

[7]The states with anti-SLAPP laws on the books are Arkansas, California, Delaware, Florida, Georgia, Hawaii, Indiana, Louisiana, Maine, Maryland, Massachusetts, Minnesota, Missouri, Nebraska, Nevada, New Mexico, New York, Oklahoma, Oregon, Pennsylvania, Rhode Island, Tennessee, Utah, and Washington. The U.S. territory of Guam also has an anti-SLAPP law.

that his lawsuit was intended to silence opposition to a hospital expansion. British Columbia then enacted an anti-SLAPP statute titled the Protection of Public Participation Act, but it was repealed four months later when a new pro-development government took power.

In Ontario, citizen groups are wary of taking on developers after a news report in the *Toronto Star*[8] that a major corporate developer asked the Ontario Municipal Board (OMB) to assess $3.6 million in fees and costs against citizens who opposed its billion-dollar resort project. That request unnerved citizens opposed to another project proposed by a subsidiary of the same parent corporation, and it brought calls for the provincial government (which appoints the OMB) to intervene. Besides the OMB request, the developer "launched four civil lawsuits seeking more than $100 million in damages," the *Star* reported, against two lawyers and two investment bankers, all opponents of the project, as well as libel suits against two citizens, one for issuing a press release against the project and the other for a letter written to a municipal clerk. There is no anti-SLAPP protection in Ontario. But because of a growing chorus of protests against SLAPP intimidation and demands that it be controlled or outlawed as in nearly half the U.S. states, there have been murmurs of change from Ottawa, where the justice minister has commissioned a study and has promised to introduce a bill to address the issue.

The United Kingdom, much like Canada, provides no statutory or decisional protection in David and Goliath cases: the law's the law. Still, membership in the European Union (EU) is sure to change some areas of English jurisprudence, as demonstrated by the much-bruited "McLibel" case,[9] the longest-running case in British history, extending for ten years through the English courts before being taken up in the European Union judicial system. In that litigation,

---

[8]Sandro Contenta, "Developer's Cost Claims Raise Fears of Legal Chill," *Toronto Star*, Toronto, Canada, Feb. 10, 2008. http://www.thestar.com/News/World/article/302135.

[9]*McDonald's Restaurants v. David Morris and Helen Steel*, [1997] EWHC QB 366 (June 19, 1997), No. 1990-M-NI. 5724. *Steel and Morris v. the United Kingdom*, European Court of Human Rights, 15/02/2005, application no. 68416/01.

the defendants started their own environmental group, called London Greenpeace, and began distributing a pamphlet critical of McDonald's Corporation, alleging a litany of complaints based on issues ranging from nutrition to animal rights. McDonald's filed a libel action against the two activists. Although the corporation won the battle, it lost the war. The pamphlet, which had been a flop before McDonald's brought suit, was soon translated into 26 languages. The case crawled through the courts over the course of seven years, embarrassing the corporation each time the press ran another story. McDonald's eventually won in the English High Court, and promptly announced it would not try to collect the £40,000 awarded. But the European Court of Human Rights (ECHR)[10] ruled that the case breached the activists' rights to a fair trial and to freedom of expression, and it ordered the U.K. government to pay them £57,000 in compensation. The European court noted disapprovingly that U.K. laws had failed to protect the public's right to criticize corporations whose business practices affect people's lives and the environment—an indication that the EU may edge closer to some sort of SLAPP standard.

---

[10]*Steel and Morris v. the United Kingdom*, European Court of Human Rights, 15/02/2005, application no. 68416/01.

CHAPTER 9

■　■　■

Reports from the Field:
Offense and Defense Case Studies

THE CASE STUDIES in this chapter illustrate how the Saint Consulting Group's approach has worked successfully for a wide variety of clients in both offense and defense land use politics campaigns. As explained in Chapter 7, a land use politics offense campaign is a political campaign that empowers and invigorates local citizens to support a project they favor in ways that effectively influence land use decisions by their local officials. A land use politics defense campaign empowers citizens to oppose a project they disfavor. The following case studies are based on actual campaigns, but details have been blurred to protect client confidentiality.

Offense Case Studies

Most often, land use offense campaigns involve a fairly straightforward approach that builds citizen support, addresses opposition issues, and wins official approval through hard work and persistence. This is easier said than done, especially when the project is controversial or unwanted.

Offense Case Study 1: Winning for an Oil Refinery

A case in point involved a Saint Consulting team's efforts to help a client build the first new U.S. oil refinery in 30 years in a rural, mostly agricultural corner of the Midwest. Saint needed to get more than five square miles of agricultural land rezoned in a county where the planning and zoning commission had recently proposed creation of an agricultural preservation district.

By the time Saint was retained, the client's real estate consultant had been in the field buying options in his own name, already creating a buzz. An enterprising reporter googled his name and discovered that he had worked for an oil company, fueling wide speculation about what was being planned for the site. When the reporter followed through with an Internet "Whois" search and found several registered Internet domains that mentioned the client, all cover was essentially blown. There was nothing to do but launch crisis management by rounding up as much local and state political support as possible and announcing the project at a press conference before opponents could characterize and define it in the public mind.

Saint staff research had shown that neighbors in the project area opposed any type of development, let alone a $10 billion, 400,000-barrel-per-day oil refinery on 3,300 acres of land. Unanswered, the swirling rumor mill and organized opposition could easily have killed the project then and there. Immediately, several opposition groups sprang up, including one that launched an exhaustive website that let the client have it with both barrels:

- The group warned that the "huge petroleum-based oil refinery and coke-burning power plant" would be placed "amid the tranquil fields and rolling hills," causing quality-of-life issues that might well "outweigh any so-called economic benefits."

- The group issued a blanket indictment of all refinery operators as bad corporate citizens, if not criminals. The opponents scoured the Internet for stories on the problems other companies had faced with accidents, spills, pollution, and health and safety issues.

What's more, they said, "fossil fuel refineries have a history of environmental violations."

- The group contended that health studies showed increased levels of asthma and other respiratory illnesses in communities near a refinery.

- The group lambasted the client for having the nerve to describe the project as a "green facility," which it called an attempt to deceive the public.

- The group raised air quality issues and argued that the project would endanger the water supply.

- The group claimed that traffic and the "constant noise" from the refinery would be an issue and asserted that "the buffer zones may not be enough to muffle the sound for those used to the quiet rural life."

- The group argued that stargazers would never again enjoy a clear, moonless night, and that light from the project "may seem more like Las Vegas than their previously unspoiled rural setting."

- The group warned that only a small percentage of the 8,000 workers needed to build the facility would be from the area, while the rest would come from elsewhere, "possibly other countries," and "would bring their families." The school system would have to expand, they asserted; there would be a rise in crime, and "a new jail and courthouse will have to be built."

- The group argued that although the newcomers' need for housing would provide a temporary boost to the local economy, they would all move on when the project ended, leaving "a glut of empty houses" as well as "a depressed business economy" and "an overburdened tax structure for the rest of us."

- The group asserted that the wage scales for jobs at the refinery would prove inadequate, and then launched personal attacks against members of the client's management team who had made political contributions, before going after the local planning and zoning commission.

- The group argued that "thousands of acres of prime agricultural land that would benefit the ethanol and bio-diesel industry will be taken out of production" and prevented from "being used to support environmentally friendly fuel production."

- Finally, the group took a swipe at their neighbors who, they said, "should not be blamed for 'selling out,'" but who would move from the area, leaving those who remained behind to deal with "the politicians and the so-called rich and powerful" to "prevent potential catastrophe."

This was strong stuff, particularly as the website operators kept a downloadable archive of all the news stories, reports, editorials, letters to the editor, press releases, and video recordings of the hearings and meetings related to the project, which they called the "Gorilla." The Saint team also knew that there would likely be national opposition to the project and that preparation for those attacks needed to be done well in advance.

Once the project was announced, Saint's project manager launched a countywide outreach program with five universes: local citizens, local elected officials not charged with making the decision, chambers of commerce in the area and region, organized groups ranging from environmentalists to tax abatement organizations, and businesses, especially those that would benefit most from the project. One day after the announcement, Saint's team was in the field, armed with a 13,000-person voter list and with a campaign manager assigned to each large town in the county. Saint invested two months in organizing support and engaging citizens, arranging house parties, developing a list of 4,000 supporters and 150 super-supporters, and preparing for the application filing and the start of the public hearing process.

Meanwhile, Saint's project manager advised the client to hire lawyers locally as well as law firms with significant experience and national presence in the petroleum business; to get environmental planners to create plans and elevations; to have permitting experts pull together numbers on emissions and pollution controls; and to have project engineers provide data on the heights and dimensions of buildings and towers so the necessary zoning relief, either as variances or as limitations in a planned unit development (PUD), could be determined. Saint was immediately charged with building the team to get it done.

The firm quickly researched national law firms, narrowed the list to six, and selected one. Saint then hosted a two-day summit, involving 15 lawyers, to rough out the language for the planned development ordinance the project needed, and began to get a draft ready to submit to the county. At this point, the client had not even met with anyone at the county level about the plans: while the project had support in the state capital, the decision would be made locally. Saint staff spent a month before the application was formally filed prepping the county board, informing the members about the plan and answering their questions, while simultaneously building a team of the project's identified supporters. Saint's project manager devised a kiosk-style forum to inform the public, where citizens would enter a large room with stations for each facet of the project and approval process, all done without speeches or presentations. Over three days, more than 1,000 people attended and left the forum mostly in support—despite opponents' efforts to hijack the event.

With the application filed, the process proceeded. The planning commission would make a recommendation, followed by the county board vote, followed in this case by a referendum vote of the citizenry that the client wanted in order to demonstrate good corporate citizenship and to provide the public officials with political cover. Opponents could hardly object to a proposal to let the people decide, and Saint's team members knew that they could run a better political campaign than the opposition could.

At the planning commission hearing, Saint's team packed the house with supporters—more than 350 to the opposition's 150. After a five-hour hearing, the project won a supportive vote of 4 to 1. At the county board meeting, Saint turned out a crowd of 300 for the four-hour hearing; no vote was taken that night because of the county board's rules. While the client waited for a vote over the following days, opponents issued a critical report drafted by a consultant at the behest of project opponents in an attempt to shatter public opinion. This report asserted that the process was moving too fast, raised questions about the project and the process, and urged delay and reconsideration.

With some amendments to the PUD ordinance that answered these concerns, the project finally won a unanimous 5 to 0 vote from the county board, and launched into the home stretch: the county-wide referendum. Three weeks after the county vote, Saint submitted more than 1,000 voter signatures to put the issue on the ballot. Over the next several weeks, the team executed the campaign strategy, building a local staff, engaging paid canvassers, covering the 13,000-person voter universe six times, issuing multiple mail pieces, and preparing for the final push to election day. In the end, the project won handily by a vote of 58 percent to 42 percent, with 3,932 voters in favor and 2,855 opposed.

Offense Case Study 2: Deploying Citizen-Soldiers

The U.K. client wanted to develop a waste disposal landfill use near a housing estate (subdivision) and primary school, a use considered certain for refusal and likely to lose on appeal. There was no sign of public or political support and no chance of organizing a citizen group to agitate on behalf of a dump. Saint's manager needed to find an existing group whose own interests could somehow be advanced by promoting the client's interests.

Saint found the project champion in the form of a small band of young mothers whose children attended the primary school. One of the kids had been hit by a car and badly injured a few months previously, and the mothers' group had pressured the school for a zebra crossing.[1] The school had refused, asserting that there was no money for a safety crosswalk—and besides, it was an issue for the

---

[1] A zebra crossing is a pedestrian crossing, used in many places around the world, with alternating dark and light stripes on the road surface. A zebra crossing typically gives extra rights-of-way to pedestrians. http://en.wikipedia.org/wiki/Zebra_crossing.

local council. The mothers had met with the council, where a bureaucrat from the highways department informed them that the quarterly road casualty statistics indicated that only 0.2 children would die on the road each year, so a zebra crossing was not a priority.

Angry, desperate, and worried for their children's safety, the mothers were receptive to Saint's offer to install a high-end, state-of-the-art children's crossing, complete with bells, whistles, flashing lights, and a full-time lollipop lady (a crossing guard who carries a stop sign shaped like a lollipop). The project instantly had their support, and Saint organized them to widen support among all of the school's parents and teachers, to form a formidable and determined group of protective adults concerned with children's safety.

Saint's team then launched a political pressure campaign. Three times an evening, every evening for three weeks prior to the planning committee meeting to consider the waste site proposal, mothers knocked on the doors of every planning committee member, delivering a compelling message: "We voted for you in the last election. We want your support now. Your council won't provide a crossing, but the waste company will. You will support this application. If you don't, we will make sure that we and all our friends vote you out of office at the next election. You will be a pariah in the neighborhood. You will be responsible for killing our children. And we will take legal action against the council and each and every member of the planning committee when the next child is injured."

At first, the message brought a strong negative response. Politicians complained to the press that they were being blackmailed. But the press knew a good story and quickly turned on the politicians, supporting the mothers and running photos of attractive, distressed young mums, the injured child, a chart showing vehicle counts past the school, and so forth. By the second week, the politicians fell silent.

At the committee meeting, posturing politicians all gave impassioned speeches, asserting that although they would not normally go against the planning officers' (staff) advice, particularly for such an intrusive waste use, they were "voting for the children!" The project was approved.

Offense Case Study 3: Overcoming Officials' Resistance

The client wanted to replace its overcrowded 35,000-square-foot grocery store with a 55,000-square-foot store a half-mile away. Approval would require a supermajority vote, two-thirds of the seven-member town board, since 20 percent of the abutters opposed the project. Neighbors of the proposed site, vehemently opposed to the development, hired an attorney to fight it. An opposition neighborhood group had persuaded three of the seven town board members to oppose the project, and a member who had a conflict of interest would not be voting—making it impossible for the client to win unless Saint changed the politics.

The Saint team used the existing store and customer base to educate local residents and build a large support base within the community. The team's efforts included production of a 20-minute video demonstrating the need for the new store, organizing citizens to telephone and write letters to key officials, and running full-page ads in the local newspaper listing the names of hundreds of supporters, thereby demonstrating that the opposition did not represent the majority sentiment, as it was claiming.

Then Saint set to work to change the politics. The team beat back the requirement for a supermajority vote by buying up more land, thereby expanding the number of abutters, and convincing more abutters to support the project. Saint project managers identified favorable votes on the board and the most likely swing vote. Saint then put citizens to work bringing intense political pressure to reconsider on that board member by publishing his home phone number in the newspaper with the message that his vote was the only thing stopping the project, and by door-to-door visits in the targeted member's neighborhood, securing permission to erect lawn signs and urging neighbors to talk with him about his vote.

On the night of the vote, the Saint team generated record-breaking standing-room-only turnout, and handed out printed baseball caps, visibly demonstrating to the board members that the majority of attendees supported the proposal. The overflow crowd burst into rousing applause as the town board voted 4 to 2, with one abstention, to approve. The board member Saint had targeted voted in favor.

Offense Case Study 4: Tailoring the Message

The client wanted to build four class A office buildings in an upper-middle-class city in which 90 percent of the land was zoned residential and development of any kind was looked on with suspicion. The client had assembled a 55-acre site, of which 14 acres were zoned for office park use and the rest for residential use, allowing development of two office buildings in one area and 47 homes in the other. The client had worked with city officials to give up the residential aspect and instead rezone the land to allow four office buildings on 26 of the 55 acres. The client agreed to turn the remaining 29 acres into a passive green-space park with running trails and picnic areas, and to donate the land to the city.

But when the planning commission hearing on the plan arrived, opponents packed the hearing and spent two hours criticizing the proposal. Although the commission voted 6 to 2 in favor of the plan, the hearing gave opponents impetus, and they quickly mobilized, adding members through a petition drive, a neighbor-to-neighbor postcard program in wealthy subdivisions, yard signs, and numerous letters to the editor, all opposing the project.

The client retained Saint Consulting to overcome the opposition. The Saint team began building a grassroots coalition to serve as the public face of citizen support, starting with business owners, adding members of two homeowners' associations whose homes abutted the site and who supported the park, and reviving a dormant environmental group also in favor of passive green space. As support built, Saint developed a mail piece to be sent from the coalition, not the client, and neighbor-to-neighbor letters from organization leaders to their members, thereby enhancing the grassroots basis of support.

Key to victory was tailoring the message, and key to that effort was identifying the audience. Using membership lists from business, homeowner, and environmental organizations, as well as signature sheets from old petition drives, Saint's team was able to identify and categorize supportive voters and tailor the message. Saint staffers had developed a voter file that identified each of the 5,500 people who had voted in a previous special election on a green-space tax. To the group who likely voted for the tax, Saint's outreach stressed the additional green space the project would provide. To those who likely voted against the tax, Saint stressed the tax revenue an office park would generate, in contrast to residential development, which would place additional burdens on the tax base. Meanwhile, with targeting completed, the Saint team was able to identify additional supporters and activate their involvement in the project's citizen group. Since commission members were elected at-large, the team was able to apply pressure on targeted members, based on intelligence from local residents and the client, by engaging citizens to generate phone calls, e-mail, and letters to the decision makers.

On the night of the commission vote, more than 225 residents packed the commission chambers. Unlike the situation at the original hearing, project supporters clearly dominated the crowd. This time, citizens from Saint's coalition rose, spoke, and presented a red-dot map of the city demonstrating that coalition members lived in every precinct in every area. After several hours of citizen testimony and debate among commission members, the board voted to approve the project by a vote of 5 to 2.

Offense Case Study 5: Overcoming Organized Opposition

The client wanted to build a 275-acre, $175 million educational theme park on a site previously used as farmland. The project required planned unit development (PUD) approval from the county commission, and the client was also seeking tax increment financing (TIF). A well-organized opposition group formed prior to submission of site plans, objecting to the park's proximity to the members' neighborhood, increased traffic and noise, and noncompliance with the community land use plan. The group had collected more than 3,000 opposition signatures over a 12-month period and had persuaded the county planning and zoning committee to recommend rejection of the application.

Following rejection by the planning and zoning committee, Saint Consulting was engaged to help secure approval of the PUD and TIF at the county commission. Within 30 days, Saint successfully accomplished the following:

- Conducted a door-to-door campaign in the neighborhood, speaking with abutters and nearby residents to understand their concerns and identify potential supporters.

- Developed a grassroots coalition in each county commission district to apply pressure to each commissioner in support of the project.

- Generated a letter-writing campaign to commission members, the mayor, and the news media.

- Created a neighborhood support group of nearly 150 local residents, and successfully staged a media event and rally in support of the project. Saint created a red-dot map demonstrating widespread support, secured more than 85 personal letters from neighbors and abutters to be sent to commissioners, turned out more than 50 citizen speakers at public hearings, and launched a citizen petition drive.

- Organized a coalition of small business owners throughout the county, held a successful press event with 18 businesses represented, and began a petition drive to expand business support.

- Hosted a countywide job fair to solicit and collect résumés from applicants seeking jobs at the theme park, thereby highlighting the economic benefit to the local economy. Saint's team used radio and newspaper ads to generate turnout and received more than 200 job applications, as well as favorable coverage from all local news media outlets.

- Turned out supporters and citizen speakers for the final public hearing (matching the opposition's speaker list one-for-one), providing political cover to commission members who had quietly voiced their support.

At the final hearing, Saint secured approval by a vote of 12 to 9.

Offense Case Study 6: Bypassing the Neighborhood Advisory Committee

The client wanted to build a seven-story mixed-use condominium building in a stylish neighborhood of a major East Coast city, where well-organized resident groups strongly opposed any commercial development. The zoning would have allowed a five-story building on 60 percent of the lot, but the client had determined that such a project would not be financially feasible, and rezoning was required. A seven-story, 60-unit building, in which views from the upper floors would make up for lower returns on lower floors, plus retail use on the first floor, was needed. The parcel was located between a bus terminal and an electrical substation, so nothing could be done about views from the lower floors, and feasibility required that the building cover the entire lot, rather than being limited to 60 percent coverage. Because of these constraints, the client had no wiggle room to negotiate the proposed height with the community.

Members of the two leading antidevelopment activist groups in the neighborhood were also the controlling members of the Advisory Neighborhood Commission (ANC), an influential elected body of community representatives to whose opinion the city zoning commission was required to give "great weight" in deliberating a land use development decision. The client's development team had met with the ANC, and the commission and audience made clear that they would rather keep a run-down used car lot on the site than accept a building taller than five stories.

Saint Consulting was then retained to develop a strategy, and quickly determined through a scope study that the ANC would never recommend approval and that there was widespread opposition in the community to development. Opponents circulated a petition against the project, collecting 500 signatures from residents within four blocks of the site, which Saint staffers calculated to mean that they had opposition signatures from 92 percent of the households in their targeted area.

But the Saint team's scope study also disclosed that the proposed project nicely fit the city's long-term goal of increasing residential density near metro train stations. Since the development was proposed as a green LEED (Leadership in Energy and Environmental

Design)–certifiable building, citizens concerned with smart growth and environmental protection would likely find it attractive. Saint therefore proposed to go around the ANC and build citizen support to influence the zoning commission. The team would work with the ANC only to the extent needed to demonstrate to the zoning commission that the ANC demands were unreasonable and its views extreme, thereby marginalizing, if not neutralizing, the commission's influence.

Although Saint strategists knew that further meetings with the ANC would help the opposition coalesce and might generate negative press coverage, the client did need to show that it had tried to work with the ANC. The key was to build coalitions of broad citizen support outside of ANC influence, and then demonstrate that support with community activism. The foundation of that support would be local smart growth groups and local members of national environmental organizations, whose members would view the project as enhancing urban density and encouraging the use of public transit. Saint staffers also identified several key community groups that could benefit from financial support as part of the client's amenities package, including a home for indigent and homeless senior citizens. Supporting that well-respected facility would insulate the client from claims that the project lacked sufficient affordable housing and place critics of the amenities package in the uncomfortable position of opposing a home for poor and homeless elderly citizens. The client also provided funding for school upgrade projects selected by the parent-teacher association, and contributed money to help fund a van to transport seniors to shopping and events.

The efforts with smart growth advocates and environmentalists produced 132 letters of support to the zoning commission, and Saint's neighbor-to-neighbor letters reached 1,000 homes surrounding the project locus. The team went door-to-door to speak with everyone who had signed the petition against the project, answer questions, and educate those who would listen, thereby suppressing opposition turnout at the zoning commission hearing. Because Saint's project manager knew that the zoning commission's practice was to send a project file to the commissioners seven days before a hearing, the team held the 132 support letters and inserted them into the record just before the file went to the commissioners, surprising the opposition with the depth and breadth of support and sending opponents scrambling to respond, while demonstrating substantial support for the project to the commissioners.

On the night of the hearing, the Saint team produced 16 well-rehearsed citizens to testify in favor of the project, equaling the opponents' presentation. The zoning commission approved the application unanimously.

Offense Case Study 7: Permitting a Planned Community

The client wanted to win approval for a 1,400-home planned community on the Hawaiian island of Maui, where concerns that an influx of new and wealthy mainland residents would dislocate locals combined with worries that the affordable housing aspect of the project would not be truly affordable. This generated arguments about overdevelopment, overcrowding, traffic, water availability, and damage to culture and natural resources. Major opposition from established preservation and environmental groups worked against approval, and a long, exhaustive schedule of public meetings and hearings would make it difficult to build and maintain supporter enthusiasm. A full strategic campaign plan was clearly needed to reassure residents, calm their fears, and generate citizen support for the rezoning request.

The campaign plan included elements to identify key messages that could be used to build support, identify key target groups whose members would be likely natural supporters, and develop strategies to implement the plan: deliver the messages, build support, and mobilize citizen activity in favor of the project. The project design included a golf course and a commercial business area, but the key feature Saint's team believed would win support from local residents was the fact that half of the 1,400 housing units were to be affordable. Gaining local support would require reversing people's initial concerns, and convincing them that the project would not dislocate local residents, but would instead provide truly affordable new housing for them. The developer would also hold a workshop informing residents how much affordable homes cost and how to get ready to buy one.

The team meanwhile identified some 7,000 Maui residents living in areas with a median income of $60,000 to $90,000, and added them to an outreach list. Each received two direct mailings and phone contact to identify supporters. This effort produced more than 300 Maui residents who supported either the project itself or development of more affordable housing on Maui. An informational Web site together with an online petition for residents to sign rounded out the initial effort.

The first affordable housing event, which drew 60 residents, resulted in two dozen residents agreeing to sign letters to the editor and testify at public hearings. The council's land use committee voted 6 to 2 in favor of the rezoning, moving the issue to the full council, and prompting Saint's team to devise an even more robust outreach plan to build wider public support and encourage council members to vote for the project.

Implementation began with an island-wide poll of residents that confirmed affordable housing as the key issue, with 54 percent identifying it as the top issue facing Maui, and 86 percent saying they supported more affordable housing. Cross-tabulations showed that top supporters included renters, newer residents of five years' tenure or less, and Filipino residents. With this information, the team was able to create a target audience of more than 10,000 renters, new residents, and people on the waiting list for another affordable housing provider, and to deliver direct mail messages to them. A further affordable housing workshop, driven by newspaper notices inviting attendance, attracted 140 residents, more than twice the original crowd, with many others expressing interest in attending future workshops, signing the online petition for the project, and responding to an online survey.

After nine months and 23 committee, community, and council meetings, the council approved the project by a 5 to 4 vote after a hearing that lasted from 9 a.m. on one day until 12:45 a.m. the next day. The development will provide $80 million in total net revenue for the county, $630 million in total wages, 900 permanent jobs, and $67 million in annual revenue for the local economy, besides $24 million in mitigation for local parks and $4 million for local school improvements. And it will provide the promised 700 units of genuinely affordable housing.

Offense Case Study 8: Double-Checking the Lawyer

For five years, the client tried to secure approval to redevelop an entire city block of retail and commercial office space. Community leaders had initially favored the redevelopment and expansion, but then withdrew their support. Several enhanced project designs had been proposed over the years, but each met with increased community resistance, particularly from a historical society seeking to preserve the existing, aging 1950s structure. By the end of the fifth year, local opposition was firmly entrenched.

Saint's two-part approach focused on assisting the client and combating community resistance. To aid the client, Saint conducted research on the ground and discovered that the client's attorney had misinterpreted the zoning regulations. The client could have built by right from the beginning, and had wasted five years in costly and unnecessary fighting. Saint subsequently discovered that the attorney was not popular in the community, and therefore had not been persuasive on the client's behalf. He was replaced.

From a political perspective, Saint assembled its own group of support within the community by collecting more than 2,000 petition signatures in favor of the project. The team conducted a community survey on redeveloping the block of stores, located in a busy urban setting. Team members took measures to characterize the opposition as unreasonable and militant, and worked closely with the mayor and city hall staff to inform the public of the project's benefits. Saint then formed its own historical society to challenge the existing group and its findings. In support of Saint's campaign program, the team conducted a media campaign, wrote letters to the editor, and developed an informational website.

Within a year from the start of Saint's involvement, the redevelopment was approved.

Offense Case Study 9: Rezoning for a Wind Farm

The client wanted to build a 100-megawatt wind farm of nearly 70 wind turbines in a U.S. rural heartland community. The land was zoned for agricultural use, and local officials were concerned about potential impacts of the project on agricultural use and the potential for construction damage to local roads. Organized project opponents claimed that the towers would decrease property values, generate harmful noise levels, and ruin the landscape. The only vocal supporters of the project were the participating landowners.

Saint's campaign team immediately began identifying a wider range of supportive residents; assessing the opponents' motivations, arguments, and criticisms of the project; and devising countermeasures to offset their impact. The Saint team developed messages to counter misinformation from opponents and spread them through outreach materials, earned (free) media, and public testimony before decision makers. The outreach team also organized community events, including a tour of an operating wind farm in the area, a picnic for supporters, and kite-flying lessons for local children. The team used these activities as organizing tools and provided participants with opportunities to demonstrate support for the project.

The team also began coalition-building with local institutions, key stakeholders, and power brokers, and then expanded the effort to include community residents. It organized a citizen group to demonstrate grassroots support and mobilized members to testify at public hearings, contact local news media, and make presentations to other community organizations. Team members drove mobilization through turnout efforts directed at identified supporters, and scripted speakers for public hearings to make sure essential points were made.

Before Saint's involvement, the local news media covered only the opposition's points about the project. Within two weeks of engagement, Saint project managers were able to induce positive media reporting through a combination of letters to the editor in newspapers, a supporters' press conference, and demonstrations of support at public meetings. Because the Saint team was able to effectively turn out impressive numbers of project supporters, local decision makers were encouraged to approve the project, and the small but vocal group of opponents, who had previously dominated the process, lost influence. The project was approved by a vote of 9 to 0.

Offense Case Study 10: Winning an Urban Street Fight

The client wanted to build an 83,000-square-foot superstore on the site of a former lumberyard. The site abutted a densely populated urban neighborhood whose activist residents opposed any reuse of the site. The project required approval by the city planning board and board of aldermen, both of whose members were already besieged by angry citizen groups and political activists who opposed redevelopment on another site nearby. Organized opposition surfaced even before plans for the new store were filed, and neighborhood activists quickly allied themselves with the already formidable opponents of the other development plan. The groups claimed that the projects would destroy the character of the neighborhood and that the resulting traffic would be dangerous.

Saint's campaign began with delivering flyers to residents living near the site, explaining the project and its benefits, followed by neighborhood meetings to address community concerns. The Saint team circulated a petition door-to-door, ultimately collecting more than 2,000 signatures, and used the contact information gathered in the petition drive to create a mail and phone list to generate support and increase attendance at public meetings. The team arranged presentations at senior housing centers, churches, and other community organizations; conducted outreach to labor unions whose members would benefit from the construction project; and met with local business owners, urging them to write to local officials in support, an effort that saw each alderman receive more than 100 letters. Saint's campaign manager convinced the client to support area community groups to gain their goodwill and vocal support, and wrote and obtained citizen signatures on letters to the editor of the local newspaper. And Saint team members successfully urged project supporters to stand up to the bullying tactics used by opponents to intimidate those who disagreed with them.

Despite a relentless campaign against the project by opponent activists—aided by three of the seven aldermen, who also introduced two measures to downzone the property—the support Saint generated overwhelmed the opposition, and provided political cover for the majority of the planning board members and aldermen to approve the project.

Offense Case Study 11: Redirecting Political Support

The U.K. client wanted to get its site allocated in the local plan for housing, but the planning officers preferred a competing site. Saint's job was to torpedo the other site and shift support to the client's site.

Research pointed the Saint team to the local town council, whose members were locked in a vociferous reelection campaign focused against another planning issue altogether. Members of the team befriended the councilors and refocused their attention on objecting to the competing housing site. Saint generated lots of media, accompanied by posters, leaflets, and petitions, and one by one the local politicians crumpled. They changed tack, supporting the client's site in preference to the competing site. But one council member, who was a cabinet member for planning, switched sides too late and lost in the election to one of the citizens involved in Saint's campaign. The client's site was approved.

Offense Case Study 12: Getting Out the Vote

The U.S. client wanted to build a retail complex with a 65,000-square-foot anchor, along with various retail out-parcels of 20,000 square feet each. The site was an open field at the center of a 12,000-resident resort community in which development had traditionally been decidedly small-scale. A citizen group funded by the client's competitor circulated a petition and filed a zoning article to limit commercial buildings to 35,000 square feet. The article went on the ballot for a town-wide referendum vote.

In reaction to the proposed 35,000-square-foot limit, the board of selectmen sponsored another ballot question to limit retail development to 65,000 square feet. Just one month before the January referendum, the client retained Saint Consulting to defeat the antidevelopment effort.

Saint's campaign team immediately began an intensive community outreach program during the holiday season—a time when residents were preoccupied with other matters. Saint recruited a steering committee to campaign against the organized and well-funded opposition group, and under the Saint team's direction, community residents became the public face of the campaign. The team conducted a poll to determine how best to convince voters that the development would not destroy the town's character, but, given the time constraints, Saint focused on one referendum issue: the proposal to limit buildings to 35,000 square feet. The other proposal would not have affected the size of the client's anchor store.

Based on the poll results, Saint developed a media campaign and schedule, including production of cable TV, radio, and newspaper advertisements; a direct mail program; a letters-to-the-editor program; and large public signs. In order to identify project supporters for election day turnout and persuade undecided voters to defeat the ballot question, Saint conducted a grassroots outreach program that included phone calls and door-to-door visits to measure community sentiment and persuade the uncertain. On the day of the referendum vote, Saint conducted an extensive GOTV (get-out-the-vote) effort to make sure supporters turned out in full force.

The competitor's ballot initiative to limit retail to 35,000 square feet lost decisively, 61 percent to 39 percent. The selectmen's ballot question to limit retail to 65,000 square feet lost narrowly, 52 percent to 48 percent. Leveraging the support base Saint had built in organizing the referendum campaign, the client won approval and built the retail complex.

Offense Case Study 13: Winning for a Limestone Quarry

The client needed permits to open a limestone rock quarry in a rural Midwestern community. The project had made no significant progress in the approval process for more than four years because of well-organized opposition, including objections to the client's plan for an 11-mile rail spur to serve the quarry. Saint's project team needed to demonstrate clear and overwhelming support for the project in order to convince local officials that they could approve it without paying a political price.

Saint's team began by identifying citizens it could organize to support the quarry and the rail spur and expanded that support base with a job fair to explain the employment opportunities the project would offer. Saint created a countywide coalition in favor of development by educating business owners about the full-time jobs the quarry would generate and the income the workers would spend locally.

Saint's team worked to publicize each step of progress on quarry approval at the state and federal levels to suggest to residents that the quarry was inevitable, an effort that succeeded when the state issued a temporary air permit allowing quarry operation. Team members identified residents who opposed the quarry but favored the rail line as an alternative to 800 trucks per day entering and leaving the site, and worked to convince them that the quarry was certain and the only choice was between trucks and the rail line.

The Saint team also recruited support from those who would gain from the project in other ways, including residents whose families would benefit from the $400,000 that the quarry would pay in school district taxes. This effort allowed the team to recruit the superintendent of schools and teachers to rally for the project and to regain support from members of the municipal board, which had once favored approval but had taken a turn against the client's interests. And Saint organized citizen pressure on the local congressman to push for expedited federal agency approval of the rail spur, rather than following the far more lengthy and expensive process preferred by quarry opponents.

Shortly before the next public hearings, Saint sponsored a barbecue and other events to attract supporters and organize them for hearing attendance, and to prepare them for holding signs and speaking in favor. This effort produced crowds of 150 vocal residents in support at the public hearings. The municipal board voted 3 to 2 to approve the project.

Offense Case Study 14: Winning an Annexation Fight

The client wanted to annex 130 acres in a large county into the neighboring incorporated town for infrastructure and financial purposes. The client proposed a 30-acre shopping center with big-box anchors and 120 units of age-restricted housing. The client had filed formal annexation plans before retaining Saint Consulting, but had quickly withdrawn them because of the uncertain political climate and because a negative vote by the five-member town council would remain in effect for a year. Local elections for mayor and three of the council seats were months away. Saint was engaged to organize and implement a grassroots community campaign to win a positive council vote when the annexation plan was resubmitted.

Saint's project manager began by conducting a survey to gauge public perception of annexation and measure persuasive arguments for and against it. Meanwhile, team members organized citizens to encourage a supportive district council member to run for mayor and create a slate of pro-annexation council candidates to fill his own district seat as well as an open seat. Saint staffers educated citizens to use county and town data to create a sophisticated file of all registered voters by precinct, advised them on targeting new and likely voters to boost turnout for the historically low-turnout election, and showed them how to build a network of campaign volunteers to support their mayoral candidate and his slate.

The team reached out to local businesses to build support for annexation and built a coalition of supportive neighbors and residents who countered opposition forces through letters to the editor, speaking at public forums, and conducting outreach efforts in advance of the election. Simultaneously, Saint's manager worked with the client to host two open forum events on the proposed development, preparing a PowerPoint presentation, brochures, and information displays; conducting media training; and creating a sense of responsiveness on behalf of the client's development team.

These efforts elevated annexation to the only issue in the town election campaign, and positioned the proposal as favorable despite initial concerns of some nearby residents and slow-growth advocates. Because Saint's team changed public attitudes toward annexation and created an atmosphere that resulted in the narrow election of a pro-annexation mayor and council, the project was able to demonstrate the public support needed to put the public officials' minds at ease, and to allow the incoming council to give the client a 4 to 1 victory.

Offense Case Study 15: Winning for Casino Gaming

The client owned and operated a racehorse track and wanted to expand the facility to include a 4,000-machine slots parlor, restaurants, and a private club. The client would not receive the slots license for several months, but meanwhile needed to secure local approvals to build the new facilities, demolish and rebuild the on-site waste treatment plant, and reformat parking options to include a new 1,500-car garage.

The municipal board, once clearly pro-client, had turned against the client's interests. Saint Consulting's challenge in organizing public support was to convince neighbors and citizens that the expansion would be good for the town and not bring additional burdens. The campaign began with a strategy focused on the abutting homeowners, holding one-on-one meetings to address their concerns and collecting petition signatures and letters of support. The message was straightforward, highlighting three important issues:

- Forcing the racetrack to tie into the municipal sewer system would overburden the town infrastructure. It would be better to let the client rebuild the on-site system.

- Traffic to and from the new entertainment facilities would be better managed if the parking situation were resolved. A parking garage would do the job.

- Additional tax revenue generated by the expanded facilities would allow the township to address other issues, such as road improvements, ball field upgrades, and sewer system extension in other areas of town, without additional burdens on existing taxpayers.

At the final hearing, the board voted 3 to 2 to approve the client's development plans.

Offense Case Study 16: Permitting Gas Stations

The client wanted to expand its existing retail footprint by adding an on-site gasoline station and to install identical expansions at seven additional locations in two states. Competing oil retailers and their association, adamantly opposed, were well-funded and hired a prominent anti-sprawl activist to organize against the expansions.

Saint's campaign team began with an in-store petition drive at the client's location, with fact sheets explaining the benefits of one-stop shopping and the competitive pricing that the client planned to offer. The Saint team also worked with the client's employees and their extended families to build a base of local political support. The team held meetings with city councilors and city engineers to provide information, emphasize associated benefits, and explain the anticompetitive motives of the opposition. Saint staffers presented facts to show that the proposed gas facility would not put existing gas stations out of business and deflected the opposition's environmental arguments by explaining the project's state-of-the-art, triple-insulated fuel storage tanks, alarm systems, automatic shutoffs, spill containment system, and other safety enhancements. As a result of Saint's successful strategy, all targeted locations were approved for expansion.

Offense Case Study 17: Making It Personal

The U.K. client wanted to develop a mixed-use project with an adult education college, essentially using a joint venture arrangement to provide new college facilities on one part of the land, with new development on the rest of the site. The local council nixed the idea because it was against policy; the land was designated solely for educational use.

Saint's project team researched the site, locality, and politics in detail and prepared a four-point strategy:

- The adult college was large, with about 1,000 students attending at any one time. Over the previous 10 years, tens of thousands of local adults had completed courses and qualified there; if Saint could round up just 1 percent of that latent support, it would have a real political movement. Saint team members met with students, college staff, past students, and past staff, and organized those who wanted to help.

- On two sides, the site abutted luxury town houses worth £3 million to £4 million apiece whose owners would strongly oppose the development. Saint's team identified likely opposition leaders; anticipated what they would do; estimated what they would have available for resources; and prepared counterstrategy: Saint would out-campaign them. This meant that the team needed to do a lot of work before the client submitted the planning application so that opponents would learn of the project late, be forced to rush to catch up, and never gain the initiative.

- One of the ward councilors was also the council leader. He and his fellow ward members enjoyed reasonably safe seats, but could be in trouble in a really bad year. Saint's project manager reasoned that if the team could demonstrate strong citizen support for the college scheme, the councilors would see that such political power would secure their seats for many elections to come. Saint deluged them with support letters for the plan from students and staff, both current and former, local businesses that sent their staff members to the college to be trained, and local employers whose employees benefited from the education. In particular, Saint found a small number of local residents who felt passionately that the college had given them their start in life. The ward council members soon became advocates for the scheme.

- None of the seven councilors who sat on the planning committee represented the affected ward or any adjacent ward, so the issue was academic for them; Saint needed to make it personal. The team therefore collected a petition with 1,400 local signatures — 200 signatures from each of the planning committee members' wards. Saint then produced a graphic map with red dots representing the 20 or so opposition residents clustered near the site, and 1,400 green dots representing the supporters. The members got the message: a small number of people who don't vote for you are opposed, and a large number of your own voters are in favor.

Planning officers called the client a month before the committee meeting and asked to talk. Having previously said refusal would be automatic, they would still have to recommend against the scheme. But they understood that the members would vote approval nonetheless. They suggested that if the project team could make some minor changes, they could reduce the grounds for refusal, thereby making the decision easier for members. The client agreed to reduce the height on one corner opposite the main opponents' homes in exchange for raising it elsewhere (which actually increased the square footage), moved the access slightly, and increased the affordable housing by a small amount. A month later, the scheme won unanimous approval over the planning officers' recommendation for refusal.

Offense Case Study 18: Winning at Hospital Permitting

The client was one of several health care providers competing for the state permit to construct a general acute-care hospital in an area already served by a well-respected facility. The existing hospital, as well as the competitors, had significant community backing and had mobilized their supporters to attend hearings and health-oriented public events and work to defeat the client's proposal. In order to gain needed approvals from local, regional, and state authorities, the client needed to identify and organize civic leaders and key activists among both residents and members of the medical community to demonstrate a critical mass of political support.

The Saint project team designed and managed an extensive outreach program to the medical community, generating more than 100 letters of support directed to state decision makers. It conducted a grassroots campaign to educate residents, community leaders, and elected officials about the unique benefits of the client's proposal, and it organized and executed a large petition drive, gathering more than 16,000 resident signatures in favor of the client's application. Team members managed and generated citizen turnout for numerous highly publicized community events, including public hearings and health fairs, and neutralized opposition by securing active support from key officials, government bodies, and community organizations.

When the client's proposal came before state regulators, the team turned out hundreds of supporters to speak in favor—overwhelming support that was unprecedented in the client's 30-year history. State and local officials voted unanimously in favor of the client's proposal.

Defense Campaigns

Most often, land use defense campaigns rely on the creativity and imagination of a professional land use campaign manager who understands that the goal is to create and nurture the perception that opponents represent the majority of citizens, the consensus. Once that perception is firmly established, stragglers and undecideds will jump on the winning bandwagon, and public officials will run to get ahead of the public in killing the project.

Defense Case Study 1: Defeating the Establishment

The client wanted to block development of a competitor's big-box store, but the small-town government establishment strongly favored the project and did everything possible to support it, including rapidly expediting the approval process. The deep-pockets developer hired prominent attorneys to manage the project outcome and launched an extensive campaign to promote approval. The site needed rezoning by a supermajority, or a two-thirds town meeting vote of approval.[2]

Saint's project manager began implementing the opposition campaign by organizing an alliance of labor unions, which opposed the competitor's anti-union posture, and small business owners, who would be hurt by retail prices they could not hope to match. The

---

[2]Town meetings are a colonial-holdover New England institution in which voters gather and decide issues, usually by majority vote. An open town meeting form of government (as in this case) allows any voter to attend, debate, and vote. A representative town meeting allows only elected town meeting members to do so. State statutes regulate requirements for the town meeting to legally act, including the level of majority necessary to rezone land, usually two-thirds.

Saint team circulated a petition opposing the project and demanding further study, and organized an opposition coalition comprising petition signers, local merchants, labor union members, and maverick town officials. Saint staffers then created a confrontational information handout, challenging the hasty approval process and posing pointed questions that the developer and his supporters had ignored. Saint republished that material in a series of ads and in letters to the editor of the local newspaper, asking why there was such a rush to get the project approved without proper review. The Saint team also coordinated local activist groups, staffed phone banks to maximize attendance at the crucial town meeting, and conducted a solid get-out-the-vote effort to make sure every opposition voter attended the town meeting.

As a result, more than 1,700 people attended the town meeting—a record turnout—and more than 46 percent opposed the rezoning, denying the project the two-thirds vote it needed. Town officials then put the issue on a referendum ballot, where it was defeated a second time. The developer finally abandoned the project.

Defense Case Study 2: Rezoning the Rezoning

A landowner filed a request to rezone 25 acres of prime real estate adjacent to an interstate highway interchange. A few citizens became alarmed; the landowner hosted a community meeting for neighbors but refused to confirm or deny suspicions that a big-box retail superstore was intended for the site. The client engaged Saint Consulting to defeat the zoning change and/or stop development of a superstore, which would compete with the client's business interests.

The Saint team secured copies of all the landowner's filings at the municipal offices, researched environmental and transportation permitting requirements at state government offices, and prepared an information package and opposition kit for project opponents. The team then conducted a door-to-door campaign to all abutters and everyone who had spoken or written against the project, and recruited support from local organized labor leaders, who shared their membership lists with the team. These efforts gave Saint a critical mass of opponents sufficient to form a citizen group, launch a direct mail outreach and education campaign to bring the issue to the general public, and drive turnout to the municipal hearings on the rezoning. After an initial one-vote loss, the project manager convinced the citizen group members to bring a legal challenge to the vote based on serious flaws in the process identified by the lawyer Saint had retained for the group.

While the legal case was pending, the citizen group proposed and won enactment of a zone change that limited retail, cutting the landowner's allowable development by 25 percent. When the landowner quietly sought city council endorsement of a new roadway configuration and highway opening, Saint discovered it. The neighbors who opposed the project brought pressure and thwarted that effort as well.

Because of the Saint team's relentless fight and refusal to cede any ground whatever, the unwanted retailer pulled out. The land was put to a different purpose, to the satisfaction of the client and the neighbors.

Defense Case Study 3: Overcoming the Planners

The client's competitor sought to construct a superstore on a commercially zoned parcel on a major state highway. Prior to Saint Consulting's involvement, the town board unanimously granted the project wetlands approval. No citizens attended the wetlands hearing.

The proposal triggered only a site plan review, a process affording little discretion to the local planning commission. The town planning staff discouraged citizens from participating, asserting that development was as-of-right and site review was merely routine.

Saint staffers secured copies of the complete wetlands files and promptly identified a stream connecting to the public water reservoir. The Saint project team then lined up support from an environmental group and obtained its expert information and analysis regarding pollution and runoff issues that would adversely affect the stream and the water supply. The team organized these materials for submission to the planning commission at the optimum moment.

The Saint team then began a targeted door-to-door outreach campaign, sharing plans and information with neighbors and recruiting opponents to organize a citizen group. When the team manager saw a resident's letter in the public file raising traffic safety issues, a Saint staffer immediately met with that citizen and used the concerns as the basis for a direct mail outreach effort to recruit more opponents. Through various outreach programs, the team organized a substantial citizen group, including a small group of direct abutters whose standing gave them both legal and political clout, and who wanted to be represented by an attorney. Saint retained an attorney and orchestrated the citizens' attendance at the public hearing, where the lawyer submitted Saint's expert analysis.

The planning commission voted to reject the site plan application because of the storm water runoff and pollution that would adversely affect the public drinking water supply. The Saint team had succeeded in overcoming the planning staff's dismissive contention that the site plan review was a rubber-stamp, zero-discretion scenario.

Defense Case Study 4: Overcoming Bureaucracy

Saint Consulting was engaged to oppose a project that needed a permit from the Department of Environmental Protection (DEP) in an eastern U.S. state, where environmentalists joked that DEP stood for don't expect protection. The bureaucracy had earned a reputation as a rubber stamp for development by ruling, in almost all cases, that no hearing was necessary as part of the permitting process. Saint strategists knew that if a hearing occurred, it would expose a real lack of understanding of the site and the impacts that the development would have on adjacent streams. There was no possibility of a hearing under the administrative rules for the permit in question, so the Saint project team set about creating one.

The team enlisted the help of environmental groups whose members were concerned with protecting local creeks and streams, and barraged all levels of the DEP with letters and phone calls demanding a hearing. The team orchestrated the campaign so each letter and call raised different problems with the site and focused on a different set of legitimate environmental problems. The team encouraged environmental groups to pass pro-hearing resolutions that could be submitted to state officials, sent letters to legislators urging them to intervene with the DEP, and prodded the legislative committee charged with oversight of the DEP to raise the issue during budget talks with agency officials.

The sheer volume of letters and calls over a three-month period brought results. The DEP called a hearing, and the developer promptly withdrew, claiming that delays rendered the project no longer viable.

Defense Case Study 5: Surgical Removal

The client wanted Saint Consulting to stop a big-box "power center" in Ontario that would compete for retailers that the client was trying to attract for its own development in the same city. In addition to the usual challenges, there was one clear operational restriction: none of the tactics used to attack the proposed power center could jeopardize the client's own development proposal. This presented a dicey situation, since the client's project was larger, was closer to downtown merchants with whom its tenants would compete, included a big-box anchor, lay less than half a kilometer from the proposed power center site, and was being subsidized with taxpayer money for contaminated brownfield site redevelopment. Delicate political management would be required to savage the competition without bringing citizen wrath down on the client's head.

While some residents were opposed to the power center, they were unfocused and completely ignorant of the local planning approval process. Saint strategists immediately analyzed the development application and identified a number of flaws and objectionable aspects on which to focus the opposition group's attention. After educating and training the abutters who would form the core of the local opposition, the Saint team concentrated on broadening the opposition base—both to gain citizen support and to keep opponents too occupied to attack the client—and dispatched citizens to apply pressure to local officials. Saint's project manager set the citizens to work organizing rallies, producing and distributing flyers lambasting the power center, and contacting public officials, among other activities, and orchestrated a busy and demanding campaign program.

Saint staffers successfully recruited local merchants, community activists, and residents who had unsuccessfully fought against an earlier big-box proposal. Saint's project manager employed this group to reach out to the larger community, identifying additional opponents and educating them on how to express their concerns about the power center to local officials. Rallies helped stimulate interest, and the community group held meetings with local officials, who admitted they had never seen such organized opposition to a proposed development.

Both the client's application and the power center application came before the planning committee on the same night. The Saint team turned out more than 250 residents intent on expressing their opposition to the power center, and none offered any comment on the client's big-box proposal. After dozens of speakers lambasted the power center with countless objections and concerns—informed and focused through Saint's efforts—the planning committee voted unanimously to deny the power center application. At the same meeting, the client's plan sailed through without a fuss. The full council later ratified both decisions.

Defense Case Study 6: Using Lawyers

A competitor planned to build a 150,000-square-foot store within a mile of the client's location. Given the projected tax revenues from the new store, the city government was eager to move quickly, and Saint Consulting was retained only after the planning commission had unanimously approved the project.

The Saint team immediately organized a citizen group to oppose the project, raising issues and hindering the development's progress for three months. Meanwhile, the Saint project manager organized a group of plaintiffs, determined the best legal arguments, and assembled a team of attorneys, traffic consultants, and environmental and economic professionals to substantiate the opposition's claims, make certain its points were on the record, and demonstrate determination. The city council approved the project, ignoring the team's input.

The developer immediately began construction, but Saint's lawyer moved for injunctive relief. The court halted construction while the case crawled through the court system. The appellate court ruled in the plaintiffs' favor, holding the rezoning and environmental actions invalid, so that the entitlement process would need to begin anew if the proponent wished to pursue the project. As of this writing, Saint has protected the client's assets and market share for eight years, and the building remains a concrete block shell.

Defense Case Study 7: Changing the Bylaw

The client had secured property intending to develop it, and wanted to stop a competing large-format retail project planned for an adjoining property. The township had recently annexed the adjoining property, and the zoning requirements were unclear. The mayor, a strong advocate of the proposed big-box development, sharply criticized the opposition.

Saint's project team researched the zoning regulations and found that they restricted big-box development, but did not specify any size limit. The team organized a grassroots neighborhood group to oppose big-box development, and worked with the local planning commission to define a big-box structure as 50,000 square feet or larger, a limit that would not interfere with the client's plans. Saint then focused its citizen group's effort on the town council and other elected officials, to convince them to adopt the new language.

Saint won approval, amending the bylaw to impose a 50,000-square-foot limit on big-box development, and the competitor withdrew his plans.

Defense Case Study 8: Reinvigorating Project Opponents

For many months, a team of Canadian lawyers and a public relations firm had been working to stop a big-box proposal in Ontario that would negatively impact the client's market share. Yet less than one month away from the final vote, the council was poised for a 6 to 5 approval of the development proposal.

Given the short lead time, Saint's project team would have to immediately develop a new strategy, integrate into the community, and swing two votes. Within hours of getting approval to engage from the client, Saint strategists put together a successful plan.

Saint's team built on the existing structure: a fatigued community group that had given up hope; a downtown insider business group that had all the answers; and a fringe activist leading a scattershot group of protestors vying for public attention. Applying tact, diplomacy, and urgency, the Saint team gave opponents new hope that victory was possible, that hard work could make a difference, and that the situation called for relentless political pressure. Over the three remaining weeks, this loose coalition gained focus, moved to a consistent message, and targeted council members whose votes needed changing.

At the public meeting, the team produced an overflow crowd of 400. The mayor berated all the people who bothered him at home about the issue, and then led the council to a 7 to 4 denial of the big-box development.

Defense Case Study 9: Educating the Public

The client wanted to prevent a competitor from developing a large landfill in the U.S. Carolinas region. The local government had taken no public position on the proposal, but referred it to a county-wide referendum. The landfill question was to be the only issue on the ballot, and the vote was scheduled to take place one week after the statewide election primary. Saint strategists knew this would mean extremely light voter turnout, since people weren't accustomed to going to the polls twice in two weeks and were focused on the election campaign. Saint strategists also knew that this scheduling gave the project proponent an advantage in turning out a favorable vote while opponents were unaware of the issue and the vote.

The Saint team immediately identified community leaders and opinion-makers who could help spread the word. The team met with them and determined that there was a significant lack of knowledge about the landfill, lack of awareness about the referendum, and lack of education on how to oppose the landfill. The team developed a strategy to convince neighbors and other citizens that the landfill would be bad for the county and bad for citizens' quality of life, placing primary emphasis on homeowners nearest to the proposed landfill site.

Saint team members created an opposition group, held rallies, met with newspaper editorial boards, carried the message door-to-door to inform citizens and identify project opponents, and developed a voter turnout infrastructure to make sure opponents got out to vote. As a result, the community voted against the landfill by an overwhelming margin, with 93 percent opposed.

Defense Case Study 10: Changing the Culture

The client owned the largest retail operation in a college town, and wanted to preserve his presence and market share. A developer planned a large-scale outlet that would have posed a direct threat to the client's business. To complicate matters, the local development culture frowned on opposition, and blocking new development was not considered acceptable.

Using a variety of political tactics, Saint's project team made sprawl the issue and organized an opposition group of nearly 500 active participants, including universities, college professors, local merchants, and chamber of commerce members. The team circulated a petition, collecting nearly 3,200 signatures opposing the development, and retained an environmental attorney to raise drainage and runoff issues. Saint also conducted an extensive local media campaign and worked with a national magazine to facilitate publication of an article on sprawl. More than 500 people attended the hearing, and the outlet was rejected by a vote of 5 to 1.

Defense Case Study 11: Debunking the Tax Mantra

The client was one of two merchants competing for the same business at a busy intersection. The client wanted to block development of a regional commerce center, which would house a direct competitor, on the third corner of the intersection. The location was in a progrowth community, where new sales tax revenue was an incentive to allow new development.

Using sprawl, overdevelopment, congestion, and traffic as key arguments, the Saint team forged a formidable coalition of community groups, environmentalists, and neighborhood associations to oppose the development, and retained a lawyer to represent the group. The team then launched a political outreach campaign that urged citizens to call and write their city officials. When the team found that the competitor's product was a nontaxable commodity under the law, it convinced the community that any tax benefits would be negligible and hardly worth the fallout from overdevelopment.

Based on the strength of community opposition, the developer withdrew his proposal for a regional commerce center, and Saint quickly moved to amend the community's general plan to restrict the number of competitive footprints per intersection to two.

Defense Case Study 12: Gaining Time

The client's ability to build market share was seriously threatened by the proposed expansion of a big-box store into a supersize big-box near the client's newly opened supermarket. The client needed 18 months to build and secure market share in this new area, which would be impossible against an entrenched opponent. Although the big-box project needed a special permit, the site had plenty of land, access, and parking, and local officials had assumed that the store would eventually be expanded. As a result, officials viewed issuing the special permit as a technicality. Local citizens generally looked on the expansion as an as-of-right addition to an existing business and viewed the project favorably.

The Saint campaign manager conducted a scope study, was able to find several local citizens opposed to the expansion, and succeeded in interesting some local union members who worked for the client and who might be in jeopardy of layoff if the competitor stole their employer's market share. The campaign manager organized the citizens, expanded the group by word of mouth, engaged a lawyer to represent opponents at public hearings, and began agitating against the project with signs, bumper stickers, mailings, letters to the editor, petition drives, and patch-through phone calls to members of the planning and zoning commission. He packed the hall with project opponents at every monthly hearing, had his citizen leader meet personally with planning and zoning members, and raised issue after issue, all directed at stopping the expansion any way possible. He was even able to recruit an employee of another competitor to come forward with standing as an intervenor against the expansion. When the special permit was eventually granted, it came with 30 conditions, including a substantial reduction in the size of the expansion. When Saint's citizen appeal was eventually dismissed and the big-box proponent's appeal of the order of conditions was finally settled, three years had elapsed—twice the 18 months the client needed to build market share.

More case studies covering a wide variety of offense and defense land use politics campaigns are available on the Saint Consulting Group's website at http://www.tscg.biz/case-studies.

CHAPTER 10

■ ■ ■

The Future of Land Use Politics

BUILT ON THE PRINCIPLES of land use politics its leaders discovered and developed, Saint Consulting has grown from a small occasional foray into land use politics 25 years ago to an international business with operations in the United States, Canada, and the United Kingdom, and with likely growth into other Western-style democracies. From a single office, it has expanded to more than a dozen; from three employees, it has grown to more than 100 spread across 10 divisions. Saint Consulting operates in nearly every U.S. state and has 250 projects in process at any one time. Saint has completed thousands of projects, and it has won 90 percent of the time. These facts are cited to demonstrate that the methods and strategies of land use politics not only work, but are becoming indispensable in a rapidly worsening atmosphere of contentious and litigious opposition to development projects.

The future of land use politics is suggested by its history. Opposition to development projects used to be concentrated in high-population areas: the East and West Coasts of the United States, the provinces of Ontario and British Columbia in Canada, and London and other large metropolitan areas in the United Kingdom. But opposition to development has grown mightily as citizens' sense of entitlement has combined with environmental concerns to reach critical mass. Today there is no suburb, no township, no village anywhere in these countries that has not heard the voice of citizen opposition to development. The old days—when citizens felt powerless to fight government and big business and held a live-and-let-live attitude toward landowner property rights—are dead and gone. Today's citizens feel perfectly confident taking on government at all levels and gigantic multinational conglomerates.

The extent and volume of opposition to large controversial development promise to grow rapidly as millions of young people, educated from birth to have strong concern for the environment, ecology, species extinction, and quality of life, join their elder brothers and sisters in the various progressive movements to make environmental sensitivity and accommodation programs such as LEED (Leadership in Energy and Environmental Design) not merely laudatory but mandatory. They will challenge not just the methods but also the very idea of mining, drilling, or other natural resource extraction in areas they consider sacrosanct. Compliance with the usual health, safety, environmental, and ecological factors will not be enough in the future. They will be mere threshold tests for approval: necessary, but not sufficient to satisfy militant opponents.

What constitutes good land use is subjective, politically unstable, and relative. Some interest groups favor a project because their members will benefit (natural supporters) and some oppose a project because their members will be adversely affected (natural opponents), while those not in any group don't much care one way or the other (the neutrals). Some in either group can be swayed one way or the other, and some neutrals can be prodded to take sides. For the most part, once these residents are accounted for, the majority of citizens are left, open to persuasion and receptive to the right kinds of argument. In the main, these are the people that land use politics addresses, while simultaneously nurturing supporters and neutralizing opponents with suitable arguments. Whatever other factors get into the mix, it's undeniable that development projects, especially large or controversial ones, do not get approved without at least the perception that they enjoy a critical mass of community support.

This is an era of situational project approval, in which discretionary political decisions are driven not merely by whether a proposed project is politically correct or acceptable, but also by whether the politicians involved feel safe in voting in favor. Without a measure of reassurance, without political cover to protect them and their hold on public office, public officials will not run the risk of approving a project that a future opponent will use as a brickbat to beat them over the head. The political cover required is the public perception—especially among those with political and legal standing—that the community and its residents will benefit from the project. This is not to require an absence of opposition to a project; that level of equanimity is hardly attainable even for the most harmless of projects. But it does mean that the politician, when criticized for his vote, needs a ready and compelling rejoinder that will resonate with the overwhelming majority of voters. The land use political consultant, in formulating a campaign plan, must identify and create such a rejoinder (sometimes, a variety of rejoinders suitable for various audiences) as an essential element of the strategy.

Barring a cataclysm, it is safe to assume that the human population will continue to increase, environmental and ecological conflicts will expand, conflicts between property rights advocates and smart growth proponents will become more heated, human incursions on threatened and endangered species' habitats will increase in number and severity, and the quest for a quiet personal domain will grow desperate as all of the foregoing put tree huggers and tree choppers at loggerheads. As the twenty-first century gets under way, growth management reformers, under whatever title, are becoming more assertive. They will certainly increase the drumbeat of their demands that humans reduce their environmental footprint, adopt sustainability, and treat land use as a privilege subject to the rules of stewardship, as written and enforced by social engineers and planners. There will be increasing regulation and constraints on how, where, and when development can occur, and how the needs of civilization for fuel, power, resources, and food will be met. These restrictions will bring counterresponses from property rights advocates, who are already demanding compensation when their land is downzoned, and they can be expected to treat other incursions on their development rights as confiscatory as well. As assaults on land use escalate, the meaning of ownership will grow in importance.

Population increases will bring expanded needs for homes, jobs, stores, and recreational facilities, among other things, and swelling of the megalopolis, the expanses of civilization that can be identified from space, especially on the U.S. coasts, in eastern Canada, and in southern England.[1] Since spread is limited by the ocean in all three cases, expansion can only move into ever-taller skyscrapers or into an ever-wider sweep of civilization. A focus of contention will be whether to force increasing density, as smart growthers and new urbanists would have it, or to allow market forces to expand a megalopolis to accommodate the increasing population. The outcome of these battles will depend on the degree to which people in Western democracies are willing to tolerate increasing population density and suffer the ever-shrinking size of their personal domains. Asians in such cities as Tokyo, Shanghai, and Hong Kong have famously acclimated themselves to high-density living, limited privacy, and confined personal space. Europeans have grown accustomed over the centuries to small living spaces and the press of urban population, escaping to the countryside greenbelt areas or to the coast on weekends to rejuvenate. But even smaller spaces and less personal privacy will mark the future if the urban ring approach to growth spreads, at least until a critical mass is reached and the masses demand more room, the dam bursts, and the spread of civilization resumes. Given growing population and limited space within an urban boundary, something eventually has to give way.

North Americans, meanwhile, are accustomed to an expansive lifestyle, including vast spaces, large living quarters, and plenty of privacy. Europeans are both bewildered and amused at North American

---

[1]French geographer Jean Gottman coined the term *megalopolis* in 1957 to describe the 400-mile stretch of cities and suburbs between Boston and Washington, D.C. The term is now applied to any extensive metropolitan region.

complaints of congestion and overcrowding; Canada and the United States each encompass roughly 3.8 million square miles and feature vast areas with little population.[2] Most of the land in both countries is vacant or, as Gertrude Stein observed, "In the United States, there is more space where nobody is than where anybody is. This is what makes America what it is." How will Americans react to increasing population density and loss of personal privacy and the personal domain? Not well, is the safe bet.

Infrastructure

The need for more infrastructure as population expands is certain to grow more contentious as new power plants are proposed and vigorously opposed. Some people despise nuclear power, noting potential dangers and pointing to laggard governments' failure to address long-term issues. Others are beginning to see nuclear power's benefits when compared to other methods of generating power. Still others have advocated it all along as clean and efficient.[3] Some abhor coal, which produces half of U.S. electricity but is blamed for acid rain, carbon dioxide, and air pollution. Others insist that abundant reserves of coal make its use essential, and that better scientific scrubbing methods are needed to address pollution issues. Some demand clean or renewable power from hydroelectric, wind, solar, ocean currents, and similar means, but they run up against the argument that such uses are not scalable to the level needed to meet expected demand, even with effective conservation programs. As with any contentious development proposal, power plants evoke the NIMBY

[2]Canada's population density is 8.3 people per square mile, while the United States, with nearly 10 times the population, has a density of 80 people per square mile. The United Kingdom, with 94,000 square miles of area, has a density 637 persons per square mile, and England alone, 50,000 square miles in area, has a density of 976 people per square mile.

[3]France, in particular, relies heavily on nuclear energy (99.8 percent), as does Ontario, Canada, the country's industrial and business heartland, where nuclear power plants produce half of the province's electricity. In the United Kingdom and the United States, about 20 percent of the power is nuclear generated.

response in residents, who all want electricity generated, but not in their backyards, and raise the defensive hackles of environmental protectionists. Barring scientific breakthroughs among the wide range of power production concepts, or a seismic shift in attitudes among opponent organizations, contentious battles over power plants—type, location, and impacts on the environment and human health—will increase in ferocity as the need presses harder and resistance stiffens.

The same is true for battles over the drilling of oil and gas wells, the laying of the pipelines needed to support them, and other industrial-level extraction processes, such as aggregate mining. Coal, aggregate, and other mining operations are generally sited far from population centers, but population expands toward preexisting operations, and a sort of reverse NIMBYism arises as newly minted neighbors complain about the long-established "nuisance" next door. Although "coming to the nuisance" traditionally has earned little sympathy in court, modern activist citizens have had some success in curtailing uses they don't like, even when the offending party was there first. Expanding population makes increases in the number and breadth of these battles inevitable.

A new element certain to be contentious will be the decommissioning process, a term commonly applied to nuclear power plants but newly relevant to the shutdown process at the close of a mine's useful life. Historically, mines were dug, played out, and abandoned. But large modern mining operations can cause huge scars in the landscape that will be increasingly contentious as civilization expands toward them, and modern empowered activists pay attention as they did not do historically. Will the mine owner spend the millions necessary to restore the site, and, if so, what level of "natural state" will be required? How will the land use politics play out? Who will own the land when the cleanup is completed? To what use will it be put? What public vetting process will be conducted, and which people and groups will have standing to appeal and litigate when the decision does not go their way? What new sets of regulations will Congress enact, and how will states deal with disputes? One aspect is certain: a mine owner who does not restore the site to the level that critics expect will find opponents waiting to attack and mount opposition to his next project.

Increasing population will also demand repair and improvement of the transportation infrastructure including highways, mass transit, and airport expansion, to mention three contentious examples, as well as facilities to process sewage, rubbish, and garbage. Until recently, such projects were largely sited through the "beggar thy neighbor" approach, in which undesirable facilities are shunted to the edge of town (and downstream and downwind), where their smoke, noise, pollutants, fumes, and ugly towers may annoy residents of an adjacent community, but are far enough away from populated and business areas in the host town to protect the politicians' chances for reelection. This approach, already falling out of vogue, will become less viable as regional solutions to waste management are proposed and as old-fashioned landfills and incinerators succumb to recycling laws and regulations.

Recycling plants are expensive to build and operate, so the economics involved usually require a wide catchment area encompassing a number of municipalities. The battle lines for such land use bloodletting are easily drawn: people who advocate recycling generally also advocate regional solutions, and people who don't, don't. Those who seek to develop major industrial undertakings such as power plants, regional waste treatment plants, or quarries prefer dealing with one regional bureaucracy rather than a dozen local boards.

But for developers, regional planning agencies can carry the threat of double jeopardy; often, the project must survive the local approval process and then face scrutiny at the regional level for compliance with regional goals. Even if the bases for review are different, the developer is forced to go through two sets of hearings, and opponents have two chances to lob objections before two different boards. There is the further issue of accountability: members of regional boards are usually appointed, not elected, and the bureaucracy (planning staff) advising the board is shielded from political influence. Planners and board members therefore have every reason to push the planning agenda, and no impetus to employ reason and cooperation in evaluating a project proposal. Unless the developer is proposing a major regional project, power plant, or quarry that the regional planning agency supports as needed—and sometimes, even if he is—the regional government agency is not his friend.

The regional planning approach advocated in social engineering circles may already be obsolete as eco-regional planning and management come to the forefront, driven by the world's largest environmental organization, The Nature Conservancy. Briefly, eco-regionalism involves conservation across entire swaths of geography to preserve functioning ecosystems. There are 91 eco-regions in the United States, 52 in Canada, and 4 in the United Kingdom, according to the widely used Wildlife Fund list, and each of them is subject to study, analysis, and preservation planning. Social engineers presume that the millions of property owners whose land is encompassed in an eco-region will be receptive to the collaborative and community-based steps that will be recommended, a doubtful proposition at best. Eco-regional management on private land is certain to involve increasing government mandates, further curtailing landowner rights and giving rise to contentious land use battles.

Medicine, Education, and Recreation

Increasing population will also demand new and expanded medical and educational facilities, again requiring regional approaches to make them economically feasible. Such facilities are less controversial than a CAFO (a concentrated animal feeding operation, essentially a huge piggery), but residential neighbors will no more want to live next to a college dorm (read "frat house") and tolerate the inevitable antics of high-spirited undergraduates than next to any other generator of noise, traffic, and nightly police calls. Like the electricity that everyone needs but nobody wants to host, a medical facility will face the same neighborhood opposition for mostly the same reasons: ambulance sirens, traffic, multiple rubbish trucks (some for trash, some for biological waste), lights burning all night long, and the unknown dangers that medical research might bring—release of chemicals or radiation into the neighborhood, for example. It is for these reasons that educational and hospital uses are usually sited next to existing educational or hospital uses, to minimize resistance from neighbors already accustomed to the downsides. But pressure for new facilities to meet the needs of an increasing population and longer-lived senior citizens will inexorably lead to intense land use battles.

Increasing population will also demand new and expanded recreational facilities and destinations, many requiring regional approaches to be economically feasible. Golf courses, once considered examples of benign and useful open space, are under attack as monuments to selfishness, as woods and meadow habitats are sacrificed to human recreation. Increasingly, they are being built on former landfill sites, appropriately lined to prevent leeching into the groundwater and capped with clean fill. Even so, golf course development remains controversial; environmental opponents oppose the loss of animal habitat, worry about nitrogen runoff from fertilizers, and see less recreational benefit in rolling lawns than in a site allowed to return to its natural forested state.

Amusement parks and racetracks, largely a failure at the local level, are returning to popularity at a regional scale. But they are controversial for the same reasons affecting any large development: traffic, noise, fumes, smoke, odors, light pollution, and so forth. Since the locus for such uses must be large tracts away from residential neighborhoods, environmental and habitat issues inevitably arise. So, too, for development of gambling casinos, which, beyond state and federal licensure issues, raise moral and ethical issues in addition to the traffic-noise bundle of complaints.

Ski resorts, once seen as harmless and health-inducing, are now condemned in some quarters as an indefensible invasion of the wilderness with adverse effects on wildlife at all levels. The Earth Liberation Front, now listed as an ecoterrorist organization, use *ecotage* (a play on the word *espionage*) to describe their habit of burning down buildings they don't like, including a $12 million ski resort in Vail, Colorado, that they evidently considered intrusive. While far more reasonable in their approach, some other environmental groups share the view that people need to leave the wilderness alone, an issue that is sure to continually erupt in controversy as population expands and people inevitably intrude farther into once-pristine environs.

New Development

As the most desirable (and properly zoned) areas for development in a community approach build-out, there will be pressure to develop virgin land farther afield, drawing the wrath of preservationists and environmentalists of every stripe. But there will also be pressure to develop less-ideal sites that were perhaps originally intended for uses that did not bear fruit. In the 1970s many communities, for example, optimistically set aside large tracts of land for industrial use, hoping that Microsoft or Wang would move to town. In most cases, this did not occur, and now these sites are under pressure from developers who want to build other sorts of projects. Likewise, disused landfills, vacant shopping centers, and old factories will become more attractive for redevelopment as development-ready sites are less plentiful, necessitating rezoning, special permits, and other forms of relief.

These parcels, it will be argued, are adjacent to similar uses, so expanding the current zoning border slightly to accommodate the new proposal should not be a problem. But opposing neighbors will argue that "enough is enough," and point out that traffic, noise, odors, and other inconveniences are already intolerable and, worse, that promises the developer made years ago were never kept. Pitched battles between developers and residents over rezoning proposals are inescapable, as residents feel more hemmed in, more squeezed, more pressured by ballooning development and population density going on all around them. They will want their personal domain preserved and protected and, since they seldom own the parcels surrounding their house lots and are not in a mood or position to buy them, will insist that development in the area would destroy the neighborhood quality of life and community character. Politicians will certainly not shrug off such assertions, and planners within urban boundaries will face clashing interests as developers seek to "infill" parcels within the zone but are confronted by neighbors who don't want their space invaded. For most cities, which don't have urban boundaries, the choice for planners is easier: join the neighbors in opposing development that doesn't measure up. The trouble for developers, of course, is not that the neighbors want something better; it is that they want nothing at all.

It's also true that zoning restrictions tend to increase over time, particularly in smaller municipalities where the easiest way to deal with a citizen's land use complaint is to adopt another regulation. Add to this the increasing volume of state, provincial, federal, and national regulation shunted onto local shoulders for enforcement, and the deferential attitude of courts toward use of the police power, which encourages increasingly restrictive bylaws, and the battlefield is ready. Once one town in an area adopts a restrictive regulation (to ban one sort of undesirable use or another), others quickly follow suit so as not to leave their taxpayers and voters unprotected. As zoning restrictions increase, opportunities for opponent mischief multiply.

The land use political wars will not leave planners unscathed, no matter how hard they struggle to remain above the fray. The expanding planner hegemony over local zoning codes is certain to escalate the war between central planning enthusiasts and property rights advocates, just as the wish for residents to be left alone is certain to conflict with the planners' vision of ideal development. This backlash is already well under way, and it promises to make things more difficult for development opponents, as well as for advocates. As developers grow more sophisticated in their responses to opposition, and as property rights advocates broadly trumpet the unfairness of denying landowners the right to use their property, opponents are likely to find their campaigns more difficult. A carefully constituted pro-development campaign, appealing to homeowners' own rights, may give traction to developers who otherwise might not get a foothold, provided the proposed project is not unreasonable. In this, planners will increasingly find themselves at odds with their own local citizens: high-density mixed-use development is fine in theory, but suburban property owners do not want it in their backyards, generating traffic and noise and invading their sylvan privacy.

Internecine Backbiting

As proponents of the smart growth, new urbanism, neo-traditionalism, form-based zoning, and other social engineering regimes expand their influence and succeed at getting their theories enacted into law, land use battles will pit faction against faction in ideological warfare. The social engineers' institutional push for regionalization, urban growth boundaries, open space preservation, mass transit, and clustered housing is growing more insistent and more urgent. The coming land use political wars will pit multiple factions against one another: local citizens, planners, developers, landowners, environmentalists, ecologists, growth control advocates, property rights advocates—each with its own agenda. Confrontations will be more pointed, hearings more contentious, and litigation more prevalent as one side works to make economic use of its land and the other works to save the planet. The era of live-and-let-live has gone the way of laissez-faire government. Gone, too, are the days of business obliviousness and insensitivity to environmental issues: more than 90 percent of global CEOs in a McKinsey survey are doing more than they did five years ago to incorporate environmental and social issues into their core strategies in response to increasing pressure from employees and consumers.[4] Another McKinsey survey found that CEOs expect the environment to attract more public and political attention,[5] a self-fulfilling prophecy as corporations tout their environmental efforts.

It's telling that the intensity of land use battles has social engineers fighting among themselves. Even among growth control advocates, there is squabbling over agendas; mutual exchanges of verbal gunfire over definitions, goals, and methods; and contention over who is the more disingenuous, schismatic, heretical, blasphemous, treasonous, or all of the above. Planners who accommodate growth

---

[4]Debby Bielak, Sheila M. J. Bonini, and Jeremy Oppenheim, "CEOs on Strategy and Social Issues," *McKinsey Quarterly*, October 2007.

[5]*The McKinsey Quarterly*, "Assessing the Impact of Societal Issues: A McKinsey Global Survey," November 2007.

instead of managing it are marked as weaklings at best, and probably traitors. Utopians who don't acknowledge that population growth is the real problem are labeled as delusional, if not disingenuous. New urbanism is nothing more than new suburbanism to snide growthers, who assert that most new urbanist development is just as bad as sprawl, consuming green space and degrading the landscape. Everybody beats the drum for sustainability, and then squabbles about what it means.

Will these rifts among the faithful lead to schism? Can they agree to disagree? Or will they raise their cudgels to beat each other? Given the simultaneous self-deprecation and moral superiority of the social engineering class, it seems doubtful that one claque of the righteous will subsume another. But if they don't speak with a unified voice, and instead send mixed messages to lawmakers, they will dilute their influence and risk stalling their own campaign. From a property rights advocate's perspective, such division among foes is welcome, and it presents opportunities for the landowner rights agenda. Whatever happens, contention within and without the various land use interest groups continues to grow, and their disputes will increase in utility for land use political campaigns nimble enough to keep their venom aimed at one another.

Land Use Policy

Land use regulation in Western republics has mostly been left to local governments, whose officials are required to follow state, provincial, or national land use policy, but are also expected to apply their own knowledge, experience, and discretion to the locus and development proposals before them. In the future, these local officials will find the job of deciding land use permissions far more demanding. Land use bureaucrats, such as planners, will enhance their influence as local officials rely on them for interpretation and advice as citizens simultaneously flex their political muscles. The result will be a complex, multilayered political struggle.

National and regional land use policies are certain to expand and grow more intricate, more stringent, and more intrusive as new forms of fuel, energy, and environmental protection take center stage. They will no longer be seen merely as national issues, but rather as international and global issues commanding the attention of nations, affecting their foreign policies, and resulting in continuous rounds of treaties, accords, and understandings between and among nations that will affect how the development business is conducted.

States, provinces, and national governments, meanwhile, will continue responding to the drumbeat of growth management with new policies, programs, and approaches. Some will try flat regulation, while others turn to economic incentives. Some will leave local discretion in local hands. Others will impose regional, statewide, or province-wide plans, and some will impose state-level or national permitting procedures for larger projects. Some are sure to expand environmental review requirements and set aside more critical areas for protection or limited development, only to face litigation from property owners whose land is suddenly included within the borders of a restricted development area and thereby downgraded in value.

At home, the attitudes and policies set at the international, national, state, provincial, and regional levels will drive local land use policies, zoning, and permit granting, and will forcefully affect how governments approach environmental problems and solutions. Inevitably, regional and local governments will be urged to handle permitting and development issues in accord with the larger worldview, and opponents of such an approach will raise sovereignty, patriotism, and self-determinism as arguments against international meddling in local affairs. The voices of contention will grow stronger, bolstered (or provoked) by new and even more restrictive government land use mandates.

Persistent struggles between environmentalists and commodities interests such as loggers (or fishermen) will continue and expand as the right to do business confronts issues of forest health (or marine health) and as those who want to manage forests (or oceans) on an economic basis argue with those who demand an ecological management basis. Environmental activism today is a multibillion-dollar industry, employing millions of people and enjoying broad political influence. Its goals conflict with those of more traditional businesses, like commodities and mining, whose activities the environmentalists seek to curtail. In their mounting clashes, the issue will be not merely the interest group's goals, but also its effectiveness in employing political principles to convey its message while short-circuiting the message from opponents. Is the interest group's goal to improve life for others or to impose its vision on society? Is it to make money (applicable to developer and enviro-business alike) or to benefit mankind? Is it to bring order out of chaos or to control and mold society into an academic theory? Is it to create utopia? Gain fame? Control access? Pursue an obsession? In this, as in other political battles, defining the issues and characterizing opponents are essential to victory. Given the enormous variety of contention over land use and preservation already, land use political battles can only multiply and intensify in the future.

In the United States, it is well to remember that the mainstays of environmental law—the National Environmental Policy Act, the Endangered Species Act, and the Clean Water Act—were all enacted in the 1970s. Their maintenance over the ensuing years has included a variety of amendments and expansions, has generated an impressive number of Supreme Court decisions, and has spawned a formidable bureaucracy. As a new generation of ecosystem manager replacements take over at the Bureau of Land Management and the Forest Service, not to mention the Environmental Protection Agency, the Army Corps of Engineers, and numerous related agencies, new interpretations are certain to pour forth, affecting agency policy. New regulations are certain to flow, and new rounds of argument and contention are certain to fill the halls of government in every branch, at every level. Further amendments, expansions, and clarifications are inevitable as experience with environmental challenges deepens and as science discovers new kinds of species, perhaps living in new kinds of habitats, to be protected. Not too great a leap of imagination is required to predict similar changes in Canada and the United Kingdom, where similar laws, regulations, bureaucrats, and environmental issues are equally pressing.

The Information Age

Increasing sophistication is driven by modern communications and the ease of acquiring information. More and more self-help websites designed to assist development opponents spring up as each enviro-business strives to seem more relevant and vigorous than the competition. Although the property rights advocates' response to the antidevelopment Web presence has not been particularly assertive or helpful in a how-to sense — relying mainly on intellectual treatises on property rights and dry reports on the latest court cases to deliver their message — the deluge of books, articles, and press items devoted to smart growth is beginning to provoke a backlash. The social engineers' demands for more aggressive growth controls, elimination of development rights, assertion of a right to roam over other people's property, elevation of animal and plant rights far above landowner rights, and sheer coercion imposed on property owners in the name of saving the planet are bringing rumbles from the traditionalist side of the battlefield. As the central planners become shriller about what they see as the failure of state, provincial, and national legislatures to act, ordinary citizens are likely to see the social engineering platform as unreasonable, excessive, and overreaching in its vision for mankind's future. When that viewpoint reaches a substantial mass, the social engineers' relevancy and influence may take an unforeseen hit.

Given the breadth and depth of land use issues and contention at all levels, in all branches of government, in the news media, and among the public, it is clear that struggles over land use are destined to grow and multiply as the finite resource of land confronts contradictory opinions of how it ought to be treated. Land use politics is replacing outmoded approaches to handling development opposition, and it is expanding rapidly because political principles apply in every aspect of citizenship and government in Western democracies. Developers faced with new and creative opposition tactics in the twenty-first century will not succeed with nineteenth-century tools like influence peddling or even twentieth-century methods such as public relations. Modern-day issues over land use will not lend themselves to facile approaches, nor will horse-drawn methods prevail in the information age. Sophisticated strategies will be required in order to overcome intractable opposition, and it is through the effective use of land use political techniques that success will be achieved.

CHAPTER 11

■ ■ ■

The Saint Index

OPPOSITION TO DEVELOPMENT is strong and growing. Virtually every land use proposal—regardless of quality, merit, or community need—now experiences some level of opposition. Who is likely to oppose real estate development, and why? What demographic characteristics are common to people likely to support or oppose a certain type of development? What are the root causes of resident opposition? The Saint Consulting Group developed the Saint Index as a research tool to analyze opposition to development.

The Saint Index was designed in 2005 by the Saint Consulting Group with initial assistance from the Center for Economic and Civic Opinion at the University of Massachusetts. A survey of 1,000 residents, it has been conducted in the United States, the United Kingdom, and Canada with a common core of baseline questions, allowing for comparison and analysis of differences between countries as well as changes and trends annually. While the core questions remain the same, approximately one-third of the questions vary each year to look at other land uses and associated issues. For example, the Saint Consulting Group has worked with George Mason Law School professor Ilya Somin to use the Saint Index to track public opinion and legislative responses to the U.S. Supreme Court's 2005 *Kelo* decision involving the taking of land by eminent domain to further economic development (*Kelo v. City of New London, Connecticut* [545 U.S. 469]).

Key Findings

Fully 74 percent of all Americans oppose any new development in their communities. This is the handicap every U.S. developer starts with on every new project. Three out of four Americans are saying "stop building in my community now." This does not mean that they are against all new development, or even that they will not shop at the new mall or grocery store if it is built. It simply means they do not want the development in their community.

The NIMBY (not in my backyard) impact is even greater in the United Kingdom, where 85 percent of British residents say no to any new development in their neighborhood. Those strongly opposed have been steadily increasing in the United Kingdom, from 13 percent in 2007, to 17 percent in 2008, to 21 percent in 2009, while active support for development remains at just 6 percent.

Canadian opposition numbers are close to those for the United States, with 75 percent against new local development.

Americans are cynical about politics and politicians, and that is reflected in citizens' view of the planning process. When it comes to deciding what can be built in their communities, 55 percent say the communities do a fair to poor job. On planning and zoning issues, 72 percent give their communities a grade of C or worse.

Opposition to All New Development
Based on 2008–2009 data.

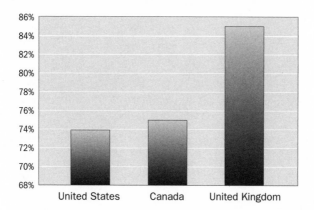

Cynicism over development runs deep. The monumental importance of campaign cash in American politics casts a shadow over
planning and zoning decisions. Sixty-nine percent of Americans believe that the relationship between developers and elected officials
makes the process unfair.

Is the fact that Americans see the process as suspect and tainted
by inappropriate relations between developers and the people trusted
to make land use decisions an election issue? A candidate's position
on growth is important to 87 percent of Americans when choosing
the candidates for whom they will cast their vote, with 47 percent
believing this strongly. This makes land use policy critical in local
elections. Candidates may run on no growth or smart growth platforms, but they instinctively know that development is a local hot-
button issue everywhere. Supporting development because it brings
jobs and new tax dollars into a community is no longer a political
benefit. Standing with the vocal, passionate, and politically active
opponents of development is now more politically expedient.

One in five Americans, or 21 percent, have actively opposed
development in their communities by attending hearings, writing or
calling officials, or gathering petitions against a new proposal. Only
one in seven, or 14 percent, has done anything to actively support a
new development proposal. Clearly, people are much more likely to
act in opposition to a land use proposal than to support one.

Active Opposition Versus Active Support

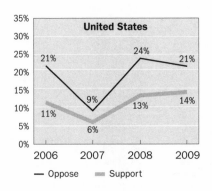
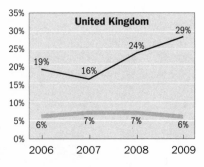

The disappointment with government may be endemic. It pervades the Canadian and U.K. results as well, with a whopping 71 percent of British residents dissatisfied with their local government's performance on planning issues and 58 percent of Canadians saying they believe their communities are doing fair to poor jobs of deciding what gets built.

The number of British residents who have actively opposed projects increased significantly from 2006 to 2009, rising from 19 percent to 29 percent, while the number of people who have taken action to support a project remained steady at 6 percent.

Most Likely NIMBYs

NIMBY activists are everywhere, and they come from every region and every ethnic, religious, and political group. The people packing hearings to stop development projects are of every age, gender, and income group; opponents cannot be easily categorized as coming from any particular demographic.

The Saint Index illustrates that the toughest region in which to build in the United States is the Northeast, followed by the West and Mid-Atlantic. The more mature and dense the market, the more intense opposition is likely to be. The Midwest is generally more supportive of new development proposals.

Active U.S. Opposition by Region

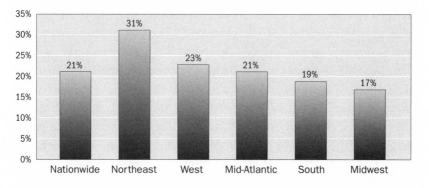

The people most likely to be NIMBY activists in the United States are between 46 and 55 years old, have college or postgraduate degrees and annual incomes of $75,000 to $99,000, and own their own homes. They are equally as likely to be from urban, suburban, or rural areas.

The most likely NIMBY activists in the United Kingdom are over age 65, are in the highest social class, vote Conservative, and live in rural areas. They are likely to be from the southeast or southwest.

The most likely Canadian NIMBY activists are also over age 65, own homes, have college or postgraduate degrees, and earn more than $75,000 annually. They are just as likely to live in urban, suburban, or rural areas, but are likely to be from the greater Toronto area or from Calgary, Alberta.

Reasons for Opposition

According to the Saint Index, U.S. residents act in opposition to land use projects to

preserve the environment (22 percent);
protect their real estate values (21 percent);
protect the character of their communities (18 percent); and
prevent additional traffic (19 percent).

But in Saint's experience, that's not the whole story. The opponents are most often fighting to protect their real estate values. Their homes are likely to be the largest investments they have ever made, and they are terrified of the changes to the community that could result if the proposed project gets built. They fear the unknown. In innumerable instances, residents have opposed the redevelopment of a blighted and dilapidated area because they were afraid of what would come. They knew the current conditions and lived with them, and they felt that they could continue to live with them. What would happen if the big new project got built? Would it worsen traffic, noise, and light issues? Would it attract a criminal element or other "undesirable" people?

In contrast, it is hard to get people excited enough to take action in support of a new development project. While they may not be opposed to the new store and will be happy to shop there once it is open, they are not willing to give up a Tuesday night to go to a town hall hearing to demonstrate their support. It is far easier to generate opposition to development than to motivate active support, so the planning process is increasingly dominated by the influence of angry neighbors and project opponents.

Opposition by Land Use

The Saint Index looks at standard land uses each year and ranks opposition to each, as shown in the graphs on pages 207–210 and discussed below.

Most Opposed Land Uses

Landfills have ranked as the most opposed land use in the United States in the Saint Index for every year thus far. They are very strongly opposed in Canada and the United Kingdom as well. Casinos are in the top three most opposed uses in all three countries. In the United Kingdom, opposition to quarries and power plants is hot and rising. The general intensity of opposition to development is significantly stronger in the United Kingdom, but there is a greater propensity for citizen activism in the United States.

Each of these uses is extremely difficult to site. Opponents are sure to fill every hearing, but supporters motivated enough to show up and demonstrate are hard to find. Elected officials are unlikely to commit political suicide by supporting such proposals in front of a

Most Opposed Land Uses

United States	United Kingdom	Canada
Landfills 78%	Quarries 85%	Casinos 83%
Casinos 77%	Power Plants 83%	Landfills 75%
Quarries 62%	Casinos 83%	Wal-Mart 63%

U.S. Opposition to Development

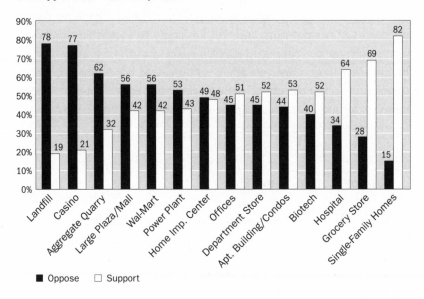

Oppose   □ Support

U.K. Opposition to Development

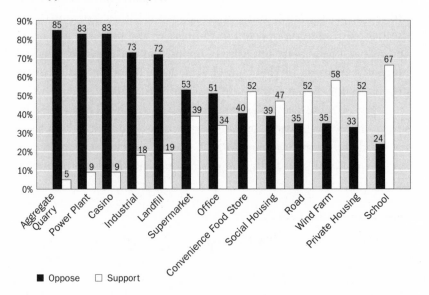

Oppose   □ Support

Canadian Opposition to Development

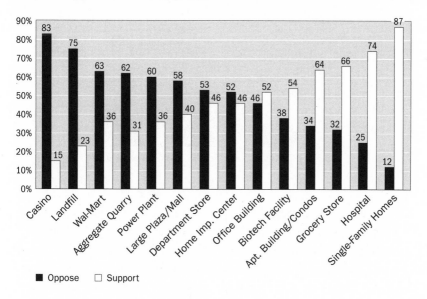

■ Oppose   □ Support

crowd of angry constituents. Developers of these uses must identify community needs with which they can assist that will leverage political support from key constituencies. The needs may involve helping the local Little League team or the historical society, but a developer must find a way to get key local activists motivated to support the proposal.

Least Opposed Land Uses

Single-family housing has been the most supported use in the United States each year of the Saint Index. Despite having a significant impact on municipal budgets because of the prevalence of school-aged children and disproportionate needs for police, fire, and other municipal services, single-family housing is not scary as long as the houses look like others in the neighborhood. Low-income housing would be another subject altogether. More houses that fit into the neighborhood are not likely to affect real estate values and generate no real fear of change.

Opposition to Single-Family Housing

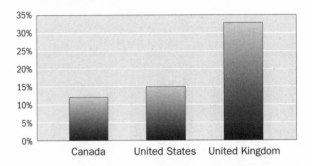

Housing is far more controversial in the United Kingdom. Fully 33 percent of British residents would oppose any new housing proposal for their community—more than double the opposition found in the United States and Canada. In the United Kingdom, 51 percent of those who opposed a development project took action against new housing. By contrast, 41 percent of those who actively supported any type of new development rose up to fight for new housing projects.

Grocery stores are opposed by just 28 percent of Americans, but many of the most hard-fought land use battles that Saint has ever been involved in have been over new grocery stores. While 70 percent of Americans support the concept of new grocery stores in their communities and would eagerly shop there, they are not showing up

Opposition to Grocery Stores

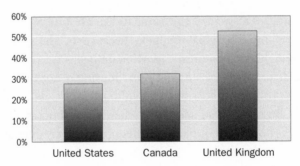

at public hearings. Only the opponents attend to strongly voice their opposition to local officials.

This one-sided view of the mind of the electorate has killed many a project. It will continue to do so until developers realize that these are truly political fights. Having a good project is not enough. Developers must demonstrate community support, but supporters, even for projects with broad community support, are very unlikely to show up.

Wal-Mart, a lightning rod for land use controversy, is opposed by 56 percent of Americans and 63 percent of Canadians. (Wal-Mart operates in the United Kingdom as Asda, a British supermarket chain.) In fact, a higher percentage of Americans would rather live near a power plant than a Wal-Mart.

Power Plants

Energy needs necessitate the development of new energy generation projects in the United States, and virtually all proposals will be met with opposition by angry and frightened neighbors. The biggest surprise in the 2009 energy numbers is the rising support for nuclear power. Sixty percent of Americans would oppose a nuclear power plant in their community, down from 65 percent in 2008. While that clearly demonstrates a majority of residents in opposition, the numbers are getting smaller. The Saint Index question is not a referendum on support or opposition for the concept of nuclear power. It asks whether people support or oppose nuclear power plants in their communities. The surprise is not the 60 percent in opposition, but

U.S. Opposition to Power Plants by Type

Type	Opposition	Amount of Change from 2008
Nuclear	60%	–5%
Fossil Fuel	50%	–8%
Bio-Fuel	37%	–1%
Hydroelectric	34%	–6%
Wind Farm	15%	–5%
Power Plants in General	53%	–4%

U.K. Opposition to Power Plants	
Type	Opposition
Nuclear	72%
Coal Fired	71%
Oil Fired	70%
Gas Fired	66%
Wind	24%
Power Plants in General	83%

Canadian Opposition to Power	
Type	Opposition
Nuclear	75%
Ethanol	53%
Bio-Diesel	52%
Incineration/ Gasification	48%
Natural Gas	38%
Hydroelectric	32%
Wind Farm	17%
Power Plants in General	60%

the 40 percent who would not oppose it. This demonstrates a great and hard-fought battle by the nuclear power industry to convince Americans of the safety of nuclear generation. If a company picks the right place and runs the right type of campaign, gaining approval for new nuclear power plants may be a winnable fight now.

While there seems to be a general understanding that the United States needs more power generation capacity, a majority of Americans oppose new high-voltage transmission lines in their communities. That opposition drops precipitously to 17 percent if those lines are delivering clean, renewable energy from wind. Support for new transmission lines leaps from 46 percent to 83 percent when Americans are asked specifically about high-voltage transmission lines delivering wind power.

Impact of the Economic Downturn

Fully 59 percent of Americans said they would be more likely to support new commercial development in light of the 2008–2009 economic recession. Although that number is encouraging for developers, the problem is that when people are presented with Saint Index scenarios for new proposals for commercial development in their communities, their support levels have not increased significantly over previous years. In fact, opposition to some uses has increased. Talking about development as a concept is one thing; actually supporting it in one's own backyard is quite another matter. Opposition to development is often an emotional reaction based on fear of the unknown.

The Effect of New Media

Today 30 percent of Americans are using the Internet for research and to stay informed, and 21 percent have used the Internet to communicate with officials, friends, and neighbors on land use issues. The staggering growth of the Internet and the introduction of new media tools are changing community organizing. It has never been easier to identify and contact like-minded people and to build and maintain an active grassroots organization.

Facebook, LinkedIn, Twitter, YouTube, MySpace, and a host of other social media websites are beginning to have a real impact on how people communicate, share ideas, and get organized. It is simple to set up a website dedicated to opposing a real estate project, and this type of medium is designed to be viral. The site's creators encourage users to pass the website on to other interested users, building a network or community of like-minded people with exponential growth potential. When properly used, such grassroots organizations can have an incredibly powerful impact on the planning and zoning process.

This highly potent form of community organizing is still new and developing. For now, project opponents tend to be far more sophisticated and active in using social media than are developers and project proponents.

The Future

Each year that the Saint Index is conducted, more data are added, the knowledge base grows, and trends emerge over time. The research area—currently the United States, the United Kingdom, and Canada—will soon increase to include France, Germany, Spain, and The Netherlands.

BIBLIOGRAPHY

■ ■ ■

David Abler, "Multifunctionality and Agricultural Policy," in Stephan J. Goetz, James S. Shortle, and John C. Bergstrom, eds., *Land Use Problems and Conflicts* (New York: Routledge, 2005).

Joyce Barker, "Opposition Does Not Equal NIMBY," Guest Opinion, *Iowa City Press-Citizen*, April 8, 2008.

Charles Barnard, "Employment Growth, Population Growth, and Electronic Technologies as Determinants of Land Use," in Stephan J. Goetz, James S. Shortle, and John C. Bergstrom, eds., *Land Use Problems and Conflicts* (New York: Routledge, 2005).

Debra Bassert, "Streamlining the Development Approval Process," Background paper for the American Planning Association's Getting Smart Project, Phase III, National Association of Home Builders (NAHB), January 4, 2007. http://www.nahb.org.

Philip R. Berke, David R. Godschalk, and Edward J. Kaiser, with Daniel A. Rodriguez, *Urban Land Use Planning*, 5th ed. (Urbana and Chicago: University of Illinois Press, 2006).

Alan Berube and Elizabeth Kneebone, "Two Steps Back: City and Suburban Poverty Trends, 1999–2005" (Washington, D.C.: The Brookings Institution, Metropolitan Policy Program, December 2006).

Debby Bielak, Sheila M. J. Bonini, and Jeremy Oppenheim, "CEOs on Strategy and Social Issues," *McKinsey Quarterly*, October 2007.

Sir William Blackstone, *Commentaries on the Laws of England*, Sixteenth Edition, Book the Second, "Of the Rights of Things" (1825).

Edward J. Blakely and Mary Gail Snyder, *Fortress America: Gated Communities in the United States* (Washington, D.C.: The Brookings Institution, 1999).

British Broadcasting Corp., "The UK Family: In Statistics," BBC News/UK. http://newsvote.bbc.co.uk.

Brookings Institution, "MetroNation: How U.S. Metropolitan Areas Fuel American Prosperity" (Washington, D.C.: The Brookings Institution, Metropolitan Policy Program, 2007).

Robert D. Bullard, Glenn S. Johnson, and Angel O. Torres, "Race, Equity, and Smart Growth: Why People of Color Must Speak for Themselves" (Atlanta, Ga.: Environmental Justice Resource Center, n.d.). http://www.ejrc.cau.edu/raceequitysmartgrowth.htm.

Bureau of National Affairs, "Exemptions: Noerr Shields Covert Sponsorship of Litigation Against Competitor," BNA Corporate Law, *Antitrust & Trade Regulation Report* 80 (1992): January 26, 2001. http://corplawcenter.bna.com/corplawcenter/1,1103,2_805.OO.html.

Meredith Burke, "Smart Growth Ignores Many Harsh Truths," *The Social Contract*, 1999.

Scott Campbell, "Green Cities, Growing Cities, Just Cities? Urban Planning Contradictions of Sustainable Development," *Journal of the American Planning Association* 62 (1996): 296–312.

"Canada's Response to the Recommendations in the Tenth Biennial Report of the International Joint Commission," Land Use section, http://www.on.ec.gc.ca/laws/tenth-ijc-response/land_use-e.html (last updated 2001).

Margaret H. Carr and Paul D. Zwick, *Smart Land Use Analysis: The LUCIS Model: Land-Use Conflict Identification Strategy* (Redlands, Calif.: ESRI Press, 2007).

John Carreyrou and Barbara Martinez, "Nonprofit Hospitals, Once for the Poor, Strike It Rich with Tax Breaks, They Outperform For-Profit Rivals," *Wall Street Journal*, April 4, 2008, p. A1.

Center for Health, Environment and Justice, "Targeting 'Cerrell' Communities." http://www.ejnet.org/ej/cerrell.pdf.

Charter of the New Urbanism, http://www.cnu.org/charter.

Cheryl Chumley and Ronald D. Utt, "National Heritage Areas: Costly Economic Development Schemes That Threaten Property Rights," Backgrounder No. 2080, The Heritage Foundation, Washington, D.C., October 23, 2007.

Sandro Contenta, "Developer's Cost Claims Raise Fears of Legal Chill," *Toronto Star*, February 10, 2008. http://www.thestar.com/News/World/article/302135.

Wendell Cox and Joshua Utt, "The Costs of Sprawl Reconsidered: What the Data Really Show," Backgrounder No. 1770, The Heritage Foundation, Washington, D.C., June 25, 2004.

David Suzuki Foundation, "Fostering a Sustainable Canada: Protecting Our Health, Environment, and Economy: Recommendations for the 2005 Federal Budget: Submission to the Standing Committee on Finance,

November 3, 2004" (Vancouver, B.C., Canada: David Suzuki Foundation, 2004). http://www.davidsuzuki.org.

John S. DeMott, "Welcome, America, to the Baby Bust," *Time*, February 23, 1987. http://www.time.com/time/magazine/article/0,9171,963617,00 .html.

Henry L. Diamond and Patrick F. Noonan, *Land Use in America: The Report of the Sustainable Use of the Land Project* (Washington, D.C.: Island Press, 1996).

Steven J. Eagle, "The Birth of the Property Rights Movement," *Policy Analysis* No. 558 (Washington, D.C.: Cato Institute, December 15, 2005).

Steven J. Eagle, "A Resurgent 'Public Use' Clause Is Consistent with Fairness," in Dwight H. Merriam and Mary Massaron Ross, eds., *Eminent Domain Use and Abuse: Kelo in Context* (Chicago: American Bar Association, ABA Publishing, 2006).

Amanda S. Eckhoff and Dwight H. Merriam, "Public Use for Peripatetic: First, Michigan Reverses Poletown and Now the Supreme Court Grants Review in an Eminent Domain Case," in Dwight H. Merriam and Mary Massaron Ross, eds., *Eminent Domain Use and Abuse: Kelo in Context* (Chicago: American Bar Association, ABA Publishing, 2006).

Amer El-Ahraf, Mohammad Qayoumi, and Ron Dowd, *The Impact of Public Policy on Environmental Quality and Health* (Westport, Conn.: Quorum Books, 1999).

Dell Erickson, "Sustainable Population Levels Using Footprint Data," March 20, 2000. http://www.mnforsustain.org/erickson_d_determining _sustainable_population_levels.htm.

Lara Farrar, "Is America's Suburban Dream Collapsing into a Nightmare?" CNN.com, June 16, 2008. http://www.cnn.com/2008/TECH/06/16/ suburb.city/index.html?iref=newssearch.

William A. Fischel, *The Economics of Zoning Laws* (Baltimore: Johns Hopkins University Press, 1985).

R. Florida, *The Rise of the Creative Class* (New York: Basic Books, 2002).

David Forbes, *Planning Law: A Handbook for Conveyancers and Property Professionals* (Birmingham, U.K.: CLT Professional Publishing, 1999).

Eric T. Freyfogle, *The Land We Share: Private Property and the Common Good* (Washington, D.C.: Island Press/Shearwater Books, 2003).

Michelle Gladden and Kim Predham, "Environmentalist NIMBY's Versus Affordable Housing Advocates," *Asbury Park* (N.J.) *Press*, April 21, 2008.

Global Real Estate Monitor, "Exploring Canada: Comparing Eastern and Western Provinces," *National Real Estate Investor*, March 2008. http:// nreionline.com.

Stephan J. Goetz, "Socioeconomic and Health Outcomes of Land Use," in Stephan J. Goetz, James S. Shortle, and John C. Bergstrom, eds., *Land Use Problems and Conflicts* (New York: Routledge, 2005).

Stephan J. Goetz, James S. Shortle, and John C. Bergstrom, eds., *Land Use Problems and Conflicts* (New York: Routledge, 2005).

Stephan J. Goetz, James S. Shortle, and John C. Bergstrom, "Contemporary Land Use Problems and Conflicts," in Goetz, Shortle, and Bergstrom, eds., *Land Use Problems and Conflicts* (New York: Routledge, 2005).

Stephan J. Goetz, James S. Shortle, and John C. Bergstrom, "Future Research Needs for Rational Land Use Decisions," in Goetz, Shortle, and Bergstrom, eds., *Land Use Problems and Conflicts* (New York: Routledge, 2005).

Jean Gottmann, *Megalopolis: The Urbanized Northeast Seaboard of the United States* (1961).

Ray Gronberg, "High Density, Smart Growth Versus Nimby 'Preservationists,'" *The Herald-Sun*, Durham, N.C., April 22, 2008.

Michael Grunwald, "Down on the Farm," *Time*, November 12, 2007.

Marci Hamilton, "A Michigan Supreme Court Decision Supports Private Landowners' Rights: Its Reasoning and Possible Nationwide Ramifications," *FindLaw Legal News and Commentary*, Findlaw.com, August 12, 2004.

Nick D. Hanley and Fiona Watson, "Land Use Problems: A European Perspective," in Stephan J. Goetz, James S. Shortle, and John C. Bergstrom, eds., *Land Use Problems and Conflicts* (New York: Routledge, 2005).

Garrett Hardin, "The Tragedy of the Commons," *Science* 162 (1968).

Erik Heinrich, "Canada: Well-Oiled Machine. With a Push from Exxon, Alberta's Tar Sands Are Poised to Increase Oil Production to Saudi-like Levels," *Time*, June 2, 2008.

Innovation Briefs, "The 'Smart Growth' Debate Continues, Potomac, Md.," *Innovation Briefs* 14 (3): May/June 2003. http://www.innobriefs.com/editor/20030423smartgrowth.html.

Thomas Johnson, "An Ideal Federal Land Use Policy," in Stephan J. Goetz, James S. Shortle, and John C. Bergstrom, eds., *Land Use Problems and Conflicts* (New York: Routledge, 2005).

Molly Kavanaugh and John Caniglia, "Dueling Developers Plan Solon Shopping Centers: City Pledges It Will Not Use Eminent Domain Powers," *Cleveland Plain Dealer*, October 2, 2007.

Barbara Kivat, "Lured Toward the Right Choice," *Time*, April 14, 2008.

Ruth Knack, Stuart Meck, and Israel Stollman, "The Real Story Behind the Standard Planning and Zoning Acts of the 1920s," *Land Use Law*, February 1966.

Regine Labossiere, "Towns Turn to Nineteenth-Century Tradition of Charrettes," *The Hartford Courant*, April 28, 2008.

Carol W. LeGrasse, "Zoning Is Not the Answer," Property Rights Foundation of America, Stony Creek, N.Y., May 22, 2006. http://prfamerica.org.

Carol W. LeGrasse, "Our Stolen Legacy: The Betrayal of the Declaration of Independence for the Cause of Landscape Preservation," Property Rights Foundation of America, Stony Creek, N.Y., July 5, 2007.

Tony Leighton, "Attention Citizen Objectors: Beware of Getting SLAPPed," *Guelph Mercury*, March 1, 2008.

Wayne A. Lemmon, "Can Sprawl Be Good?" The Sprawl Guide, www.plannersweb.com, undated.

Lawrence W. Libby, "Rural Land Use Problems and Policy Options," in Stephan J. Goetz, James S. Shortle, and John C. Bergstrom, eds., *Land Use Problems and Conflicts* (New York: Routledge, 2005).

Lori Lynch, "Protecting Farmland," in Goetz, Shortle, and Bergstrom, eds., *Land Use Problems and Conflicts* (New York: Routledge, 2005).

Niccolò Machiavelli, *The Art of War*, Book 7 (1520).

Niccolò Machiavelli, *The Prince* (c. 1505, orig. pub. 1513). XXIV, "Why the Italian Princes Have Lost Their States." http://www.constitution.org/mac/prince00.htm.

Carla T. Main, "How Eminent Domain Ran Amok: Kelo and the Debate Over Economic Development Takings," The Hoover Institution, *Policy Review*, October/November 2005, Stanford University, Palo Alto, Calif.

Jeff McGoff, "Exploring the Boundary of the Noerr-Pennington Doctrine in the Adjudicative Process," *University of Memphis Law Review* (Winter 2004).

The McKinsey Quarterly, "Assessing the Impact of Societal Issues: A McKinsey Global Survey," November 2007.

Robert I. McMurray and Dwight H. Merriam, "How to Kill a Development Project in 10 Easy Steps," *Real Property Section Review* (Los Angeles: Los Angeles County Bar Association, Summer 2004).

Stuart Meck, "Model Planning and Zoning Enabling Legislation: A Short History," in *Modernizing State Planning Statutes: The Growing Smart Working Papers*, Vol. 1, American Planning Association, Washington, D.C., 1996.

Stuart Meck, "APA, Brookings Panel Sparks Debate on Zoning Reform," APA News and Features, American Planning Association, Washington, D.C., 2003.

Michael Mehaffy, "A Conversation with Andrés Duany," *Katasxis* no. 3, December 2002, http://www.katarxis3.com/Duany.htm.

Dwight H. Merriam and Robert I. McMurray, "An Addendum on Grassroots Lobbying," July 23, 2004.

Dwight H. Merriam and Robert I. McMurray, "Organizing Support for a Project," ALI-ABA Course of Study, Land Use Institute: Planning, Regulation, Litigation, Eminent Domain and Compensation, Boston, August 26–28, 2004.

Dwight H. Merriam, *The Complete Guide to Zoning: How Real Estate Owners and Developers Can Create and Preserve Property Value* (New York: McGraw-Hill, 2005).

Dwight H. Merriam and Mary Massaron Ross, eds., *Eminent Domain Use and Abuse: Kelo in Context* (Chicago: American Bar Association, ABA Publishing, 2006).

Elaine Misonzhnik, "Land on Shaky Ground," Retail Traffic online magazine, November 28, 2007. http://www.clickability.com.

Stacy Mitchell, *The Home Town Advantage: How to Defend Your Main Street Against Chain Stores . . . and Why It Matters* (Minneapolis: Institute for Local Self-Reliance, 2000).

Adam Mossoff, "The Death of Poletown: The Future of Eminent Domain and Urban Development After *County of Wayne v. Hathcock*" (Michigan State University College of Law, *Michigan State Law Review*, 2004), Research Paper No. 03-02.

Naples Daily News Editorial, "Florida Property Tax Amendment: Good for Homeowners, Good for Our Economy," *Naples* (Fla.) *Daily News*, January 12, 2008.

National Association of Home Builders, "Streamlining the Regulatory Process," April 14, 2008. http://www.nabh.org.

National Charrette Institute, "What Is a Charrette?" (Portland, Ore.: National Charrette Institute). http://www.charretteinstitute.org/charrette/html.

National Readership Survey, http://www.nrs.co.uk/about_nrs/data_available/definitions_of_social_grade.

National Specialty Foods Memo blog, "Retail Memo Special Feature: Wal-Mart, Inc., Might Have Found a Solution or Two to Much of the Opposition to Its Mega-Supercenter Stores in the USA," April 25, 2008. http://naturalspecialtyfoodsmemo.blogspot.com/2008/04/retail-memo-special-feature-wal-mart.html.

New Rules Project, "The Government Sector: Devolving Authority and Democratizing Decisionmaking: New England Town Meeting" (The New Rules Project, 1996). http://www.newrulesproject.org.

New York Law Journal, "An Unfair Fight—Noerr Permits Opponents of Zoning Changes to Deceive," *New York Law Journal*, July, 26, 2000.

John R. Nolon, *Well Grounded: Using Local Land Use Authority to Achieve Smart Growth* (Washington, D.C.: Environmental Law Institute, 2001).

Erica Noonan, "Moms for More Taxes: Women Lobby for Overrides as Mass. Towns Struggle," *Boston Globe*, March 2, 2008.

Al Norman, "Wal-Mart Cancels 45 Superstore Projects: 'Cannibalization Factor' Eating the Company's Future," *Huffington Post*, March 20, 2008. http://www.huffingtonpost.com/al-norman/walmart-cancels-45-super_b_94112.html.

Ontario Municipal Board website. http://www.omb.gov.on.ca/english/ OMBinformation/OMB_Municipal_role.html.

Ontario Municipal Board, "Your Guide to Ontario Municipal Board Hearings," Queen's printer for Ontario, 2004.

Ontario Municipal Board, "Here's What You Need to Know If You Disagree with an OMB Decision," Queen's printer for Ontario, 2004.

Optimum Population Trust, "Britain's Major Parties Environmentally Illiterate," April 25, 2005. http://www.optimumpopulation.org/ opt.release25Apr05.html.

Optimum Population Trust, "UK Overpopulated by 70 Per Cent," February 18, 2008. http://www.optimumpopulation.org/opt.release18Feb08.htm.

Andrew Oswald, "Theory of Homes and Jobs," working paper preliminary for Part II paper, University of Warwick, Coventry, U.K., September 18, 1997.

Randal O'Toole, "The Folly of Smart Growth," Thoreau Institute, *Regulation* magazine, Fall 2001.

Randal O'Toole, "Debunking Portland, The City That Doesn't Work," Policy Analysis No. 596, Cato Institute, Washington, D.C., July 9, 2007.

Randal O'Toole, "Why Government Planning Always Fails" (Washington, D.C.: Cato Institute, September 29, 2007). http://www.cato.org/pub _display.php?pub_id=8831.

Randal O'Toole, "The Planning Tax: The Case Against Regional Growth-Management Planning," Policy Analysis No. 606, Cato Institute, Washington, D.C., December 6, 2007.

David Palubeski, Mark Seasons, and Steven Brasier, "Toward a Canadian Urban Strategy: Framework for Government of Canada Involvement in Urban Affairs—Submission to the Prime Minister's Caucus Task Force on Urban Issues by the Canadian Institute of Planners," March 11, 2002.

Neal Peirce, "Zoning: Ready to Be Reformed?" Washington Post Writers Group, Washington, D.C. http://www.postwritersgroup.com/archives/ peir0127.htm.

Eduardo M. Peñalver, "The End of Sprawl?" *Washington Post*, December 30, 2007.

Rolf Pendall, Robert Puentes, and Jonathan Martin, "From Traditional to Reformed: A Review of the Land Use Regulations in the Nation's 50 Largest Metropolitan Areas," August 2006, Metropolitan Policy Program Research Brief, The Brookings Institution, Washington, D.C.

Michael Penn, "Taming the Suburban Wasteland," *On Wisconsin* (1998): 28–34, 54.

Iver Peterson, "Suffolk County Resists Public Housing Projects; Suffolk County Is Resisting Public Housing Project Rise," *The New York Times*, April 25, 1977.

Pew Research Center, "Inside the Middle Class: Bad Times Hit the Good Life," Pew Social & Demographic Trends, April 9, 2008. http://pewsocialtrends.org/pubs/706/middle-class-poll.

Max J. Pfeffer, Linda P. Wagenet, John Sydenstricker-Neto, and Catherine Meola, "Value Conflict and Land Use Planning," in Stephan J. Goetz, James S. Shortle, and John C. Bergstrom, eds., *Land Use Problems and Conflicts* (New York: Routledge, 2005).

Rutherford H. Platt, *Land Use and Society: Geography, Law and Public Policy* rev. ed. (Washington, D.C.: Island Press, 2004).

Trip Pollard, "Greening the American Dream: If Sprawl Is the Problem, Is New Urbanism the Answer?" *Planning* 67 (9) (2001): 10–15.

Douglas R. Porter, *Breaking the Development Logjam: New Strategies for Building Community Support* (Washington, D.C.: Urban Land Institute, 2006).

Lori Potter, "Strategic Lawsuits Against Public Participation," SLAPP Resource Center. http://www.slapps.org/bios/potter.htm.

Eyal Press, "The New Suburban Poverty," *The Nation*, April 23, 2007.

George W. Pring and Penelope Canan, *SLAPPs: Getting Sued for Speaking Out* (Philadelphia: Temple University Press, 1996).

Property Rights Foundation of America, "NYS DEC's New Open Space Conservation Plan Finalized: Unbridled Radical Preservation," Stony Creek, N.Y., 2007.

Jeremy Rabkin, "Dangers of Designations: Regional, Federal, State and International Land-Use Intrusions: National/American Heritage Areas, UN Biosphere Reserves and UN World Heritage Sites," testimony before the U.S. House of Representatives, Committee on Resources, September 12, 1996, on the American Land Sovereignty Protection Act, Property Rights Foundation of America, Inc., Albany, N.Y.

John Randolph, *Environmental Land Use Planning and Management* (Washington, D.C.: Island Press, 2004).

Richard C. Ready and Charles W. Abdalla, "The Impacts of Land Use on Nearby Property Values," in Stephan J. Goetz, James S. Shortle, and John C. Bergstrom, eds., *Land Use Problems and Conflicts* (New York: Routledge, 2005).

Rob Roberts, "Of Developments, Lawsuits and the 'Chill Factor,'" *Posted Toronto*, May 2, 2008. http://nationalpost.com/np/toronto/archive/2008/05/02/of-development-lawsuits-and-the-chill-factor.aspx.

Sacramento Bee Editorial, "CEQA's Being Hijacked: Where Are the Enviros? Environmental Groups Watch Silently as Special Interests Misuse the State's Key Statute," *The Sacramento Bee*, February 2, 2008.

Salt Lake Tribune Editorial, "Taking the Initiative: Legislature Exempts Land-Use Laws from Ballot Tests," *The Salt Lake Tribune*, March 14, 2008.

Robert J. Samuelson, "The End of Entitlement," *Newsweek*, May 26, 2008, p. 39.

Marshall Sayegh, "Twenty-first Century Carpetbaggers and Privateers: The Booty Is Your Property," speech presented at the Eleventh Annual National Conference on Private Property Rights, Property Rights Foundation of America, Inc., Albany, N.Y., October 13, 2007.

Adrienne Schmitz and Deborah L. Brett, *Real Estate Market Analysis: A Case Study Approach* (Washington, D.C.: Urban Land Institute, 2001).

Heather Schofield, "Canada's Oil Wealth Strategy Questioned," *Globe and Mail*, Toronto, June 21, 2008.

Andrew F. Seidl, "Falling Markets and Fragile Institutions in Land Use," in Stephan J. Goetz, James S. Shortle, and John C. Bergstrom, eds., *Land Use Problems and Conflicts* (New York: Routledge, 2005).

Christopher Shea, "A Handout, Not a Hand Up: A Popular Approach to 'Sustainable Development' Doesn't Work, Critics Say," *Boston Globe*, November 11, 2007.

Roger M. Showley, "Building in Changes: Planning for 'Compact' Living Can Be a Solution," *San Diego Union-Tribune*, April 20, 2008.

Sierra Club, "Sprawl: The Dark Side of the American Dream," 1998. http://www.sierraclub.org/sprawl/report98.

Sierra Club, "Stop Sprawl: Sprawl Overview," http://www.sierraclub.org/sprawl/overview.

Sierraclub.com, "Sustainable Population Development Solutions." http://www.sierraclub.org/population/sustainable-development-solutions.

Jane Silberstein and Chris Maser, *Land Use Planning for Sustainable Development* (New York: CRC Press, 2000).

Sean Silverthorne, "Putting Entrepreneurship in the Social Sector" (Cambridge, Mass.: Harvard Business School, Working Knowledge for Business Leaders, February 4, 2008).

Alvin D. Sokolow, "The Smart Growth Approach to Urban Land Use: Implications for Farm Land Protection," in Stephan J. Goetz, James S. Shortle, and John C. Bergstrom, eds., *Land Use Problems and Conflicts* (New York: Routledge, 2005).

Thomas Sowell, "War on Poverty Revisited," *Capitalism*, August 17, 2004.

Donald R. Stabile, *Community Associations: The Emergence and Acceptance of a Quiet Innovation in Housing* (Westport, Conn.: Greenwood Press, 2000).

Dean Starkman, "Condemnation Is Used to Hand One Business Property to Another," *Wall Street Journal*, December 2, 1998.

Richard C. Stedman, "Sense of Place as an Integrated Framework for Understanding Human Impacts of Land Use Change," in Stephan J. Goetz, James S. Shortle, and John C. Bergstrom, eds., *Land Use Problems and Conflicts* (New York: Routledge, 2005).

Debra Stein, "Charrettes: Not Always the Right Answer," *Land Development*, National Association of Home Builders, Washington, D.C., Winter 2001.

Debra Stein, "The Ethics of Housing and Nimbyism," *Affordable Housing Finance*, Northbrook, Ill., February 2006.

Debra Stein, "Preparing Your Lobbying Plan," *Land Development*, National Association of Home Builders, Washington, D.C., Fall 2004.

Debra Stein and David Stiebel, "When Neighbors Refuse to Negotiate," *Land Development*, National Association of Home Builders, Washington, D.C., Spring/Summer 1993.

David Streitfeld, "The Food Chain: As Prices Rise, Farmers Spurn Conservation," *New York Times*, April 9, 2008.

Richard L. Stroup, "The Endangered Species Act: Making Innocent Species the Enemy" (Bozeman, Mont.: Property and Environment Research Center, 1995). http://www.perc.org.

Matthew Sturdevant, "Residents Worry Complex Will Bring Crime," *Daily Press* (Hampton, Va.), January 11, 2008.

Sun Tzu, *The Art of War* (circa 500 B.C.E.), Richard D. Sawyer, trans. (Boulder, Colo.: Westview Press, 1994). Also see http://classics.mit.edu/Tzu/artwar.html.

"The Sustainability Report: Canada's Population, 2000," Sustainability Reporting Program, Canada. http://www.sustreport.org/signals/canpop_ttl.html.

Kathryn W. Tate, "California's Anti-Slapp Legislation: A Summary of and Commentary on Its Operation and Scope," *Loyola of Los Angeles Law Review* 33:801 (372) April 2000.

Evan Thomas, "The Closing of the American Mind," *Newsweek*, December 31, 2007/January 7, 2008.

Alexis de Tocqueville, *Democracy in America*, Vol. 2 (1840), the Henry Reeve Translation, revised and corrected, 1899.

United Kingdom Charities Direct website. http://www.charitiesdirect.com.

United Nations, "Report of the World Commission on Environment and Development," General Assembly Resolution 42/187, December 11, 1987. http://www.un.org/documents/ga/res/42/ares42-187.htm.

United States Census Bureau, Statistics Abstract of the United States, 2008 ed. http://www.census.gov/compendia/statab/cats/geography_environment/land_and_land_use.html.

United States Department of Commerce, "A Standard Zoning Enabling Act Under Which Municipalities May Adopt Zoning Regulations" (SZEA), 1926.

United States, Environmental Protection Act of 1999, Part 2, "Public Participation," and Part 4, "Pollution Prevention." http://www.ec.gc.ca/CEPARegistry/the_act.

Urban Land Institute, *Mixed-Use Developments: New Ways of Land Use* (Washington, D.C.: Urban Land Institute, 1976).

Carl von Clausewitz, *On War* (1812), Principles of War. http://www .clausewitz.com/readings/OnWar1873/TOC.htm.

Loretta Waldman, "Charrette Proposal Derailed by GOP; One Selectman Questions Magnitude of the Project," *The Hartford Courant*, March 6, 2008.

Wall Street Journal Editorial, "Review and Outlook: Eminent Reality," The Wall Street Journal Online, January 30, 2008. http://online.wsj.com/ public/article_print/SB120165400238627033.html.

Westchester County Business Journal, "Developer Claims Tactics Thwart Retail Center Plans," August 3, 1998.

Wikipedia, "Development Control in the United Kingdom." http://en .wikipedia.org/wiki/Development_control_in_the_United_Kingdom. Updated December 5, 2007.

Wikipedia, "Mixed-Use Development: Drawbacks." http://en.wikipedia.org/ wiki/Mixed_use_development.

Wikipedia, "Mixed-use Development: History." http://en.wikipedia.org/ wiki/Mixed_use_development.

Wikipedia, "Noerr-Pennington Doctrine." http://en.wikipedia.org/wiki/ Noerr-Pennington_doctrine.

Wikipedia, "Principles of Intelligent Urbanism." http://en.wikipedia.org/ wiki/Principles_of_Intelligent_Urbanism.

Wikipedia, "Regional Assemblies in England." http://en.wikipedia.org/wiki/ Regional_Assemblies_of_England, July 18, 2008.

Wikipedia, "Sustainability: Definitions," citing the conference highlights and overview of issues report of the Organisation for Economic Co-operation and Development (1997) on the Government of Canada's conference on sustainable transportation, Vancouver, March 24–27,1996. http://en.wikipedia.org/wiki/Sustainability.

Wikipedia, "Town and Country Planning in the United Kingdom," last updated February 23, 2008. http://en.wikipedia.org/wiki/Town_and _country_planning_in_the_United_Kingdom.

Wikipedia, "Urban Growth Boundary." http://en.wikipedia.org/wiki/Urban _growth_boundary.

World Fertility Rates. http://www.pregnantpause.org/numbers/fertility.htm.